HELPING BEREAVED PARENTS

The Series in Death, Dying, and Bereavement
Consulting Editor
Robert A. Neimeyer

Davies—Shadows in the Sun: The Experiences of Sibling Bereavement in Childhood
Harvey—Perspectives on Loss: A Sourcebook
Klass—The Spiritual Lives of Bereaved Parents
Leenaars—Lives and Deaths: Selections from the Works of Edwin S. Shneidman
Lester—Katie's Diary: Unlocking the Mystery of a Suicide
Martin, Doka—Men Don't Cry…Women Do: Transcending Gender Stereotypes of Grief
Nord—Multiple AIDS-Related Loss: A Handbook for Understanding and Surviving a Perpetual Fall
Roos—Chronic Sorrow: A Living Loss
Rosenblatt—Parent Grief: Narratives of Loss and Relationship
Werth—Contemporary Perspectives on Rational Suicide

FORMERLY THE **SERIES IN DEATH EDUCATION, AGING, AND HEALTH CARE**
Consulting Editor
Hannelore Wass

Bard—Medical Ethics in Practice
Benoliel—Death Education for the Health Professional
Bertman—Facing Death: Images, Insights, and Interventions
Brammer—How to Cope with Life Transitions: The Challenge of Personal Change
Cleiren—Bereavement and Adaptation: A Comparative Study of the Aftermath of Death
Corless, Pittman-Lindeman—AIDS: Principles, Practices, and Politics, Abridged Edition
Corless, Pittman-Lindeman—AIDS: Principles, Practices, and Politics, Reference Edition
Curran—Adolescent Suicidal Behavior
Davidson—The Hospice: Development and Administration. Second Edition
Davidson, Linnolla—Risk Factors in Youth Suicide
Degner, Beaton—Life-Death Decisions in Health Care
Doka—AIDS, Fear, and Society: Challenging the Dreaded Disease
Doty—Communication and Assertion Skills for Older Persons
Epting, Neimeyer—Personal Meanings of Death: Applications for Personal Construct Theory to Clinical
    Practice
Haber—Health Care for an Aging Society: Cost-Conscious Community Care and Self-Care Approaches
Hughes—Bereavement and Support: Healing in a Group Environment
Irish, Lundquist, Nelsen—Ethnic Variations in Dying, Death, and Grief: Diversity in Universality
Klass, Silverman, Nickman—Continuing Bonds: New Understanding of Grief
Lair—Counseling the Terminally Ill: Sharing the Journey
Leenaars, Maltsberger, Neimeyer—Treatment of Suicidal People
Leenaars, Wenckstern—Suicide Prevention in Schools
Leng—Psychological Care in Old Age
Leviton—Horrendous Death, Health, and Well-Being
Leviton—Horrendous Death and Health: Toward Action
Lindeman, Corby, Downing, Sanborn—Alzheimer's Day Care: A Basic Guide
Lund—Older Bereaved Spouses: Research with Practical Applications
Neimeyer—Death Anxiety Handbook: Research, Instrumentation, and Application
Papadatou, Papadatos—Children and Death
Prunkl, Berry—Death Week: Exploring the Dying Process
Ricker, Myers—Retirement Counseling: A Practical Guide for Action
Samarel—Caring for Life and Death
Sherron, Lumsden—Introduction to Educational Gerontology. Third Edition
Stillion—Death and Sexes: An Examination of Differential Longevity Attitudes, Behaviors, and Coping
    Skills
Stillion, McDowell, May—Suicide Across the Life Span—Premature Exits
Vachon—Occupational Stress in the Care of the Critically Ill, the Dying, and the Bereaved
Wass, Corr—Childhood and Death
Wass, Corr—Helping Children Cope with Death: Guidelines and Resource. Second Edition
Wass, Corr, Pacholski, Forfar—Death Education II: An Annotated Resource Guide
Wass, Neimeyer—Dying: Facing the Facts. Third Edition
Weenolsen—Transcendence of Loss over the Life Span
Werth—Rational Suicide? Implications for Mental Health Professionals

HELPING BEREAVED PARENTS

A Clinician's Guide

Richard G. Tedeschi
Lawrence G. Calhoun

Brunner-Routledge
New York and Hove

Published in 2004 by
Brunner-Routledge
29 West 35th Street
New York, NY 10001
www.brunner-routledge.com

Published in Great Britain by
Brunner-Routledge
27 Church Road
Hove, East Sussex
BN3 2FA
www.brunner-routledge.co.uk

10 9 8 7 6 5 4 3 2 1

Library of Congress Cataloging-in-Publication Data

Tedeschi, Richard G.
    Helping bereaved parents : a clinician's guide / Richard G. Tedeschi &
Lawrence G. Calhoun.
        p. cm. — (The series in death, dying, and bereavement)
    Includes bibliographical references and index.
        ISBN 0-415-94748-0 (alk. paper) — ISBN 1-58391-364-5 (pbk. : alk. paper)
    1. Children—Death—Psychological aspects. 2. Bereavement—Psychological
aspects. 3. Parents—Counseling of. I. Calhoun, Lawrence G. II. Title. III. Series.

    RC455.4.L67T435 2003
    155.9'37—dc21

                                                        2003011094

CONTENTS

Foreword   ix
Preface   xiii
Acknowledgments   xv

Chapter **1**   **The Experience of Grieving Parents**   1

Chapter **2**   **Grief Perspectives, Models, and Myths**   15

Chapter **3**   **A General Framework for Intervention**   37

Chapter **4**   **Bereaved Parents and Their Families**   71

Chapter **5**   **Circumstances of the Loss**   101

Chapter **6**   **Spirituality and Religion**   125

Chapter **7**   **Issues for the Clinician**   145

Chapter **8**   **Resources for Bereaved Parents and**   167
                   Their Expert Companions

References   175
Index   181

FOREWORD

Now numbering over 60 books published over a period of twenty years, the Brunner Routledge *Series on Death, Dying and Bereavement* aspires to bring the results of the most important contemporary research to professional readers, providing authoritative but readable reports of leading edge scholarship on the human engagement with grief, loss, and end-of-life issues. By synthesizing, analyzing, and interpreting the wealth of studies that are opening new vistas of understanding into the human engagement with death, previous volumes have offered a trove of valuable information, tools, and perspectives to practicing clinicians of many disciplines confronting such problems as life-threatening illness, death anxiety, suicide, and bereavement in its many forms. Although well grounded in research, series authors have above all attempted to speak practically to fellow professionals, translating sometimes-abstract findings into "news you can use" in the crucial crucible of the clinical context.

In this respect, *Helping Bereaved Parents: A Clinician's Guide* succeeds admirably. Between its covers the reader will encounter the frank advice and practice wisdom of two of the bereavement field's leading contributors, Richard Tedeschi and Lawrence Calhoun. What distinguishes this book is its remarkable blend of research sophistication and clinical acumen, bridging two worlds that are too often isolated from one another. Thus, Tedeschi and Calhoun begin by disabusing the reader of many time-honored assumptions about the experience of bereavement based on older theories, assumptions having to do with the stage-like progression of "healing," the universal need for "grief work," the danger of "denial," and the eventuality of "recovery," none of which is well-supported by contemporary research. But rather than leave the reader adrift from old conceptual anchors, they then help the informed clinician chart a new and more helpful course in working with bereaved parents, complementing a realistic assessment of the dangers of the journey with a hopeful, growth-oriented perspective that profound learning can arise from profound tragedy. Speaking frequently in the words of the parents themselves, chapter after chapter teaches the clinician to acknowledge the former perils, and to accentuate the latter prospects.

Although they are clearly consummate clinicians, Tedeschi and Calhoun are well aware of the dangers of presumptive expertise in a terrain as daunting as that of parental bereavement. As an alternative to the "clinician knows best" stance that might be conferred by some schools of clinical practice, they advocate eloquently for a humble form of "expert companionship," in which bereaved parents themselves are regarded as the primary authorities on what they need at any given moment. Far from fostering clinical passivity, however, this stance empowers the clinician to join the parent in a search for meaning and coherence in a life story that has been severely challenged or perhaps entirely shattered by traumatic loss. This is nowhere clearer than in the numerous transcripts of actual clinical exchanges, which convey more subtly than any theory could how one might draw on the potential inherent in the client's own language, support network and belief system to plant the seeds of hope in a terrain that initially appears barren of possibility. In passage after passage, Tedeschi and Calhoun do not merely tell the reader *what* to attend to and *when* to intervene, they demonstrate *how* to do it in richly realistic portrayals of actual clinical practice.

The scope of coverage of this book, although focused on parental bereavement, is broad. In clear, practical terms, the authors discuss how to address problems and mobilize resources in clients' family systems and cultural groups, evaluate social-ecological constraints on change, and recognize and remedy complications arising from a mismatch of client and therapist worldviews or spiritual convictions. They address the unique challenges of suicidal, homicidal, accidental, and illness-related bereavement. They offer hard-won, in-the-trenches insights about the perils of legal and media involvement in the violent deaths of children, the hazards of parental guilt, and the appropriate use of rituals of remembrance. And with admirable reflexivity, they turn their attention to the person of the clinician, moving beyond platitudes about compassion fatigue or burnout arising from working with traumatic loss, to address specific countertransference issues that can compound the difficulty of such work and suggest equally specific solutions. Consistently and commendably, Tedeschi and Calhoun convey the sense of having "been there" in countless individual, family, and group sessions with grieving parents, as they offer research-informed counsel on how best to serve this vulnerable population.

To me, the most inspiring "take-home message" of this compact clinical guidebook is the recognition that traveling through the landscape of loss changes both bereaved parents and those professionals who journey beside them, in ways that can be both deep and durable. Contending with one of the most horrendous forms of loss can in this sense lead to significant, if unsought gains, including a more developed sense of compassion, insight into the mysteries of life and death, tolerance for human difference, and philosophical recognition of what has meaning and purpose. Tedeschi and Calhoun have clearly traveled this terrain and found these treasures, and in this guidebook have had the generosity to share them with us.

Robert A. Neimeyer, Ph.D.
University of Memphis
Series Editor

PREFACE

This was a difficult book to write. Although both of us have extensive clinical experience with persons facing major life losses, and one of us (RGT) has for many years provided clinical support services to bereaved parents through a nonprofit agency, we still wondered if we were indeed qualified to write about an experience that life has, so far (and hopefully forever), spared us. To use the metaphor that Robert Lipsyte used in describing his experience with life-threatening illness (Lipsyte, 1998), parental bereavement is a "scary and strange," painful, difficult country (Riches & Dawson, 2000). This is a country we have visited indirectly, but to which we have not traveled and in which we do not reside. We have read about it, have had many conversations with people who live there every day, we have done academic research about it, and have been to similar locations, but we have not been in that particular place. So, we lack the direct and painful experiential knowledge about parental bereavement. We have relied on those many people we have known who have this knowledge. This was also a difficult book to write because it immersed us again in the suffering that we encountered, in the words and experiences of bereaved parents themselves.

But this was as well a highly satisfying book to write. We were able to draw on our own clinical experiences and personal reactions, on our own scholarly work on responses to crisis and loss, and on the growing body of literature on grief in general and parental bereavement in particular. Very good work has already been done on parental bereavement, and we have relied greatly on the work of those scholars, clinicians, and parents who already made major contributions to this area. Our intent has not been to supplant, but instead to build on, add to, and perhaps provide some useful recombinations of what has already been done. We also hope that we have provided ways that will help clinicians listen to, understand, and constructively engage bereaved parents. We use the term "expert companion" in describing our approach to helping these parents.

We have written with one broad audience in mind: the general clinical practitioner who is not a specialist in the area of parental response to the loss of a child. These clinicians include social workers, psychologists, pastoral counselors, counselors, psychiatrists, family practice physicians, nurses, and others who are placed in the position to be of potential help to grieving parents, but whose clinical practice is not focused primarily on those persons. Because we are writing primarily for clinicians, citations are primarily intended to illustrate the literature, rather than to cite it exhaustively. Our judgments about this matter may lead some scholarly oriented readers to wish we had been more comprehensive in citing references, and may lead some readers who are less interested in the scholarly data to wish we had perhaps exercised even more "judgment" and made even fewer citations—we hope we have struck a satisfactory balance. In order to help our audiences see how we attempt to be expert companions to bereaved parents, we have included many examples from individual sessions and from support group meetings with parents. These are altered in terms of names and some details to protect identities, but the interactions are preserved in substance.

Finally, a word about general perspectives and cultural contexts. We provide in this book a discussion of some elements to consider to understand grieving parents in their own multicultural contexts. The scholarly research and the clinical and personal experiences that frame our own views in this book are primarily those of a North American and Western European "developed country" tradition. The examples, recommendations, and programmatic ideas we present are most likely to be directly applicable to similar cultural contexts. However, the general underlying foundations of the ideas we present (e.g., focus on understanding individuals in cultural context) may well be usefully applied, with appropriate modifications, in other cultural arenas.

Note

Richard G. Tedeschi and Lawrence G. Calhoun can be reached at the Department of Psychology, University of North Carolina at Charlotte, Charlotte, NC 28223.

ACKNOWLEDGMENTS

We acknowledge our gratitude to those parents who, either in the course of our studies or through our clinical work, have freely and generously shared their experiences, their views, and their stories with us. What we describe in this book is their country, not ours, but we are grateful to those parents who have been willing to help us understand it better. We also appreciate the professional and personal support of the staff at KinderMourn. To Kelly Hamilton, for creating a climate where we can flourish, and especially to long-time colleagues Martha Ausman, Dan Busch, Chris Crawford, Lura McMurray, and Elizabeth Pearce, who have shown so clearly the way to be an expert companion to bereaved parents, we also express our gratitude.

We also thank our professional colleagues who have added so much to the enjoyment of our work and to our understanding; Arnie Cann, our good friend and faculty colleague, who has collaborated with us on many projects, and freely lent us his expertise on so many more; Ryan Kilmer and Rick McAnulty who have helped us broaden our understanding of coping and human behavior. And, to the two colleagues whom we lost much too early, Dr. Jim Selby and Dr. Margaret "Peg" Stanley Hagan, our thanks for the measure of time we had with you. Many of our students have helped in recent years, adding to the contributions of those students who have helped us in years past: Dottie Fulmer, Cheryl Cryder, Deborah Proffitt, Sherry Brabham, Eric Quidley, Dominica Harlan, Amanda Cobb, Kelli Evans, Jennifer Baker, Erin Mills, and Jessica Bryant.

Special thanks to the Department of Psychology and our chair Brian Cutler, and to the College of Arts and Sciences of UNC Charlotte, and to our dean and friend Schley Lyons, who supported our work with a reassignment of duties leave for the first author.

The Experience of Grieving Parents

A voice is heard in Ramah,
lamentation and bitter weeping.
Rachel is weeping for her children;
she refuses to be comforted for her children,
because they are no more.
                    Jeremiah 31:14–16

In the United States in 2000 over 33,000 children under 5 years old, and more than 38,000 between the ages 5 and 24, died (Minino, Arias, Kochanek, Murphy, & Smith, 2002). If we extrapolate from those numbers and think about the numbers of parents, siblings, grandparents, and others with strong psychological connections to the child who has been lost, the number of persons in the United States annually affected by the loss of a child becomes large indeed. Because many bereaved parents will seek help following miscarriages and stillbirths, national statistics may significantly underestimate the number of persons affected by the death of a child. The loss of a child can cause pain that can persist for a lifetime, so the cumulative total number of persons who are at any one time survivors of this tragic loss becomes immense. And, if consideration is given to adults 25 years old and older who die, who are still viewed as children by older parents, the numbers of persons in parental roles affected by the death of children grows even larger.

Although the general focus of this book is on the loss of persons whose chronological age would lead us to designate them as "children," even the death of persons whose age places them well into middle age will represent the loss of a beloved "child" to older persons. Many of those who are touched by the loss of a child may seek support from clinicians in a variety of contexts, even when the loss itself may not be described to the clinical worker as the primary presenting problem.

This book is for clinicians and other people who have an interest in being of help and service to bereaved parents. A reasonable place to start is to try to understand what it may be like to lose a child. It is quite clear that there are limits to such understanding. Even those who have themselves lost a child may, in some instances, have difficulty truly understanding the reactions of other parents whose responses may be different from their own. One general assumption that we will make throughout this book is that bereaved parents are the best source of understanding about their own lives and losses. But we also think that sensitive and careful researchers in the best traditions of trustworthy psychological investigations can also offer helpful information. Some of the most helpful work about grieving parents is reported by careful investigators whose primary goal is to summarize what they have learned from parents in ways that can be helpful to professionals and laypersons alike. (As we mentioned in the preface, however, our citation of supporting sources will be illustrative rather than comprehensive.)

"If you have never been there, you can't possibly know what it is like and I cannot possibly get you to understand." It is not possible for one person to fully inhabit the experience of another. In no context may this be more accurate than when the person we are trying to understand is a bereaved parent, and we are not. Even if two people have shared a "similar" tragedy, individual contexts and responses may differ to such an extent that very little commonality of experience exists. But it is still important to try to understand, to the extent possible, what some of the experiences of bereaved parents may be. When engaged with individual persons, clinicians can rely on their ability to fully attend and empathize to help them in the sometimes difficult task of understanding the experience of their clients. But it is probably also helpful to have some general information about some of the common experiences of grieving parents.

Our focus in this chapter is on providing a broad overview of what grieving parents say their experiences have been like. Although there may well be some universal human responses to the loss of a child, our major sources of information are parents from the industrialized countries of the Northern Hemisphere, and this may place some limits on how these experiences are reflective of other people in other places. In this chapter we try to let parents speak for themselves about the impact of the death of a beloved child.

☐ The Circumstances: Examples

Eddy's Mother

Eddy was not yet a year old when my little cousin got really sick and they didn't know what was wrong with him. They had him tested all over. And finally, they took him to Dr. Reynolds, and he was diagnosed with muscular dystrophy. We didn't know anything about it. My husband read about it and said that it was a hereditary disease and when I saw that, my heart just sank. Once we found out that it was hereditary, both sides of the family were tested, and we found out that it came from our line, and then we were tested, the kids and me. And, well, it only went to boy children; the girls were carriers, but the boys were the ones who got the disease. So we tested Eddy when he was a little over a year old and it came back positive. They told us that kids with this disease could live a normal healthy life until about age seven or eight, then they would get the illness.

And we lived those years, not telling many people about it because we never wanted to be treated differently. And then, almost to the day when he turned seven, he began to act oddly. It's a disease that's so complicated.

. . . So he had to have a tube put in his stomach, and after that anesthesia, he never spoke again. You know, I'm really tearing up and crying here. It is hard for me to think about this because when I talk about it. I . . . I . . . when I talk about it it all just comes back, and it's [pause] it's a tough tough thing. . . .

Three or four months before he died he started having a lot of trouble with his breathing. It was affecting his respiratory system. We knew that's what would happen one day, but he was just not breathing.

The night before he died it was three o'clock in the morning, and I heard her [private duty nurse] call my name. Then I heard her say, "Karen" [mother's name], and then again, I heard my name. I went into the room and I said, "Kirsten [nurse], what's the matter?" And she said, "Nothing, I didn't call you. Go back to sleep." And I said, "I heard you call me twice." And she said, "I didn't call you, you must have been dreaming, just go on back to sleep." And he was really laboring with his breathing. So I said to her, "Go on downstairs and take a nap on the sofa." And so she did, and I got in the bed and stayed with him.

I was just holding him and praying with him, and talking to him. And he was just breathing real hard. About seven o'clock in the morning, she came up and she said she was ready to go, and that she'd see me that night. And I said, "I don't think you will." And she said, "Oh, don't be silly, he's going to be around for a long time yet." I think she thought when she said that that it comforted me, but I didn't want to hear that about the so-called life he was living. . . .

Of course I wanted him to be with me forever, but not like he was. But anyway, I said, "I don't think he'll be here." And she said, "Yes he will. I'll see you tonight." And at eight o'clock the day-shift nurse came. It was Sunday, and we were getting dressed . . . , and I said to her, "He's really breathing funny. I think something's going on." She had my pager number and I said, "Page us immediately if something goes wrong."

And we were just heading out the door, I was coming downstairs and the nurse yelled and I ran back upstairs, and he had stopped breathing. And, thankfully, we were all here, my husband and my daughter, and my best friend from college had come in from North Carolina to visit me that weekend. I hadn't seen her in probably six or seven years and she just came up to visit me. And we were all here and I was with Eddy; and I was glad. I had prayed that that would happen, that we would be with him, that he wouldn't be alone. And he died peacefully. I could never regret or feel guilt over our care for him, or even his life. But even so, [sighs heavily] this is a hard, tough, awful thing to put a human being through.

Gary's Father

It happened real fast. We got a call from one of his real close friends and he came knocking on our door and said that Gary had been in a real bad accident. He tried to comfort us because I think he already knew it was serious. He wanted to know if he could take us. So I just got into my own car and we went there and of course, they wouldn't let us near the scene. But we knew it was real bad.

As far as the circumstances, he had left one Friday afternoon about 7:00 to go out to meet some friends at school for a birthday. He got a call that one of the other friends wanted him to come by to pick her up. So he did and they stopped to get pizza on the way. Coming back from the pizza place they hit a tree. We don't know exactly what happened. I never did ask because I really didn't want to know. I didn't really want to see the car and I didn't want to know what happened. But anyway, what they told me was he went around this curve and hit a tree; it killed both of them. Instantly, I think.

It was very hard to even deal with it. I guess I sort of blocked it out; I really didn't accept it for a long time. I just sort of survived, I guess. . . .

We're always grabbing at something to help us cope. And even after this many years [it has been 11] I still can't really handle it sometimes.

☐ **Shock and Disorientation**

Although certainly responses vary with circumstances, a common experience of grieving parents is to feel some degree of disorientation and shock on learning of a child's death. Following are the responses of several different parents on first learning of their loss.

I know when it first happened [son's death] I went into shock. . . . I had a hard time breathing. Some friends of ours came over at about 2:00 in the morning to sit with us and I was saying things like it's okay, Bobby's gone to heaven and we're going too. He'll be there when we get there. I was saying things like that but I was still in shock.

I think the suddenness of it, well, it was really difficult. I know that when it first happened [son's death in automobile accident] I know I went into shock because I studied a course about that. I had diarrhea and I had a hard time breathing. I was really in shock.

It was just a horrible day, as you can imagine. The worst possible day. It was a God-awful day. The hardest day you can imagine. In fact, *you can't* imagine it, there's nothing can ever prepare you or make you think that you'll ever go through a day that bad.

W. B. Yeats's familiar words seem to express the same sense of disorientation that many newly bereaved parents experience:

Things fall apart; the centre cannot hold;
Mere anarchy is loosed upon the world.

Finkbeiner (1996) quotes one parent, Chris, who said, "I remember for several weeks after she [her daughter] died, whenever I went out in public, I felt like I didn't belong there. I felt like I maybe had come from another world or something."

The death of a child can destroy the parent's understanding of the world and how to make sense out of it. "After a child dies, many beliefs, goals, routines, commitments, and relationships" (Rosenblatt, 2000b, p. 16) simply no longer are applicable. The natural order of things is for the old to die before the young, the parent before the child. The natural order of things is for children to bury their parents, not the other way around. For many bereaved parents, not only is the death of their child unnatural, it is also inconceivable and incomprehensible. Like the devastating earthquake that reduces a city to a pile of amorphous and formless rubble, the death of a child can shatter the parents' understanding of the world and their place in it.

Tom Crider, writing eloquently about his "passage through grief" following the death of his daughter Gretchen said:

I am not who I was. My reason, judgment, and all my defenses have dissolved, leaving me confused and terrified in a world turned suddenly strange. (Crider, 1996, p. 7)

He is like a beggar in winter, clawing through box after box of old coats, looking for one that fits. (Crider, 1996, p. 6)

☐ Exiles

In the preface we described the use of the metaphor of a different "country" (Lypsite, 1998; Riches & Dawson, 2000) to speak of what it is like to become a bereaved parent. An experience of many bereaved parents is a sense of being sent into exile. The death of a child deports parents to a place where they did not want to be. A place characterized by a constellation of experiences and difficulties that are unfamiliar, disorienting, and deeply painful. "We [bereaved parents] are *here*, but those who have not lost a child are *there*. They are alive but we are in the land of the dead."

Rosenblatt (2000b) speaks of how the death of a child creates a "vast chasm" between parents and the rest of the world. One bereaved parent says that "you feel like you're in another dimension that other people can't relate" (Rosenblatt, 2000b, p. 93). Another parent also speaks of feeling disconnected from other people: "How could anyone understand . . . What did people know about losing a child?" (Donnelly, 1982, p. 113). Bereaved parents may experience themselves as being cut off from other people, of being in a different place from which they simply cannot meaningfully connect to the people who are not in the same country, who are on the other side of the chasm.

The experience of being in another place may sometimes be accentuated by choice. Donnelly (1982), for example, describes a couple who voluntarily stayed away from other people, including their close friends. Their need was to be together, with each other, but to avoid other people. After several months the couple made a decision to reconnect with their friends, but ironically this proved difficult, because, in the words of one of the spouses, "[They] were kind of uncomfortable about how to act." The friends did not seem to know the rules for interacting with bereaved parents.

Individuals who share common cultural traditions tend to learn a common set of rules for interacting in certain contexts. These rules are not necessarily formally taught, but as people have repeated exposure to the same general kinds of settings, they tend to develop an understanding of what kinds of behaviors are expected. For example, in the United States standing and yelling is considered appropriate during major sporting events, but not during the performance of a classical ballet in a concert hall. For contexts such as these, most North Americans could readily reach consensus on the social rules that apply. But lack of familiarity with what one is allowed to do, what one is expected to do, and what one should not do in a particular social context can lead us to be uncertain about how to behave (Calhoun, Abernathy, & Selby, 1986). In no context may the lack of clear guidelines be more inhibiting than when encountering another person who has recently undergone the death of a family member.

What are the social rules for interacting with bereaved parents? Few, perhaps none, of the friends of bereaved parents are fully confident about what they should or should not do. The bereaved parent's experience of being in a different place may be due in part to the sense of awkwardness that those who wish to be supportive may feel. Bereaved parents may sense the awkwardness of friends who lack the certain knowledge about how to provide comfort, and the bereaved parent's sense of alienation from the rest of the world is further reinforced. In a more extreme response, lack of knowledge and confidence about how to approach the grieving parent may lead a potentially supportive friend to think:

> "I don't know what to do to help them, so maybe I just won't do anything right now. It's better to do nothing than to do something that would turn out to be wrong."

And the bereaved parent's sense of being on the other side of a vast chasm from their friends is reinforced.

☐ Pain and Suffering

The death of a child is a devastating loss, and to point out that it typically involves severe pain and suffering may well be unnecessary. Although many parents are able to survive and to continue with their lives, at least in some fashion, the experience of excruciating pain is almost universal among bereaved parents.

> He wanted a strenuous climb to release the terrible tension in his body, . . . When he had climbed . . . above the tree line, he decided to perform a ceremony . . . He left the trail . . . He sat in the snow next to a scrub pine and picked one of its weathered cones. With his pocketknife he cut his wrist and covered the pinecone with his blood. He let his tears fall on it before he scratched a hole in the earth and buried it. "Good-bye, Gretchen, good bye. . . . peace, peace, peace." (Crider, 1996, p. 15)

> My body ached, my heart ached. That was the first time that I ever . . . physically felt a broken heart. And I had this . . . pain in me. . . . It was . . . an emotional thing. It was a very, very physical thing, too. (bereaved parent quoted by Rosenblatt, 2000b, p. 84)

There is perhaps no greater pain than that experienced by bereaved parents. Metaphors for the loss and its resulting pain are surely inadequate, but they are plentiful (Klass, 1988; Rosenblatt, 2000) and can help express in images what descriptive words alone cannot. A common metaphor for grief in general, and the loss of a child in particular, is the description of the loss as a kind of amputation.

> The parent, just like the amputee, must begin the long, arduous task of accepting the loss. . . . For the amputee, the raw bleeding stump heals and the physical pain does go away. But he lives with the pain in his heart knowing his limb will never grow back. . . . We bereaved parents must do the same. (Klass, 1988, pp. 12–13)

The metaphor of something cut out or amputated may also be less specific, with parents describing feelings of "emptiness and holes" (Rosenblatt, 2000b, p. 77). Rosenblatt (2000b, p. 77) quotes a bereaved mother identified as Hannah:

> It's like somebody has got into your body and pulled a piece out, and you really don't need it to survive, but you know that hole is there. . . . It's always there, always . . . there's something missing.

A parent, describing her experience with the death of her son, said:

> I just hurt so bad I felt like there was this great big hole in the middle of my chest. It felt like somebody was just twisting my heart and trying to rip it out.

Another metaphor for the loss is the experience of part of the parent dying (Rosenblatt, 2000b) or an even more general sense that in some ways the parents themselves are already dead:

> Part of us died. . . .

> Part of me died when Blake did. (Rosenblatt, 2000b, p. 79)

> It just kind of kills you. You are dead inside. You just can't live again like you used to.

☐ Loss of Daily Functioning

The experience of loss of ability or interest in fulfilling the demands of everyday life is a common one for all types of grief, and not surprisingly it happens for bereaved parents too.

> I could not function . . . I could not do anything to my house, I couldn't cook, I couldn't buy groceries. I could do my job, but even that was sort of automatic, I really didn't have to think about it and I could go and do that. Sometimes I could come home and cook dinner, but I didn't do anything for maybe a year, I guess.

> I was paralyzed. It seemed like I just couldn't do anything. My mind was either blank or filled with thoughts about what happened. I had to drag

myself to do things. I think there is some poem that talks about a head filled with straw. That was how I felt—no brain, just kind of an empty head and a lot of pain. It was months before I felt that I had some ability to think and do things.

This loss of efficiency in meeting the demands of daily life should not be seen by the clinical worker as an indicant of psychopathology. The parent is responding normally to an extremely disorientating and painful circumstance. And loss of efficiency is neither unusual nor a sign of psychiatric symptomatology.

It Never Quite Goes Away

Most bereaved persons, including parents, tend to report a reduction of psychological distress as the months and years pass. But a common experience for parents is that the loss of a child never quite completely recedes from consciousness. Time *may* reduce the intensity and frequency of the grief experience and the distressing thoughts and feelings, but at least periodically many parents experience the reality of the loss. This persistent return of the hurt may continue for years, and perhaps for the remainder of the parent's life. One woman, who in her twenties had experienced the neonatal death of a son who was named Daniel, could never hear the familiar folk tune "Danny Boy" without crying for her lost child; this continued throughout her life—she lived to be 91 years old.

Another parent, speaking 6 years after a son's death said:

> You're never, no matter how good a time you are having, are ever that happy. It is not possible ever again. It just isn't when you have lost something that close to you.

> You'll never get over it. . . . It's just life, but you're so damn down over something like that. . . . You never get over it affecting your life. (Rosenblatt, 2000b, p. 117)

> It's not something that goes away. . . . You don't move on in the same ways that people expect . . . it hurts every day . . . it's just right there on the surface, and it always will be. (Rosenblatt, 2000b, p. 117)

☐ Continuing Connections to the Child

Given the influence of the ideas developed by John Bowlby (which we examine in the next chapter), the parent's experience of a continued connection to the lost child may also be referred to as continued *bonds* or continued *attachments*. Whatever label it is given, this sense of the continued presence of the child, or of the parent's continued psychological connection to the child, whether it is meant literally or metaphorically, is a common theme in the experience of grieving parents.

> We would bring pictures [to the bereaved parents support group] . . . you could just feel everybody feeling more comfortable. My friends would still talk about him [deceased child] and that's the best thing to do is talk about your child. Everybody wants him to be somewhat alive. Not somewhat, but you have to keep him alive for you.

> I needed to know that he was in Heaven . . . and I struggled with this. . . . I opened up my Bible and it opened up to Psalm 73. . . . And the whole time I was reading it, it was like he [deceased son] was just standing there saying it to me.

Klass (1999, pp. 41–42) quotes the father of a stillborn child as follows: "I know that for me you are born still; I shall carry you with me forever, my child, you were always mine, you are mine now."

☐ Growth Amid the Struggle and the Pain

We have done a good bit of clinical and research work on the psychological growth that can come from the struggle with very difficult life circumstances (Calhoun & Tedeschi, 1999; Tedeschi & Calhoun, 1995). And whenever one is discussing posttraumatic growth it is important to repeat that the experience of growth is not the same as the absence of suffering. For most parents the loss of a child produces great pain, and for some the pain experienced and the struggle to survive may be accompanied by an experience of growth. The experience, for example, of seeing oneself as a more compassionate person as a result of coping with loss should not be expected to displace the suffering the parent experiences from the loss. Rather, it may be best to think of the possibility of growth from the struggle, on the one hand, and the reality of suffering on the other hand, as separate domains—a grieving parent may experience both at the same time.

It is also important to remind ourselves that in some circumstances the mere suggestion of the possibility of growth from the struggle can seem insensitive and ignorant. As one person responding to a discussion of the growth that sometimes can arise from the struggle with trauma emphatically said:

> I don't want to hear any bullshit about this being a good thing. It is not a good thing, damn it. This is horrible and there is no way anybody is going to convince me there is the slightest bit of good in any of this.

This unambiguous response is a useful reminder to clinicians. There is *nothing* good about the death of child.

But it is also true that as they proceed in their painful journey of grief, some parents do experience growth arising from their difficult struggle with unbearable loss. It is important to indicate clearly that any growth experienced is viewed as arising from the *struggle* to cope, the struggle to simply survive. Growth from the struggle with suffering can manifest itself in several ways: changes in the self, in relationships with others, in life priorities, and in the domain of spirituality. Following are some of the things bereaved parents have told us that fall into these general categories.

Self

Before people would walk all over me and I would have never said anything back to them. . . . I realize I've been hurt as bad as I can be hurt and had no control over that [child's death] hurt. Other hurts I do have control over. When someone does something to hurt me, I let them know how I feel. (Klass, 1988, p. 35)

I've become more empathetic towards anybody in pain and anybody in any kind of grief. I think that is one reason why I went into oncology nursing.

I can handle things better. Things that used to be big deals aren't big deals to me anymore. Like big crisis problems, they will either work out or they won't. Whichever way it goes, you have to deal with it.

I have changed . . . not that I was a bad person. Maybe I grew up.

There are situations that go on and people say "I can't deal with it." I have never said that. Because I have been through the worst, the absolute worst that I know. And, no matter what happens, I'll be able to deal with it.

There's one other thing I'd like to say, because I feel that it really helped someone and I have been drawn to help when I've found somebody close by who has lost a child. I will contact them and let them know that I'm here for them to talk to if they need me.

Relationships

Our relationship [with spouse] has grown closer and I realized why he was doing what he was doing, because he saw me hurting so bad and he didn't know how to comfort me.

In fact I feel closer to some of my friends than I do my family. . . . When he died people just came out of the woodwork . . . I realize that relationships with people are really important now.

. . . and I cherish my husband a lot more.

Priorities

Your family becomes more important to you [and] your friends. It totally changes your outlook on life.

It has affected the way I look at life. You realize that life is precious and that we don't take each other for granted.

Most definitely I have changed. As a friend of mine would say, "just don't sweat the bullshit." I find myself calmer where before I was sort of Type A personality. Oh, everything bothered me and if everything wasn't just so it bothered me . . . [now] the only things that really concern me are my child and everything sort of takes care of itself one way or another . . . [if] it's not going to change my life I'm not going to worry about it.

Spiritual Matters

Well, God became real to me because I came face to face with Him. And I also know that my son is with Him.

You think about getting through something like that and it's downright impossible to even conceive of how you ever could. But that's the beauty of the thing . . . it's gonna have to be said because I believe that God got me through it. Five or six years ago I didn't have these beliefs. And I don't know what I would do without Him now.

Somebody was watching us, I think to help us. I probably think that more than him, but we had to get the strength from somewhere. (Rosenblatt, 2000b, p. 214)

The experience of growth may well be part of a bigger picture for some parents. However, clinicians should take care not to assume that, because some parents describe growth in the areas described earlier, this is necessarily typical, or there are not negative experiences in these domains—either of these assumptions would be incorrect.

For example, in describing their experiences with spiritual matters, parents with preexisting religious beliefs may well question the reality of a God, or the wisdom of God, or may struggle to reconcile their immeasurable loss with a belief in a just or loving divine being. As one parent told us:

I used to think that God was in control and that if I prayed about something it would probably happen . . . that whole belief was shattered. And so I sorta lost confidence in that faith. . . . I depended on God to keep it [child's death] from happening. So, when it happened, I thought, well, God must have let me down . . . it was so hard to maintain scripture reading and a belief in God.

☐ Parents' Reactions

It is clear that the parent's response to the loss of a child includes strong emotional elements. The intensity of the experience, and the ease with which the parent's internal experience may be noticed by others, may be greater in the first few months after the child's death. But, for many parents, "the pain never quite goes away." And, like an unwanted intruder, the distress associated with the parent's loss may break in unexpectedly for many years. Sadness, yearning, unbearable pain, a sense of having been abruptly disconnected from a previously familiar world—in sum, a general constellation of difficult and painful emotions characterizes the experience of most parents.

Especially in the earlier stages following the child's death, grief can manifest itself in certain cognitive ways too. Shock and disorientation, more likely for sudden or unexpected losses, are common experiences. A reduction in the ability to think clearly, make decisions, and meet the routine demands of everyday life can be present too. The general ways in which the parent makes sense of life and his or her place in the world are disrupted, with some parents experiencing a major shattering of their assumptive worlds. This disruption can increase the sense that parents are "exiles," now disconnected from the known, the safe, the predictable, and the familiar.

The experience of "exile" can also be reflected in the disconnectedness toward others that some parents may feel. The sense of being disconnected from others may be attributable, at least in part, to the parent's own sense of now being different from others who have not lost a child. The perceived difference from others who are not similarly bereaved may, in some instances, make social contact less helpful than it might otherwise be. The sense of being in "exile" may also be partially a result of the general lack of an existing social structure to guide potential comforters in how best to help and support a grieving parent. Others may simply be ignorant about how to approach, talk with, and interact with a bereaved parent. And parents may see others as meaning well, but also as not knowing how to go about providing comfort, or even how to act and behave in the presence of one from the "exile" community.

For most parents, initial feelings of shock and disbelief, the most intense feelings of sadness and loss, the degree of loss of efficiency in daily living, and the experience of disconnectedness from other "non-exiles" decrease in intensity and frequency over time. However, it is also the case that for many parents, although typically occurring with less ferocity as time passes, the sense of yearning and sadness at a great loss will never quite go away. To paraphrase the ancient Hebrew prophet Jeremiah, Rachel cannot be comforted, because her children are no more.

What do these descriptions mean for clinicians? Clinicians should use these general descriptions of the responses of grieving parents only as general guidelines. Although it is likely that most bereaved parents will present with many of these kinds of responses, the clinician should always respond to the individual parent, within the individual social and cultural contexts in which the parent is immersed. The clinician needs to be prepared to see a wide array of individual differences in how grief is experienced and expressed. *Clinicians need to be particularly on guard not to assume* that, when parents' responses deviate from what the *clinician* believes to be the typical parental grief response, the divergence is indicative of something wrong with those individual parents or with the way they are responding to their loss.

In this introductory chapter we have described some of the general and common responses of bereaved parents. This summary is indeed illustrative of the typical responses of many bereaved parents. It is important to keep in mind, however, that what is statistically typical is not necessarily reflective of individuals. The stories and experiences of each parent are different, and the potential helper should listen for the individual's own unique account and attend to each person's individual response.

Grief Perspectives, Models, and Myths

Give sorrow words: the grief that does not speak
Whispers the o'er-fraught heart and bids it break.
Shakespeare, *Macbeth*

Our human struggle with loss is nothing new. Some of the most ancient remnants of modern humans are archeological sites related to death and burial. Ancient texts, some of which still have great meaning for many people today, speak powerfully of the impact of the death of a loved one. For example, the Jewish Bible, also called by Christians the Old Testament, records the tragic story of an attempt by one of King David's sons, Absalom, to seize the throne. The son is assassinated and he is found hanging from a tree branch. David's words, on hearing of his son's death, still speak for many contemporary grieving parents:

> The king was deeply moved and went up to the chamber over the gate and wept. And thus he said as he walked, *"O my son Absalom, my son, my son Absalom! Would I had died instead of you, O Absalom, my son, my son!"*

However, the systematic attempt to understand the grief process, and to employ that understanding in a way designed to best assist mourners, is a relatively modern undertaking. It is also a useful undertaking in two broad ways. General theories about grief can provide guidance to researchers who wish to study the reactions of bereaved persons about how to accomplish their task. In a similar vein, applied theories of grief can provide

15

the clinician with a helpful framework to use in making decisions about how to provide the most helpful response to bereaved persons who seek their help.

In this chapter we first examine some of the earlier modern formulations that influenced the course of our understanding of the bereavement process, and then we then look at two contemporary models of grief. Our overview of perspectives and models is selective, with a focus on those that seem to have had the most impact on how clinicians think about grieving clients, and that appear to be supported by research and deeper understanding of the grief process. (More research-focused, comprehensive reviews of models of grief are available elsewhere [e.g., Stroebe, Hansonn, Stroebe, & Schut, 2001a].) In addition, we look at some of the assumptions about grief that may not be completely accurate, that is, the "myths" about loss and mourning that may still have significant influence on the expectation many mental health professionals have about how grief does, or should, unfold. We begin first, however, with a brief discussion of what the words *perspective* and *model* mean in the present context.

☐ Perspectives and Models

We use the word *perspective* to mean what is usually meant when the word *theory* is used—a general conceptual framework that helps the scholar or clinical worker organize information about something. The word *perspective* communicates more explicitly that one is looking at something from a particular point of view. Just as in the old anecdote about the wise men and the elephant (in which one focused on the trunk, another on the leg, and yet a third on the elephant's side, with each drawing a very different conclusion about the nature of the beast), trying to understand something from a particular perspective is going to influence, as well as possibly limit, what we can understand about that something. Whether we call the framework a perspective, theory, paradigm, or school of thought, essentially the same thing is meant. A *perspective is a set of assumptions* that scholars or clinicians rely upon to tell them *what to observe and pay attention to* and *how to observe and how to make sense out of what has been observed.* The word *model* means pretty much the same thing, although it tends to be a word that is applied to a more restricted range of things. One might speak of a theory or perspective on human behavior on the one hand, and might speak about a model of parental grief on the other. For our purposes, however, we regard the words *perspective* and *model* as roughly synonymous. In this chapter we look at some of the perspectives on grief and bereavement that have influenced counselors' understanding of grief and some of the best ways to be of help to grieving persons in general, and bereaved parents in particular.

☐ Earlier Modern Perspectives on Mourning and Grief

Many readers will readily identify the name of the individual who articulated what is viewed as perhaps the first widely influential modern perspective on mourning: Sigmund Freud. Freud is today one of those writers who is still often referenced, but rarely read anymore. Although modified and sometimes considerably diluted, Freud's ideas are still powerfully influential, often in unrecognized ways. His influence is certainly present in the assumptions that many clinical workers make about the grief process and how they should approach bereaved clients.

Freud's Perspective

Sigmund Freud developed his theories about human behavior in general, and therapeutic interventions in particular, based on a limited sample of clients, primarily 19th century, middle-class European women. He never did what psychologists in the 21st century would call systematic research. However, the comprehensive theory that he formulated, and his paper, *Mourning and Melancholia* (Freud, 1917/1957), still have an impact on how many clinicians think about the grief process. It is always a challenge to try to identify the main assumptions of Freud's perspective, because he not only wrote extensively, but also revised his ideas over his many years of writing. But there are some of his ideas that are important to specify, because either directly or indirectly (for example, through revisions of his original ideas by others) they influence what many clinicians still assume about grief.

One of Freud's core ideas was that human psychology was strongly influenced by forces outside of the individual's conscious awareness. A key assumption of Freud's was that *much, if not most, mental activity goes on in the unconscious*. The individual's conscious experience and feelings, and whether or not that person exhibits signs of psychological problems, are a direct result of what is happening in the unconscious domain of psychological activity. This general assumption is a key component of his most influential paper on the grief process, *Mourning and Melancholia*, originally published in 1917. In that paper Freud's primary focus was on trying to explain melancholia, that is, clinical depression, by utilizing what he assumed was the typical process that occurred when an individual experienced a serious loss, such as the death of a loved one. He provided a brief description of the typical components of grief, and some of these were feeling of pain, loss of interest, loss of the ability to develop meaningful intimate connections with "new" people (his terminology was new "love object"), and a tendency to think a lot about the deceased loved one. Freud also suggested that mourning "passes off after a certain time has elapsed" (Freud, 1917/1957, p. 163).

But Freud's most influential idea may well have been his suggestion that *in order successfully to adapt to the loss, the grieving person's psychological systems need to engage in an active processing of the loss.* This "work" needs to be done if the person is to adapt satisfactorily to the loss. He referred several times to what we today would call grief work. He talked about "the absorbing work of mourning" (p. 155), "the work of mourning" (p. 157), and "the work of grief" (p. 169). The general idea was that the external signs of grief are the surface manifestations of the internal, mostly unconscious, processes that the individual's psychological systems are employing to eventually eliminate the psychological investment in the deceased loved one, making it possible for that psychological investment then to be transferred to new intimate relationships. When the work of grief was successfully completed, then the person would have succeeded in successfully adapting to the loss.

At least two of Freud's specific ideas about grief seem to still have considerable, if often modified, influence in how many clinical workers understand the grieving person. One idea that is still highly influential is the assumption that a significant amount of the individual's psychological activity in response to loss occurs out of conscious awareness. For example, when a bereaved person is described as being "in denial," the speaker is articulating a point of view quite compatible with Freud's assumption that people can be quite unaware of their own mental processes. An assumption that some counselors still make represents an extension of this idea of Freud's. It is the idea that the unconscious responses to grief occur in all bereaved persons, and that the absence of surface expression of the emotions experienced may be evidence that the "work of grief" is not progressing satisfactorily. The clinical worker may make the assumption, then, that the grieving person may need some form of therapeutic encouragement to access the internal state that is assumed to indeed be present, but beyond the person's full conscious awareness. As we show later in this chapter, this is an assumption that may not necessarily be accurate in most, perhaps even in all, instances of parental bereavement.

A second, and still current, assumption that reflects Freud's ideas about the work of grief is the clinical belief that individuals who are grieving the loss of a loved one may *need* to engage in the complicated psychological process of the "work of grief." The hypothesis is that if the individual does not actively engage in "grief work," psychological difficulties will result later on. This assumption can sometimes lead to an additional idea, that clinicians need actively to encourage grieving clients to consciously experience and to overtly express highly distressing emotions. Clinicians who assume that "grief work" is necessary to cope successfully with bereavement also owe a debt to Freud, and to those who have developed his ideas about the grief process. One of them was Erich Lindemann.

Erich Lindemann's Perspective

On November 28, 1942, fire destroyed the Cocoanut Grove nightclub in Boston, Massachusetts. There were about 1,000 occupants in the club and almost half, 492 persons, lost their lives. Lindemann became involved in providing psychiatric services to some of the survivors (Lindemann, 1979), and he subsequently conducted interviews with 101 bereaved persons, some of whom were bereaved survivors of the Cocoanut Grove disaster or their close relatives. His observations on grief were published in 1944, and they became perhaps the clinical description of grief that had the greatest influence on clinicians in the United States in the 20th century.

Lindemann's (1944) descriptions greatly influenced subsequent assumptions about grief in at least three broad areas: what constitutes "normal grief," what the course of normal grief is, and what constitutes abnormal grief. In what today might be regarded as a slightly contradictory heading, Lindemann described the "symptomatology of normal grief." "Normal" grief included a preoccupation with the deceased, problems with daily functioning, feelings of guilt and hostility, altered sense of experience (e.g., depersonalization), and somatic distress. In describing the course of grief, Lindemann echoed some of Freud's ideas when he indicated that the course of grief depended on the success with which the bereaved person successfully had done "the *grief work*" (p. 143). Successful grief work resulted in adjustment to the world without the deceased loved one, with the formation of new relationships.

Lindemann identified two general categories of what he termed "morbid," that is, abnormal, pathological grief reactions. One he called "delayed grief," in which he described an absence of the expression of the distress and discomfort of "normal grief." At some later time, perhaps even years later, the individual would then experience significant signs of psychological distress caused by the failure to work through the past loss. Delayed grief was expected to manifest itself by signs such as those he observed in an adolescent who had lost both parents and her boyfriend in the Cocoanut Grove fire: "marked feelings of depression, intestinal emptiness, tightness in the throat, frequent crying, and preoccupation with her deceased parents" (p. 144).

A second category of abnormal grief Lindemann labeled "distorted reactions" and among these he listed overactivity without a sense of loss, furious hostility, and agitated depression. Such distortions of normal grief were viewed by Lindemann as "surface manifestations of an unresolved grief reaction" (p. 144). This is another way of saying that grief can become problematic when the individual does not successfully complete "grief work." Lindemann's assumption that people engage in grief work, and that such work is necessary for successful psychological adjustment to the loss of a loved one, has been highly influential. Although there is now some debate about whether this assumption is correct, the matter has not been entirely settled, as we show when we discuss some of the possible "myths" about grief.

John Bowlby's Attachment Perspective

John Bowlby also was trained in the psychoanalytic tradition, but greatly revised many of the main assumptions of that perspective, as he developed *attachment theory*. Bowlby's attachment theory was designed to apply to a much broader arena than grief, but his views have had a major impact on the conceptualization of the grief process (Fraley & Shaver, 1999). A central assumption of the attachment perspective is that because they have enhanced the chances of species survival, attachments, strong connections, develop between infants and their primary caregivers, typically, but not always, their mothers. When very young children and "mother figures" are separated, there is intense distress and protest, and the child anxiously "searches" for the missing caregiver.

One of Bowlby's key observations was that the responses of persons who are grieving are similar to those of young children separated from their primary caregivers. Just as a young child may go through a series of rather predictable responses, in trying to reestablish contact with the parent from whom he or she has been separated, Bowlby suggested that a similar set of phases tends to occur in the grief process (Bowlby, 1980; Bowlby & Parkes, 1970). There is an initial sense of numbness after the loss, followed by highly distressing yearning and "searching" for the deceased person, with subsequent disorganization and despair, and finally psychological reorganization. This idea that grief occurred in "stages" was highly influential, and perhaps because Kübler-Ross (1969) at about the same time identified the stages of dying, the assumption that grief occurs in a series of predictable, identifiable, and sequential stages became part of the way many people thought about grief (Sanders, 1999), a somewhat more restrictive conceptualization than Bowlby probably originally intended. The assumption of stages of grief subsequently led to significant debate about the accuracy and utility of viewing grief as occurring in sequential stages (Wortman & Silver, 1989), and we look a bit more closely at this debate a bit later in this chapter.

From the attachment perspective, an important assumption is that how the individual processes the attachment with the deceased loved one is a key ingredient in how well that person can cope, and eventually satisfactorily come to terms with, the loss of a loved one. The perspective also allows for the possibility that attachments to the lost loved one can continue, even after the loved one's death. More recent elaborations on this theme suggest that a sense of attachment to the deceased is not unusual (Rosenblatt, 2000b; Talbot, 2002), and, unlike some other perspectives (such as Freud's, for example), such attachments can be viewed as a component of adaptive grieving. Bereaved parents may continue to experience a deep and meaningful connection to the child who has been lost. This continuing attachment can be a helpful one for many parents.

Parkes's Perspective

Colin Murray Parkes, who early in his career worked with John Bowlby, has made contributions in both the theoretical understanding of the grief process and the research on the experience of grief. A major contribution to the understanding of grief was his development of the concept of "psychosocial transitions" (Parkes, 1970), which he applied to many kinds of difficulties in life, including the death of a loved one. Central to the understanding of psychosocial transitions is the concept of the *assumptive world*. The assumptive world represents the totality of what the individual knows or thinks he knows. "It includes our interpretation of the past and our expectation of the future, our plans and our prejudices" (Parkes, 1970, p. 103). The assumptive world includes our general understanding of who we are, the organizing beliefs that we use to make sense out of what happens to us, our general expectations about our daily lives, the expectations we have and the assumptions we make about the world around us, such as our general sense of safety, our sense of control over what direction our lives take, and our general expectation of predictability in our lives (Janoff-Bulman, 1992).

With a major life change, such as the death of a loved one, significant components of the assumptive world are affected. The psychosocial transition makes many of the assumptions previously held invalid. For example, the woman whose beloved husband has suddenly died of a heart attack can no longer view her world as predictable or safe, her understanding of herself as part of a couple is no longer valid, and the ideas she had about the way that she should plan and organize her days will likely no longer be completely applicable. The phrase "her world was shattered" directly applies from this perspective, because the death of a loved one may very well create major damage to the individual's assumptive world. As Crider wrote, "[I am] confused and terrified in a world turned suddenly strange" (Crider, 1996, p. 7).

At the center of this point of view is the assumption that coping with the loss of a loved one involves coping with the changes in the assumptive world. Coping with the change, such as the death of a loved one, means that individuals are called on to make changes in the assumptive world. It is this process of rebuilding the assumptive world that is assumed to be at the heart of dealing with bereavement. The central component of grief involves the complicated rebuilding of the damaged assumptive world. The new, changed, and rebuilt assumptive world can be a "healthy" one (Parkes, 1970, p. 106), leading to a satisfactory transition through grief. Or, the revised assumptive world can be an unhealthy one where the assumptive world is distorted or maladaptive in some way, leading to grief-related problems, such as "chronic grief" (Rando, 1993). Clinicians whose interventions contribute to the client's rebuilding of an adaptive assumptive world will have done much to assist the bereaved individual who has sought professional help.

Models Still Have Influence

These earlier models of the grief process still influence the assumptions that many clinicians make about bereaved parents. The general views of Freud and Lindemann, that individuals *must* engage in a process of painful confrontation and experience with their loss, is one that is still influential. Clinicians will indeed need to be willing to listen to the painful self-disclosures of bereaving parents, and sometimes it may indeed by appropriate to gently encourage parents to talk about matters that may be distressing. But it may be unwise to encourage painful emotions, simply because the clinician makes the assumption that the experience of pain represents what these earlier models suggested were requirements—the painful process of "grief work." It is likely that most parents do indeed struggle with coming to terms with their loss, but the absence of what has been termed "grief work" is not necessarily a sign of pathology, as we explore later in this chapter.

☐ Two Contemporary Models of Grief

As we have indicated, the word *model*, as it is typically used in social and behavioral research, describes a set of assumptions and fundamental ideas that tends to be somewhat more limited than a "theory" or a "perspective." A "model" is in a sense a miniperspective, and in the present case a perspective on grief, and grief only. Although there are several different models of grief that have been proposed (Rubin, 1981; Sanders, 1999; Stroebe & Schut, 1999; Walter, 1996), there is no single one that has been widely adopted. As illustrations of contemporary models of grief, we briefly describe the "two-track model" of bereavement (Rubin, 1981) and the "dual process" model of grief (Stroebe & Schut, 1999, 2001).

The Two-Track Model

Rubin (1981) described two main antecedent models of the grief process. One model was the psychodynamic view articulated by Freud (described earlier), and the other he called the "personality change" model. In his proposal for a "two-track" model, Rubin synthesized these two points of view and added some elements of his own. One of the two tracks involves the general impact of the loss on the individual's general level of functioning, and the other track involves how the individual processes the psychological attachments to the deceased. The two-track model included a description of the stages through which grieving individuals are assumed to progress, on each of the two tracks, as they respond to the loss (Rubin, 1981). Soon after the loss the individual needs to begin accepting the reality of the loss, and to begin the difficult process of detaching the affectional bonds to the deceased. In addition, changes in functioning also are likely to occur. Then, both personality changes and the process of detachment from the deceased continue, and may mutually influence each other. Finally, the detachment process reaches a conclusion and whatever changes in personality functioning have occurred become stabilized.

This particular model, then, suggests that two main areas are involved in what happens to grieving persons. A main point of focus is the psychological bonds the individual had with the deceased, and how those bonds are revised as times goes by. As with Freud's idea, the eventual goal is for the psychological investment that the individual had with the deceased to be ended, and for that psychological energy to be invested elsewhere. A second main point of focus is on the individual's general level of functioning, and how well grieving persons do in restoring, over time, some sort of psychological balance in lives.

The Dual Process Model

As its name implies, the dual process model includes two major components (Stroebe & Schut, 1999). One component is the kind of coping in which the bereaved person engages, and the other is the degree of oscillation in the coping process over time.

The first component is the "loss versus restoration orientation" (Stroebe & Schut, 1999, p. 209). Individuals who have lost a loved one may focus on aspects of the loss itself, engaging in psychological work that is similar to what Freud and Bowlby described as necessary in grief. This process of thinking a lot about the deceased, trying to understand the events that led to the death, missing and yearning for the deceased, reflects the "loss orientation." When the individual is oriented to the loss, he or she is in the process of coming to terms with what has happened. Coming to terms with loss, although it certainly can involve significant distress and emotional pain, can also include remembering the good times and focusing on positive interpretations of aspects of the loss—for example, being relieved that the deceased no longer has to suffer. "Restoration orientation" describes the focus on secondary stressors occurring as a result of the loss. In a sense, it describes the focus on "what do I have to do now that he/she is gone?" This restoration orientation includes, for example, the development of a new identity (no longer wife but widow), new tasks that must be performed (need to learn how to cook or do the income taxes), and addressing any issues that have arisen as a result of the loved one's death (what is to be done with the vacation cottage).

The second component of the dual process model is "oscillation." Clinicians who have significant experience with grieving clients, and persons who have themselves faced the challenge of bereavement know full well that bereaved persons "oscillate," but it is surprising that previous models of grief have not explicitly included this component. According to this model, grieving persons can oscillate between coping by having a loss orientation at some times, and by having a restoration orientation at others. In addition, the bereaved person may oscillate between openly confronting the loss and at times avoiding active engagement with the loss. Sometimes the grieving person actively engages in what needs to be done to cope (e.g., dealing with implementation of the will) and at other times the person prefers to be distracted from what needs to be done (e.g., "let's not think about this anymore right now, let's go to a movie"). An important additional assumption of this model has direct relevance to clinical practice: "Oscillation is . . . fundamental to adaptive coping" (Stroebe & Schut, 2001, p. 58). Bereaved persons would be expected to fare better psychologically if they engage in restoration-oriented coping at some times and loss-oriented coping at others, and if they sometimes directly work at confronting what needs to be done, but at other times engage in some protective distracting avoidance of the realities of the loss, perhaps even accepting the possibility of good coming from the struggle with loss. Although this assumption is intriguing, and some data appear supportive, it is not a proposition for which there is clear and unambiguous empirical support (Stroebe & Schut, 2001).

☐ Myths About Grief?

In 1989, Camille Wortman and Roxanne Silver published a paper that began quite a bit of controversy that continues until the present. The main focus of their article was on the "myths of coping with loss." Relying on empirical studies of the psychological impact of the death of a loved one and other forms of loss (e.g., losing the ability to walk as a result of injury), the authors identified assumptions that they believed were widely held, but which were either not supported or were actively contradicted by research studies. In this section we look at some of the possible myths that clinicians may hold about bereavement and the grief process, building on and expanding a bit on the ideas of Wortman and Silver (1989, 2001).

Is Severe Psychological Distress Universal?

Is it a myth that *all* persons who lose a loved one experience a rather predictable set of distressing psychological responses? The answer appears to be yes, it is a myth. But if the question is slightly rephrased, the answer may change. Do *a significant majority* of bereaved persons in general, and bereaved parents in particular, tend to experience high levels of psychological pain and distress? The answer is yes (Stroebe et al., 2001a). For example, a large percentage of grieving parents report significant levels of distress, at least on some occasions, after the death of a child (Leahy, 1992–1993).

In the previous chapter we presented a composite picture of the grief experiences reported by bereaved parents. On average, most grieving parents will experience many of those responses. But clinicians do not work with averages, they work with individual people, couples, and families, and one must be extremely cautious when relying on group averages to make decisions about how best to help in individual cases. The research data appear quite convincing in contradicting the belief that all bereaved persons will experience intense distress. Even if intense distress is typical, and in most circumstances it is likely to be, it is important to remember that severe distress is *not* inevitable, even in the most tragic circumstances. If clinicians assume that severe distress is inevitable and absolutely universal (although it is indeed very common), they may inadvertently allow this assumption to guide their clinical responses in ways that are not helpful to the client. Although low in probability, it is indeed possible that some parents may not experience extreme levels of pain and suffering. Or parents may, because of the cultural contexts and social factors that influence how they respond to their loss, present themselves in ways that may not evidence the level of emotional distress clinicians expect. And, to the extent that clinicians fail to respect and accept either the level of suffering the parent is actually experiencing, or that the parent is able comfortably to express, then in their desire to "push" parents to experience or express their pain, clinicians may inadvertently engage in responses that are not helpful, or may indeed be hurtful to the client. We discuss this pitfall in chapter 7, where we address issues that clinicians who serve the bereaved are likely to face.

In addition, practicing clinicians are quite aware that even when people are dealing with the same general sets of circumstances, individuals differ in the particular kinds of responses they will have and in the pattern of their responses over time. For example, it is quite common for grieving parents to experience very high levels of psychological pain. Different people will experience the pain in different ways, and some parents will experience less intense pain than others. Following are descriptions from grieving parents.

> [At first] I was in shock for a long time and had trouble sleeping. Every time I would lie down to go to sleep I couldn't sleep and my heart would start pounding . . . I was so sad and hurt and in so much pain. I can't even begin to describe the pain.

> I just didn't want to accept it. I would come home from lunch just knowing he was going to write. You just knew this was going to happen, but, of course it didn't. . . . I guess I decided he wasn't going to come home. There are so many questions, and I was just angry. Your heart hurts so bad.

> She did have leukemia and suffered for years and then died. So you have to put it in perspective. No, I didn't want this to happen but you know it did and the outcome was not what I wanted. But it's easier to a point knowing where she is [with God].

> Right now [her child died some years ago] we're in a real good place in our lives. My husband's job is good and the boys are healthy and starting new lives in college and I am excited about that. . . . We were all here [when she died] and I was with her and I was glad. She died peacefully. . . . She was a great kid. She had a good, short life.

To a degree, the question at the beginning of this section may be of primary interest to academic researchers. But it has great importance for the practicing clinician as well. How do *you* expect grieving parents to act? If the parent whom you are trying to support fails to show great pain and distress, what conclusions will you draw about the parent, about what the central aim of counseling should be, and about the potential presence of psychological problems that go beyond grief alone? The available data suggest that there will indeed be some bereaved persons who fail to show the overt signs of intense distress that have traditionally been associated with grief, especially in modern European and North American traditions: crying, dressing in particular ways at certain times and places, and showing general signs of sadness and distress.

In addition, bereaved people do not experience the same psychological states all the time. As Stroebe and Schut (1999) remind us, oscillation occurs in bereaved persons, with difference kinds of responses and concerns becoming salient at different times. As we have often heard bereaved parents say, "I have some bad days; I have some not so bad days."

Does the Absence of Distress Indicate Psychological Problems?

In June 2001, a woman in the United States was arrested and charged with drowning her five children. The woman's husband, the children's father, later spoke with reporters for the first time after learning the horrible truth. Although his eyes appeared red, he spoke calmly and without displaying a great deal of emotional distress. His voice did not break, he did not cry, and he communicated clearly with the reporters present. To some he must have appeared "cool and collected." If you viewed this man on television, knowing the extent of his recent loss, what inferences would you make about the appropriateness of his response? What would you infer about his psychological functioning?

One bereaved parent described the following responses, which also do not reveal much about the individual's inner pain.

> Well, going back to that point in time. Of course I had to be really strong for the other two [children]. I stayed really busy. I started playing tennis a lot more. I just started doing things. I'd go to civic functions and things like that so I wouldn't be sitting at home.

To the extent that clinicians in such cases find themselves making automatic inferences about "denial" or "absent grief," then those clinicians may be accepting one of the myths of coping with loss. We have discussed the issue of "denial" in the context of traumatic losses elsewhere (Calhoun & Tedeschi, 1999), but it is also appropriate to discuss the matter here. The phrase "in denial" has become part of popular culture, perhaps as a consequence of books that have been written to help persons who experienced significant abuse as children or persons who have problems with substance use.

Denial is a psychological defense mechanism through which elements of experience that are intolerable in some way are rejected from consciousness (Sarason & Sarason, 2001). In contemporary use, the words *suppression* and *repression* may be used interchangeably with the word denial (technically these words differ in their meanings). In order for the clinician accurately to describe someone's response as "denial" the clinician must know what the objective reality is (e.g., knowing that a woman's child has died) and also have reliable knowledge that the person is not capable of consciously accepting that reality (e.g., the woman gives clear evidence that she is not aware that her child has died). Although denial as a response to the death of a child is possible, it is not at all typical, and the clinician needs to have a lot of reliable information before accurately identifying a person's response as evidence of denial.

Furthermore, we have the corrective of research on grief that informs us that there are indeed people, although usually not a majority, who experience great losses and who do not show signs of, and perhaps may actually not experience, extreme degrees of psychological pain and distress (Wortman & Silver, 2001). Given what the research tells us and what practicing clinicians know, it is not unreasonable to expect grieving persons, particularly grieving parents, to be highly distraught about their loss. However, *unless there is clear and strong evidence to the contrary, the clinician should not assume that the absence of clear distress is indicative of psychological distortion or psychopathology.*

But what about "delayed grief"? Are not bereaved persons who show little or no grief response at the time of loss at risk for significant problems later on? Or as one student once asked—"if they don't get in touch with their feelings then, won't they surely have troubles as a result later on?" The short answer is no. And, recalling our definition of perspective at the beginning of this chapter, the answer depends on what assumptions we make about how best to understand grieving people.

The idea that individuals can experience delayed grief is based on an essentially psychodynamic (i.e., in the general tradition of Freud) perspective. The assumption is that grief is a universal phenomenon, that everybody who loses a loved one undergoes a significant amount of upheaval in the internal psychological systems, and a lot of that upheaval is out of the individual's conscious awareness. The expectation is that if the grieving individual does not show clear signs, through the overt expression of grief, that the internal psychological systems are working toward readjustment, then that individual will not reach a satisfactory resolution of the loss. And, at some later point, that failure to resolve the loss will erupt in some form of psychological difficulties, perhaps, as Lindemann argued, in "delayed grief."

In general, however, the available information from longitudinal studies of bereaved people indicates that if they occur at all, such delayed grief reactions are quite rare. It seems more reasonable to assume that delayed grief reactions, caused by failure to experience sufficient levels of distress in the time soon after the loss, will not occur at all (Wortman & Silver, 2001).

The implications for clinical practice seem clear. When the client is *a bereaved parent who may not be showing clear and strong signs of distress, it is better for the clinician to accept and respect the parent's mode of grieving.* The cultures that influence the client's expression of grief may differ from those of the clinician (we discuss the importance of understanding the parents' cultural contexts in a later chapter), and, in addition, the available research indicates that there are some people who will not overtly exhibit clear signs of psychological distress. Our recommendation is that the clinician accept that. *When the bereaved parent is not showing clear signs of distress, the clinician should proceed with great caution before trying to create a context in which the client is coaxed into "experiencing" highly distressing emotions.* Although there is no clear consensus on the matter, the data suggest that the experience of severe distress in early bereavement may predict greater distress for the future (Wortman & Silver, 1989, 2001). This suggestive data should give the clinician pause before goading clients into experiencing painful psychological states during therapy sessions in order to break through what the clinician has determined to be "denial."

Is It *Necessary* for Bereaved People to "Work Through" the Loss?

The idea that people "work through" a loss is derived from the ideas of Freud, Lindemann, and Bowlby. From these points of view, it is assumed that the psychological investment (Freud's word for this was *cathexis*), or attachment, that the bereaved had for the deceased must be satisfactorily modified. The grieving person, as we have previously discussed, was expected to do the "grief work" of reestablishing psychological equilibrium by detaching the psychological investment in the deceased, and shifting that psychological investment into new relationships. The work of grief was assumed to be difficult but also necessary. From this perspective, if the bereaved person does not "work though" the loss, then psychological difficulties will be expected to arise later. Failure at working through the loss was expected, for example, to produce depression, delayed grief, and other problems (Lindemann, 1944).

The idea of the necessity, and if not the necessity at least the great desirability, of "grief work" is one that seems to still be part of the way many mental health professionals think (Wortman & Silver, 2001). How would the clinician decide if an individual were indeed working though the loss?

It appears that one of the practical ways in which psychotherapists make a rough evaluation of the presence of active and successful "grief work," is by observing the degree to which the grieving person expresses reactions culturally associated with grief. More particularly, the clinician may look for the expression of grief emotions considered appropriate by the standards of the clinician's own professional culture. To decide if a client is appropriately processing the loss, clinical workers may look for the bereaved persons' expression of feelings related to the loss and to their current psychological state, signs that the person is thinking frequently about the deceased and the loss, indications that the grieving person feels sad, greatly misses the deceased, and is actively trying to accept and "come to terms with the death" (Wortman & Silver, 2001, p. 411). Some counselors may think more in terms of the "tasks" (Worden, 1991) that the bereaved person needs to complete in order to satisfactorily adapt to the loss. The general assumption is the same: certain "tasks," certain kinds of "grief work," need to be completed, and the clinician will try to determine how successfully the grieving person is engaging in those tasks.

Must the grieving person engage in "grief work" or must the person satisfactorily complete certain "tasks" as part of the grief process? The answer appears to be a cautious no. Congruent with one of the central themes that we articulate in this book, no single set of responses should be expected from every grieving person. Clinicians need to respond to the individual person, couple, and family, doing their best to understand those persons in the context of the many social and cultural factors that influence them, attending to the unique ways in which individuals can satisfactorily come to terms with tragic loss. And some of those unique ways of coping with loss may very well differ from the general ideas that clinicians either have explicitly been taught or have adopted based on the influences that have shaped their own perspective on the process of grief.

We will repeat this admonition, but it seems useful to articulate it here too. *The assumption that all grieving persons must go through the same process of "grief work" appears to be incorrect.* The psychotherapist must therefore be very cautious before engaging in deliberate attempts to get clients to experience certain kinds of distressing emotions or psychological states in order to help them "work through" their grief. Sometimes helpful therapeutic interventions can lead individuals to temporarily experience some distress (e.g., bringing in a photo and telling about the deceased child). But these should not be done merely to encourage the grieving person to experience painful psychological states, on the assumption that this will encourage "grief work." Such "therapeutic" manipulations may accomplish the opposite of their therapeutic goal by actually making the grief process more painful and difficult for the bereaved individual (Wortman & Silver, 2001).

When Will the Parent "Recover"?

You have heard it too. The newsperson reporting on a tragedy in which school children were gunned down by a classmate may use phrases such as "so that the healing can begin," or "counselors will be on hand to help students come to terms with . . ." Laypersons and clinicians alike may make an assumption that after a certain period of time the bereaved person will eventually reach a state of recovery in which they are psychologically back to normal. The expectation may be that grieving persons will eventually "heal," "come to terms with," or "reach closure." Clinicians who assume that "grief work" is either necessary or helpful may assume that once the work is satisfactorily completed, that the bereaved will once again be functioning "normally."

In the past many clinicians tended to assume that grieving persons would be "recovered" within 6 months to 1 year after the death of a loved one (Calhoun, Selby, & King, 1976). There are indeed studies that suggest that people who have been bereaved for shorter periods tend to report higher levels of psychological distress than people whose loss occurred several years in the past (Rubin, 1981). But on the other hand, there are also many people who either may never return to the preloss baseline, or may take many years before their experience of distress related to the loss is significantly diminished (Wortman & Silver, 2001). So although some grieving persons may return to some form of preloss emotional baseline, there are also others who will retain some of the pain of their loss for the rest of their lives. *Should, then, grieving people be expected to "recover"? Especially with bereaved parents, universal expectations of "recovery" or "closure" are unreasonable.*

What kinds of expectations should clinicians have, then, for the psychological functioning over time of their clients for whom grief is a central source of pain and distress? Should clinicians not be concerned about painful grief that persists for years? Certainly we should, because helping clients cope is one our main jobs. But it is important to maintain a perspective that recognizes that *for some grieving parents, a return to a preloss level of functioning will simply not occur.* And further, even when the pain of loss persists for years, it is not necessarily desirable to consider that persistence as a sign of pathology or psychological maladjustment. While maintaining the general point of view that for many people "recovery" will not occur, doing one's clinical best to help grieving persons come to terms with their loss and to experience less pain and distress in their daily lives is also highly desirable. It is not necessary to regard long-lasting grief as a disorder in order to try to help clients come to terms with the loss of a loved one.

Does the Grief Process Unfold in Stages?

As previously indicated, the assumption that the grief process unfolds in stages has been held by many mental health practitioners. In his book *No Such Thing as a Bad Day* (Jordan, 2000), Hamilton Jordan describes his life, with a focus on his experiences dealing with three major types of cancer. Early in the book he tells how he is awaiting the results of medical tests, including a biopsy of a mass in his chest. A friend who is a counselor comes to visit him. She describes the psychological stages (based on Kübler-Ross's ideas) through which people are assumed to go when facing a serious illness: denial, anger, bargaining, depression, and finally acceptance. Interestingly, however, Jordan proceeds to tell the counselor that he has gone through none of those stages:

> "Look," I said, "I'm not trying to be different and maybe I am just hiding my real feelings, but what you describe is not the way I feel. Denial? Deny what? . . . Angry? At whom?" . . . "Bargaining with God?" . . . "I don't think that God has to sit down and negotiate with his creations." (Jordan, 2000, pp. 8–9)

The counselor appropriately tells him that his response has contradicted her theory and that his attitude "is terrific."

Hamilton Jordan was not dealing with the death of a loved one, but his response is similar to what happens in bereavement. Grieving persons do tend to have, on average, similar sorts of responses and psychological experiences. But the idea that certain kinds of responses occur first, to be followed in a predictable way by a second set of responses, and so on, does not accurately reflect what grieving persons actually experience (Stroebe et al., 2001a).

There are indeed some kinds of responses that are quite common in the early days of grief for people facing certain kinds of loss. For example, sudden and unexpected deaths such as suicide are probably more likely to produce some early disbelief and shock than deaths that are expected and anticipated (Calhoun, Selby, & Selby, 1982). And, on average, the intensity and frequency of psychological distress tends to become diminished over time. However, as we have seen, for some people it can take many years before the pain significantly diminishes, if it ever does.

As Stroebe and Schut (1999, 2001, Stroebe et al., 2001a, 2001b) suggest, it is better to view grief as characterized by oscillation rather than by a linear progression through predictable stages. It seems unlikely that significant numbers of practicing clinicians still assume that their grieving clients are going to go through a series of discrete and separate phases. But some practitioners may still have a general notion of a less distinctive series of stages through which they expect grieving people to go. *Our view is that the assumption that a grieving client is going to go though certain phases or stages in a predictable sequence is not helpful in clinical work.* In addition, the longitudinal research on grief is not supportive of the hypothesis that grief unfolds in a series of specific stages (Wortman & Silver, 1989, 2001).

The idea of possible phases could be regarded as correct, but only in a very general and imprecise way. It is accurate to say that for some people, dealing with certain kinds of losses, certain emotions are more likely in the early days of grief—on average. It is also accurate to say that many people, as the months and years pass, tend to report a reduction in the intensity of the pain. But these are generalizations that are accurate for group averages and they are based on comparisons between the early days with times much later in the grief journey. These generalizations about what is typical "on average" fail to tell the clinician about two very important qualifiers. First, they do not tell the clinician about the great variability in the responses of different people. Different people will react differently even to situations that seem to be quite similar. Second, generalizations of this kind do not tell the clinician about the great potential variability in the experiences of the same individual from day to day and month to month. As the grieving parent we quoted earlier said, "I have some bad days; I have some not so bad days."

☐ Is Positive Change from the Struggle to Cope Possible?

In the last 10 years there has been a great increase of interest in the possible ways that the struggle with difficult situations can lead some people to experience significant psychological growth, and we have contributed some of our ideas to this area (Calhoun & Tedeschi, 1999, 2001; Tedeschi & Calhoun, 1995; Tedeschi, Park, & Calhoun, 1998). The observation that the struggle with major difficulties can produce positive psychological changes is not new. It has been around for hundreds if not thousands of years. But there currently is a much greater interest in the possibility of psychological growth in these circumstances. Practicing clinicians, particularly those who work with persons facing major life challenges and loss, have begun to talk and think about the possibility of growth arising from the struggle with crisis and loss. Is the assumption that the struggle with major loss, such as the death of a child, can produce significant psychological growth just another myth of coping with loss?

The short answer is no, it is not a myth. Psychological growth can be experienced by people dealing with all sorts of life difficulties, including the death of a loved one, even a beloved son or daughter. The research on what we call *posttraumatic growth* suggests that many people report at least some growth resulting from their struggle with major losses (Park, 1998; Tedeschi & Calhoun, 1995). The growth that individuals report arising from their attempts to handle major life crises tends to fall into three broad areas: changes in self-perception, changes in relationships with others, and changes in the existential or spiritual domain (see Calhoun & Tedeschi, 1999; Tedeschi & Calhoun, 1995, for more extensive descriptions).

Changes in individuals' understanding and perception of themselves can be summarized with the phrase "I am more vulnerable, but I am also stronger than I thought I was." Being confronted with the death of a child clearly shows a parent that bad things can happen—the loss shows that he or she is individually vulnerable to losses in life. But at the same time, many persons experience their struggle with loss as proof that they have what it takes to survive major life difficulties. Struggling and somehow making it through from day to day leads them to see themselves as stronger and more capable than they had previously thought. As another bereaved parent said:

> All of a sudden, since this has happened I have become very bold, very outspoken. And I feel that what I have to say is important.

People struggling to cope with difficult circumstances *may also experience an increased sense of connection to other people*. This increased sense of closeness to some people may come at the price of feeling greater distance from others. "Now I know who my real friends are." When greater intimacy with others occurs, it is often in the context of couples and families. As one bereaved man said about his relationship with his wife:

> Our relationship has grown much closer. I realized why she was doing what she was doing. [It was because] she saw me hurting so much and she didn't know how to comfort me. Overall our relationship is much closer now.

This sense of connection to other people may also manifest itself in a greater sense of compassion for persons who also experience great pain or tragic loss. Bereaved parents, for example, may become particularly compassionate toward other parents who experience the loss of a child. And many will turn this increased feeling of compassion into compassionate actions.

> . . . I have been more drawn to help when I've found out somebody close by has lost a child. I will drive up and contact them and let them know that I'm here for them to talk if they need me. [describes a specific instance of offering help] . . . I went to her and I told her I'd just heard what had happened to her daughter. That it was the 5th anniversary of my [child's] death and that I'm here for you, right across the way. And we started talking, she started opening up and we've talked a lot since. I get to help people.

Another way in which *some people may experience posttraumatic growth is in the general domain of spirituality*, and for some this change is in their religious lives. This is not to say that the individual's original set of beliefs is necessarily strengthened. For some people, the loss of a child may also lead to the loss of religious beliefs or to a weakening of their spiritual lives. Many persons, however, including grieving parents, may come to experience the spiritual domain of their lives as more important to them, more meaningful, and richer than it was before they were forced to face tragedy. What they believe and assume about the world and their place and purpose in it may be different, but for many persons their spiritual lives become deeper and more meaningful than they were before they struggled with loss. Changes in this area can include a *greater appreciation* for what one still has and *changes in one's life priorities*. Changed priorities where the individual moves "the really important things" (spending more time with my surviving children) to the top of the hierarchy.

> It [struggling with the loss] has just really changed my whole life. Things that seemed important before were just so insignificant. . . . All of a sudden you realize it and your family becomes more important to you—your friends. . . . God became real to me because I came face to face with him. And I also know that my son is with Him.

The possibility of growth in the struggle with the death of a loved one is real (Calhoun & Tedeschi, 2001; Riches & Dawson, 2000). But the assumption that such growth is universal can also become a myth—*growth does not occur in all grieving persons*. Some grieving persons simply do not experience growth resulting from their struggle with bereavement. In addition, even when the individual experiences positive change, the changes may occur in some areas (e.g., enhanced compassion and altruistic behavior toward other parents who also lose a child), but not in others (e.g., no change in self-perception), and some areas of functioning may actually show a decline from their preloss levels (relationships within family have become more strained and difficult between some people).

☐ Conclusion

To be an expert companion for bereaved parents, a clinician must be able to provide accurate information about the experience and process of bereavement when parents wonder about what is happening to them and what may lie ahead. Some clinicians still cling to outmoded models of grieving that confuse bereaved parents unnecessarily. In this chapter, we have alerted you to what clinicians and researchers have come to recognize about bereavement that you need to keep in mind while you work. We encourage you to remember that grief does not occur in neat stages, and is not concluded in a set period of time. Instead, it is more accurate to think of it as a recursive process that involves multiple concerns that vary from parent to parent, and that need much time for consideration. Also remember that changed, but enduring, attachments to a child who has died are common for parents, and that, for some parents, experiences of personal growth mix with their grief, and do not represent denial of grief. Finally, the process is idiosyncratic, and it is useful to be able to see bereaved parents' varying attempts to comprehend their situation and survive it as the "new normal" rather than anything pathological.

A General Framework for Intervention

Today, the road all runners come,
Shoulder high, we bring you home,
And set you at your threshold down,
Townsman of a stiller town.
A. E. Houseman, "To an Athlete Dying Young"

With some knowledge of models of the grieving process and the experience of grieving parents, the reader is ready to learn some basic principles of intervention with this population. In this chapter, we first describe the general approach and processes involved in the central clinical stance we suggest should be taken when working with bereaved parents. We also describe how clinicians can adopt a growth perspective and we identify some of the specific issues that can emerge when providing assistance to bereaved parents.

☐ The Central Clinical Stance: Expert Companionship

Given how bereaved parents respond to their loss, as described in chapter 1, it is important for the clinician to maintain a way of relating with them that promotes a sense of safety and trust. Remember that bereaved parents often feel isolated, misunderstood, and feel great despair, especially as the realization gradually sets in that for them the pain of grief may extend for a very long time. We have found in our clinical work that *it is generally best to approach parents as companions in this journey, and downplay professional clinical expertise.* Even if you happen to be a bereaved parent yourself, this is a good stance to take. We call this clinical style "expert companionship." It is focused on the clinician's understanding of the bereavement experience, and it allows bereaved parents to feel safe and validated, when so many others seem to misunderstand them.

The Primacy of Expert Companionship

Unlike much other clinical practice where you might be working with people with certain psychiatric disorders, most bereaved parents are psychologically healthy people who have been struck by tragedy. Therefore, as a clinician, you will find that you can trust them to find their own way to grieve and survive. You usually will not have to provide psychological treatment in the same sense you might with depression, anxiety, and other kinds of similar difficulties. However, there are parents who have had preexisting psychiatric disorders, including substance abuse and personality disorders, and this will demand a more active style of intervention. In addition, there are parents whose children have died in circumstances that produce posttraumatic stress symptoms for the bereaved parent. These are usually situations where the child's death was the result of a violent cause, when the parents have witnessed elements of the child's death, or when they create their own horrific images of what they think might have happened. Some elements of effective treatments for posttraumatic stress might be indicated in these cases. We suggest becoming familiar with trauma treatment approaches (e.g., Herman, 1992) in order to be prepared for these clients, but most of this chapter focuses on the situations clinicians are most likely to face with bereaved parents. We also suggest that *expert companionship* is of primary importance for these clients and is the most suitable style to employ with most bereaved parents.

There are several reasons why this clinical style of expert companionship may be the best one to adopt. First, by being a companion, you do something that many others are unwilling to do: stick with parents as they talk about their children's lives and their deaths. Some people are willing to do this in the immediate aftermath of the loss, but few friends and family can do this for the long haul. Bereaved parents usually have the feeling in short order that the world has gone on functioning as if nothing has happened, and even those who are most concerned become less solicitous as time passes. Parents may also assume that they may wear out their welcome with people who have been particularly helpful and sensitive, and they do not want to lose the support they have. Therefore, *as a clinician, your greatest gift is to be there for the long haul, always showing clear signs of willingness to listen to and actively engage the parent in every session.* This can be a tough task for clinicians who usually operate in a short-term therapy model. Current therapeutic paradigms (e.g., "brief therapy") may emphasize rapid and efficient intervention, and larger social and economic forces (e.g., managed care) can push clinicians in the direction of short-term work as well. Therefore, as time wears on, clinicians may start to doubt their effectiveness, or the appropriateness of their work with bereaved parents. We recognize that some clinicians operate in settings where long-term contact with such clients is not supported financially or philosophically. It is best in these circumstances to acknowledge the truth. Say to the bereaved parent,

> Your tragedy may take a long time to heal. Unfortunately where I work, we aren't able to work with you for the length of time you might need. It would probably be best for you to work with someone who can stick with you over the long haul.

Be ready to refer parents to a person or agency that does just this. We believe that without urgency to terminate work with bereaved parents, both the clinician and parent can settle into their best work. It is a therapeutically safe environment from the start.

There is another reason why it is good to downplay the expertise of facts and interventions, and emphasize expert companionship. This is because every life or death is different, and clinicians will find that parents appreciate therapists who take the time to get to know what is special about their child, and their specific circumstances. It is most important to get to know the child through the parent's eyes in order to appreciate the particulars of what the parent has lost. Instead of a generic understanding of this loss, find out the special qualities of the child that made him or her unique. Find out what the character of the parental–child relationship was. Find out what the problems might have been in the relationship, that the parent may be regretting or feeling guilty about. Find out about special talents and interests, that now are reminders, both painful and comforting, of the child's death and life. Find out about the specific circumstances that made the death difficult, or perhaps a relief, and how these circumstances continue to be played out after death. We discuss these kinds of circumstances later in this chapter.

Parents will feel close and safe with you as a clinician if they have a sense that you knew their child, and the parent indeed can introduce you. Remember that here again, you are not the expert, but the companion. *The parents are the experts on their children, so have them teach you.* Say something like,

> In order for me to get an understanding of your grief, I need to know about who you lost. I would appreciate it if you could tell me more about Bobby.

Ask them to bring photos, even if the parent cannot bear to look at them. We have not run into any parents yet who are not willing to share photos, even if they have difficulty looking at them. They may get someone else to choose some, or they will grab a framed picture they are familiar with and bring it with them, hardly looking themselves. But they will do it because they want you to know their child. Photos from all different ages are helpful, from baby pictures to those taken in recent times. Some parents will bring those that are less painful for them to look at, perhaps those from long ago rather than recently. Look carefully at these photos, and try to imagine the personality of that child, and talk together with the parents about what you see in their child. Notice the expression, the action of the picture, who else is there, how they are dressed. Much information may be revealed about the child and the parent's relationship in such a conversation. The talk about the child's life can also be a bit of a relief from the pain of their death. For a moment there may be a pleasant memory. The parent may tell an amusing story. The two of you may laugh together. This in particular may be a revelation for a parent. For example, one parent said,

> When we looked at Danny's picture and laughed together about that day at camp, I realized that I hadn't laughed since he died. I guess it was more than I couldn't, it was that I didn't want to. Someone might think I no longer hurt. But I knew you knew that wasn't the case, so I guess it was safe to laugh with you.

Some parents might wish to bring in videotapes, so it is good to have equipment to view them. Videos seem to be harder for most parents than photographs. Their child's movement and voice make what has been lost even more painfully clear. At the same time, these videos can show a clinician even more about the child, so it is useful to let the parents know that they can bring them in when they are ready. Some parents have given us videos to watch outside of clinical sessions, because they cannot bear to see them yet. We have honored such requests, and then talked with the parents about what we viewed, just as with still photographs. Other ways parents introduce their deceased children to us include their children's writings and drawings, eulogies and poems written about them, and other pieces of memorabilia. All these things have a story behind them, and encouraging this storytelling is a great way to build your relationship with bereaved parents, to help them feel emotionally secure with you, and to advance the healing process. Sometimes you may feel that you are going slowly by focusing on such things, but it is all helpful. *Avoid short-cuts*. Bereaved parents can be quite sensitive and vulnerable, and can pick up slights and disinterest, especially if they sense that you are not wanting to know about their children. The expert companion is patient with this process.

☐ The Expert Companion in Multicultural Context

The expert companion must also learn how to accompany people from different cultures, who have differing expectations regarding the grief process and professional help. Recognizing and appreciating cultural differences will become increasingly important in order for clinicians to be effective in helping bereaved parents.

The United States and other countries in the Northern Hemisphere have become, and will to continue to become, increasingly diverse. Greater variations and changes in the ethnicity, religion, skin color, and primary language of the population are expected to continue well into the 21st century. Although not new (e.g., Kanfer & Saslow, 1969; Lewin, 1936), by the end of the 20th century there was a welcome emphasis on the importance of understanding individuals, especially clients, as part of a diverse and multicultural world (American Psychological Association, 1993).

Although definitions of culture vary, it can be thought of, at least in a rather general way, as the behavior that individuals acquire as part of their membership in a social group. Multiple *cultural influences and cultural contexts*, then, can be thought of as the means through which individuals are shaped and influenced by their participation in social groups. In this section we suggest some of the cultural elements that can be useful to consider in order to better understand grieving parents in their own unique multicultural contexts. Although accurately identifying and attending to the static demographic characteristics (e.g., gender, nationality) of the individual parent is important, it is even more useful to obtain a good understanding of the dynamic cultural factors that are of importance to and have influence on the individual parents a clinician is trying to assist.

Identifying Primary Groups: Reference and Support

Primary reference groups are those groups that have social influence on an individual. An easy way to assess primary reference groups is to consider, "Who does the individual want to please or whose opinions does the person value?" For most individuals, the answer would include many persons belonging to several different social groups: the person's close friends, family members, teams, clubs, religious organizations, gangs, and so on. In colloquial language, primary reference groups tend to be those whom the person "identifies with." Although not universal, persons who belong to demographic groups that are minorities or who lack significant social and political power may also see themselves as belonging to the broader, more abstract group that constitutes a particular social class, ethnicity, or nationality. So, in trying to understand a particular parent, it is useful for the clinician to listen for clues indicating the persons and groups that are important to parents, and who have the ability to yield social influence over them.

Many bereaved parents see themselves as belonging to an additional reference group: bereaved parents. As fellow citizens of this particular "country," other parents may become important sources of information, guidance, support, and comfort.

There can be much overlap between the groups that can have influence and the groups from which support can come in times of difficulty. It is also highly useful for the counselor to understand who the parent's *social support groups* are. Which important groups can provide useful services, and emotional, informational, and perhaps even material help for the parent? When individuals experience a loss, social groups can be a powerful source of comfort. An excellent source for parents is other persons who have experienced a similar loss. For some parents the most appreciated source of support will be other parents who have lost a child under similar circumstances.

A very helpful thing that clinicians can do is to make the grieving parent aware of groups of other parents who have themselves lost children. Although we address the issue of support groups in more detail in other sections of the book, it is good to be reminded that something very useful a clinician can do is to help a grieving parent connect to other parents who have lost a child. To do this well, however, the clinician must have accurate information about the quality and availability of such resources.

Social Rules and Norms

We tend to regard the words *rules* and *norms* as interchangeable, although in more technical writing significant distinctions are drawn between the meaning of these two words. *Social rules or norms* are the guidelines that tell an individual what should be done, what can be done, and what should not be done in particular social situations. For example, what rules do you assume to be in place when you meet for the first time with an adult friend who has recently lost a parent? What do you think you are supposed to do or say, what are you not supposed to do or say, and what do you think it would be acceptable to do or say, even though it is not required by the situation? Many of us in North America probably assume the first time we see a friend after the death of a parent that we should, in some way, express condolences by saying something explicit, such as "I was sorry to hear about your mother's death." And in this same context, we probably also believe it is against the rules, and inappropriate, for us to ask direct questions about the cause of the parent's death. The rules we assume to be applicable may tell us that we should *not* ask a question as direct as "Could you tell me exactly what caused your mother's death?" It is very helpful for clinicians to understand the social norms that guide the individual's behavior, particularly those social norms that parents share with members of their primary reference groups.

Social rules regarding funerals and death rituals are highly relevant, especially when the parent comes for help in early bereavement. There are variations in if and how the parent is expected to have contact with the child's body, who "prepares" the body, the conditions under which the family is expected to "receive" those who wish to express condolences, and a wide variety of other matters. For some religious groups, there are clear prescriptions about how a body should be prepared, who should do it, and the time frame within which rituals or funerals must be completed.

Social rules governing the expressions of the emotions associated with grief can also be of great importance, and their relevance can last long after funeral and death rituals have been completed. There may be general expectations about the expression of emotions in general, but there may also be separate rules for different members of particular subgroups. For example, among some cultural groups it is expected that women will cry and wail, whereas men are expected to maintain a quiet stoicism. In other contexts, which may be the predominant ones in many regions of North America, some expression of emotion is tolerated and even anticipated, but adults are generally expected to express their emotions, if they do so at all, with some degree of decorum. As one person described it: "I think they [survivors] should try to control their emotions. . . . It could be a more proper way. . . . Try to keep themselves under control" (Perry, 1993, p. 58).

Parents immersed in some sociocultural groups may experience a great need to appear "strong," much as the person just quoted who wishes mourners to be controlled. In other social settings, for example, among some Mexican communities, "the emotional response . . . is perhaps more open and demonstrative than it is in" many Anglo communities (Younoszai, 1993, p. 77).

Social rules governing the behavior of members of the parent's wider social group can also have an impact on the parent. It is not uncommon for persons in the United States to express some degree of social discomfort about interacting with bereaved persons, in part because of the lack of clarity of the social rules for the provision of comfort and support. This particular discomfort may be aggravated when the potential comforter is considering how best to interact with grieving parents. Many potential comforters probably ask themselves: "What can I possibly say or do when I talk to them? I have no idea what to say, how to act, or what to do. I certainly do not want to say the *wrong* thing." In turn, this potential discomfort on the part of members of the parent's primary social groups may somehow get communicated to parents, making their already extremely difficult situation a bit more awkward and stressful for them. This sense of social awkwardness, enhanced by the lack of clear social rules indicating how potential comforters can provide support for grieving parents, may in turn lead the parent to feel even more disconnected from persons who might otherwise be perceived to be the source of bountiful help and support.

The Clinician's Status and Social Role

> Doctor, you are an expert on sadness and loss. I feel very bad. Tell me what I should do so that I may begin to feel less sadness over my loss.

This was a request from a client from a country other than the United States, in which "doctors" are expected to utilize their expertise to offer an expert solution to the patient. For this client, the clinician was seen as having high status, because of his education and knowledge, and his role was seen as that of a wise and knowledgeable person who could offer a potential solution for this man's deep sadness. The clinician's style of expert companionship may need to differ for parents in different cultural contexts.

There are variations among sociocultural groups as to what the role and status of the "psychotherapist" or "counselor" is, and each clinician should develop a general awareness of how he or she is viewed by individual parents, and also how mental health professionals in general are viewed by the parent's primary social groups. In contrast to the high status accorded to the psychologist in the illustration just given, many practicing clinicians have experience with clients who describe members of their social groups as assuming psychological interventions are ineffective and a waste of time. Clinicians must make a decision about the degree to which their approaches may be changed, given different assumptions clients have about what their status is and what their roles should be. But it is important to at least try to understand what those assumptions and expectations are—both what the parent's view is and the views that predominate among the parent's primary social groups.

A very important element for understanding the cultural context of clinical work is *for clinicians to remember that they themselves have reference groups that influence them and how they approach the task of trying to be of help to grieving parents*. In addition to the typical primary reference groups that we all have—for example, families and friends—practicing clinicians, trained in typical North American and Western European psychological traditions, tend themselves to share a subcultural set of assumptions about what "good" therapy should be in general, and how to assist grieving persons in particular. For example, clinicians tend to see accurate and intimate disclosure, by the client, of emotions and thoughts as a desirable component of the therapeutic process. Many clients, and in North America these may be more likely to be men (Shay, 1996), may have strong sociocultural influences that discourage or inhibit such disclosure. Such cultural influences on clients tend to stand in opposition to what the subculture of clinicians typically regards as the best way for the therapeutic process to unfold. The clinician should respect parents' ways of thinking about death and bereavement, and the particular ways in which the parents choose to express, or not, their grief during counseling sessions.

Clinicians may also have some sociocultural assumptions about the appropriate and desirable ways in which grieving parents should behave in the world outside the confines of the treatment session. It is important to be aware of the potential differences between how bereaved parents in their sociocultural contexts, and practicing clinicians in theirs, view the clinician's role, the grief process, and the therapeutic relationship.

Assumptions about What Helps

As a psychologist, counselor, social worker, or whatever professional training you have, *what main assumptions do you make about what the helpful ingredients of the psychological interventions you provide to bereaved parents are*? Most clinicians can readily articulate some general ideas about this. However, if we were to ask each bereaved client, particularly parents, with whom you work this same question, to what extent would there be agreement between you and each of your clients?

The parent's view of what may or may not be helpful about psychological interventions is influenced by the sociocultural groups and communities to which the parent belongs. The assumption that counseling and psychotherapy are about "getting in touch with your true feelings" is one that is common in popular culture and may represent, at least in some ways, the views of many practicing clinicians as well. But some parents may have significantly different expectations—they may be seeking expert advice, reassurance, words that they hope may directly provide comfort and solace, or, in a more general sense, wisdom. It is useful to be aware of what ideas parents have of how counseling can be helpful to them, and how those ideas may differ from the ideas the therapist has.

Sociocultural Consequences of Change

To the extent that psychological interventions produce good results, those results usually involve some kind of change on the part of the client. Although the desired ends of intervention may differ between client and counselor at the beginning of the counseling relationship, greater congruence of goals is likely to occur over time. Another important aspect to consider then, in order to understand the parent's grief in sociocultural context, is the social consequences of therapeutic change. How will the parent's primary social groups respond to the changes the parent undergoes as a result of counseling? Consider, for example, a "reluctant male" (Shay, 1996, p. 503) bereaved parent who learns to value self-disclosure and expression of emotion as a result of his experience in psychotherapy. We might well imagine that this new skill will be highly appreciated by some of his important others, but in some of his cultural contexts—for example, with his male friends who are also reluctant to engage in self-disclosure—ready expression of intimate feelings may result in awkwardness at best and perhaps significant social sanctions (such as derision or ridicule) at worst.

Although a therapeutic process that encourages the expression of inner states and painful feelings may be a good choice, even for a highly reluctant man, the clinician should try to obtain the best understanding possible of what may happen if the man does indeed practice his new-found skills outside of the therapeutic session.

Religion and Spirituality

In the United States a very large percentage of the population identifies itself as having a belief in God, and a lesser, although still considerable, percentage identify themselves as religious in some ways. Although many North American psychologists view "spirituality" as an important part of life, they are less likely than their typical clients to regard themselves as religious. The beliefs of North American psychotherapists, even when they include a belief in some form of higher power, are not likely to conform to the traditional assumptions of the world's major religions (Calhoun & Tedeschi, 1999). It is helpful for clinicians to identify and understand the spiritual and religious ways of thinking and doing that bereaved clients have. Such beliefs can include various versions of the major religions of the world, but in the Western "developed" countries such beliefs are also likely to include agnosticism and atheism (Parkes, 1998). Given the ever-increasing multicultural and pluralistic demographics of countries in Western Europe and North America, it is highly likely that clinicians' views on the spiritual or religious elements of grief will differ from many of the bereaved parents they see.

Some, perhaps many, clinicians may have assumptions that can be called secularism or secular humanism (Dees, 2001; Parkes, 1998). Secularism is characterized, in part, by agnosticism or atheism, a reliance on logic, reason, and empiricism, and a general disinterest in, and sometimes direct antipathy toward, traditional beliefs about gods and an afterlife. Some clinicians who are secularists may regard beliefs about God and the afterlife as "wish-fulfilling nonsense" (Dees, 2001, p. 19). In the United States there is also a minority of clinicians whose views are in many ways the opposite of those held by secularists. Such clinicians hold strong religiously orthodox views, which they incorporate directly into their clinical practice, making the assumption that the best clinical interventions represent a direct implementation of their religious orthodoxy. For example, some North American clinicians identify themselves as "Christian counselors" who specialize in implementing their own interpretation of the Christian Bible as part of psychological treatment.

In understanding bereaved parents and their spiritual assumptions (or lack of them), the viewpoint that we prefer is what we have called *pragmatic religious constructivism* (Calhoun & Tedeschi, 1999; see also Pargament, 1997, for a detailed examination of this and other issues). Bereaved parents will have a variety of beliefs, held with differing degrees of certainty and conviction, about the prospects of life after death and the continued existence of the child, possibilities about maintaining bonds and contact with the deceased child, possibilities about contacting the child, and the general role of God or gods. A similar statement about the variety of beliefs among clinicians can also be made. *Pragmatic religious constructivism* assumes quite simply that "it is desirable for the clinician to enter, respectfully, into the client's religious worldview and help him or her utilize . . . spiritual understanding to recover, grow, and develop" (Calhoun & Tedeschi, 1999, p. 110). It may be a challenge to put such abstract goals into practice, but we believe it is useful for the clinician to try.

Such an approach to the bereaved parent's religious and spiritual life does not leave room for the imposition on the client, by the clinician, of rigid orthodox views, whether they are religious, spiritual, or completely secular. But in order to respectfully work within the parent's worldview, the clinician must make systematic efforts to include this dimension in the framework for understanding the individual parent's way of trying to come to terms with the death of a child. Listening carefully to parents' use of language to describe their experience will reveal much about their spiritual and religious context.

Idioms of Distress, Death, and Grief

Different sociocultural groups tend to develop particular ways of talking about and conceptualizing death and the associated distress and grief. Although not specifically referring to death, some cultures talk about psychological distress as reflecting "bad nerves" or in Portuguese, "ataque de nervos." Even as clinicians who have extensive experience in the area of loss and grief, we are experiencing some degree of idiomatic constraint, now, as we write this very book. Look back to the last paragraph before the current heading on idioms. We have avoided using any version of the word *death* in association with the word *child*, at least in part because the phrase "dead child" seems cold and harsh, given the particular sociocultural groups in which we are ourselves currently immersed.

Clinicians need to exercise significant cultural sensitivity about the ways in which bereaved parents think and talk about their particular loss. This is another way to be the expert companion, rather than merely the expert. *Listen carefully to the language of grief that parents use, and judiciously join them in this form of communication.*

A phrase that is quite common in some groups in the southeastern United States is the verb "to pass" as a way of talking about a person's death. "Their child has passed," for example, is the typical way in which some social groups describe a child's death. "He's gone to be with the Lord," "God just called him home," "she's in heaven with her Gramma," and "she has left us" are examples of some of the phrases used by some social groups to talk about a person's death.

Generally, the term "died" may be the safest for a clinician to use, because it is virtually universally accepted. But the clinician should be highly sensitive to the ways the death of a child is conceptualized and the words and idioms used to talk about it. If the parent says that the child returned to her maker, for example, this might invite you to say,

> I notice that you said that Maria 'returned to her maker.' I gather that this means you have a clear sense of her relationship with God and where she might be now.

Then, you will probably develop a discussion about spiritual matters that are important to the parent. This kind of discussion is explored in depth in chapter 6. But we wish to point out here that it is important that you show you are willing and able to talk about such matters, and learn the parent's cultural perspective on them in relationship to their child's death. With regard to spiritual matters, we can recall a few parents who had a strong reaction to the use of the word "lost" to mean that their children had died. For them, this term had an important religious significance. One parent said,

> I didn't "lose" my child. I know just where he is; DeShawn is with God. God has him safe at home with Him.

There are other words commonly used in relation to the grief experience that can produce strong reactions in some bereaved parents. One of these is often used by media people: "closure." We have found that many bereaved parents hate that word. To them it means that their child's death has been put aside, and that there is no longer a recognition or emotional memory of them. Many bereaved parents do not believe this is possible or desirable. It is also important to appreciate the variability among parents in reaction to certain words and phrases. When you are the expert companion who listens carefully, you can avoid offense by using these phrases only when you understand their meaning and impact. For example, just as the mother quoted earlier was comfortable with the idea that her son was with God, another said,

> I hate it when people say Carlo is "in a better place" or that God is caring for him. I'm his mother, and I'm supposed to be caring for him. I'm sorry, but I still think that's my job, and I want to be doing it.

We are not suggesting that the clinician parrot back the particular phrases that a parent uses. We are suggesting that the clinician should attend to how each parent speaks about grief and loss, and that the clinician respect those concepts and idioms and, to the extent that it is reasonable and appropriate, also speak to the client within the general framework of those words and concepts.

The Parent's Sociocultural Context: Summary

All persons are immersed in a complex network of social influences. The various cultural and subcultural groups from the individual's past and present have the potential to influence him or her in a variety of ways. The diverse, pluralistic, multicultural worlds of contemporary bereaved parents may be quite different from those of the clinicians to whom they come for help and support. Knowing what the bereaved parent's primary social groups are, the social norms the parent shares with those groups, the linguistic traditions used to talk about distress, death, and grief, the assumptions the parent makes about the clinician's status and social role, what the clinician is expected to do to be of help and support, understanding the social consequences for the parent of experiencing therapeutic change and the parent's spiritual and religious perspective—these can provide the clinician with a good grasp of the parents' experiences within their unique social contexts.

General knowledge about the general cultural patterns of people belonging to broad categories such as nationalities or ethnic groups can be very useful. It is important, however, to keep in mind that even for familiar and well-established broad conceptual categories (e.g., men and women), where general characteristics and average statistical differences may have been described by reliable observations, clinicians should always follow an admonition that is widely acknowledged and quite familiar: *Focus on the individual parent and his or her unique experience and sociocultural context, not the group(s) to which that person belongs.* It is important for the clinician, in order to provide the best help of which he or she is capable, to learn about the individual parent and that parent's *unique* sociocultural influences and environments, and to acknowledge, understand, and respect the differences between the world of the client and the world of the clinician.

☐ The Expert Companion in the Uniqueness of a Parent's Grief

Another reason to avoid trying to be the "expert" on matters of cultural context is that there is so much to learn about bereaved parents' particular situations that might play a role in their reactions. For example, predicting with any confidence when they will be feeling better is fraught with difficulties. Some parents do not want to feel better, because they feel that this would be a betrayal of their children, and the world might take this as an indication that it is all right to forget them. Some parents are in the midst of legal battles that require them to be careful about what they say, limiting their ability to express grief in a way that might be helpful to them. Some parents have children die under mysterious circumstances, prompting them to spend much time being detectives, finding out what these circumstances really were. Who murdered them? Could the physician have saved them? Did the seat belt fail? Being the companion as the parent goes through such searching, wondering, questioning, and data gathering is an important service. Again we repeat—avoid shortcuts. Even though you may think parents are torturing themselves by pursuing such questions, the vast majority seem to have a good sense of when this is necessary, and when they are satisfied with the answers or ready to give up, accept what they know, and decide what to believe about the rest.

For those of us who are not bereaved parents, it is dangerous therapeutically to claim expertise in this area, given how many parents are clear that only another bereaved parent truly understands. We believe that they are right. It is probably impossible to know the particulars of this pain without going through this, even if you have heard many stories as we have, or try your hardest to be empathic. Even if clinicians themselves are bereaved parents, their own experience and cultural contexts can diverge from that of other parents. There is no reason to invite the reaction, "I don't think you really understand, you've never gone through this." Although the same might be said about many clinical problems, like substance abuse, obsessive compulsive disorder, or bipolar disorder, because parental bereavement deals with the loss of the most precious person, empathy born of direct experience is usually more of an issue for the client.

Given this stance of expert companionship, rather than expertise, is there any place where expertise in facts and interventions comes in? After all, you are probably reading this book in hopes of becoming more expert in helping bereaved parents. *Yes, there is expertise involved in this work.* We are making the case that the expertise is primarily involved in being a high-quality companion in bereavement, and that the expertise is woven into your interactions, rather than revealed through knowledge of facts or intervention procedures that heal the pain of grief. However, there are ways to help parents with some facts, suggestions, and the like from time to time. Indeed, they will ask for this kind of knowledge sometimes. You will be asked such questions as, "Should I read the autopsy?" "Should I tell his little sister the truth about how he died?" "Is it OK that I don't wish to visit the grave?" "What should I do on her birthday?"

In responding to such specific questions, we acknowledge that the real experts are parents who have survived this grief. Their experiences have informed us enough that we felt drawn to and capable of writing this volume. All of what we know about this process, and what is helpful, comes from listening to parents directly, or by listening to them through our research or that of others. So, we often find ourselves introducing suggestions and facts with:

> Some bereaved parents have told me that. . . . Has that been the case for you?

First, such a statement says that we do not know this through personal experience, and admit that. Second, it says that some parents have this perspective, but that it is not the only one—the parent's personal experience may be different, and just as valid. We find that bereaved parents are usually eager to learn from others who have been enduring similar circumstances, and by invoking the perspectives of other bereaved parents, we can give credibility to the information we share. In chapter 8 you will find some recommended resources that will help you learn about various ways that bereaved parents handle the situations and decisions they face. But all of this must be tempered with a consideration of the parents before you—what are they ready for, what fits their cultural context, and what just feels right for them.

Of course, another way to handle the problem of expertise and credibility is to conduct mutual support groups for bereaved parents. But these parents also recognize the limitations of their hard-won "expertise." One mother had friends whose son was killed about five years after her own son had died in a similar accident. She said:

> We got up the next morning and went to them. And it was really strange from the standpoint that I thought that I should have some great words of wisdom here. I've been there, I should know something. And I found myself sitting there thinking I have no clue, as most people do not have a clue who want to say something to somebody in a similar situation. And if I could tell anybody anything if they are faced with a friend who is going through this, all you can do is say "yeah I'm here, if you talk, we'll talk, if you don't, we won't." That's all you can do, you cannot take that pain from another person.

☐ A Growth Perspective

In addition to expert companionship, another part of the clinical stance that we recommend is a growth perspective. We have been working since the early 1980s investigating how people report that the struggle with difficult life crises has changed them in positive ways. We coined the term *posttraumatic growth* to represent these changes. As we described earlier, we have discovered that posttraumatic growth can be expressed in one or more of five domains: improved interpersonal relationships, new life paths, a greater appreciation for life, a sense of personal strength, and spiritual development (Tedeschi & Calhoun, 1996). Some of our research has focused on growth in the aftermath of bereavement (Calhoun & Tedeschi, 1989–1990; Tedeschi, Calhoun, Morrell, & Johnson, 1984), including bereaved parents (Calhoun, Tedeschi, Fulmer, & Harlan, 2000; Tedeschi & Calhoun, 2001). We have heard parents say frequently in the midst of their grief that they recognize certain ways they have changed for the better. These parents are unaware of our research into posttraumatic growth, and they volunteer such statements without being prompted from us. Our research and clinical experiences have convinced us that the reports of growth in bereaved parents are valid and important for the healing process, and we encourage clinicians working in this area to include this perspective in their central clinical stance.

To illustrate how bereaved parents refer to the five domains of post-traumatic growth in their reports of their bereavement experience, we again let some parents speak for themselves.

Spiritual Development

If I had any question about heaven, it has been strengthened because of Kim's death. And I don't know I'm not sure if that's wishful thinking on my part, I don't think it is. And people who are not as fortunate as I am, there's got to be something better for them. In life hereafter, there's got to be purpose for them. So all of that has kind of come together for me in that I don't have any question about life hereafter. And I have no question about Kim being there. So that's the assurance that has come through this experience.

New Paths

After spending all that time in the intensive care unit with Katie, I recognized how hard those nurses worked. I appreciated how they took care of us, and I guess I figured, since I did a lot with my own child, I could do it for someone else's. And I felt so empty after taking care of Katie all that time, it was like I had become a nurse already, but had no job. So I went back to school, and here I am, doing for others what was done for me.

Stronger Interpersonal Relationships

Although we had a pretty good marriage before, I think this forced us to look at what we meant to each other. And even if we didn't grieve the same way, we both loved Mario so much that we had to share that. It was like if we let this break us up he would be diminished somehow. We sort of vowed to make ourselves a better couple for the other kids, like a vow to Mario, as much as to each other. And it has helped us stay on track, and reminds us each day about what we are doing to be good partners and parents.

Appreciation for Life

I sure don't assume anything anymore. I know now that in an instant it all can change horribly. I mean I still plan for the future, but I don't take it for granted, either. I see other people operating like it'll be OK, and I think, they just don't realize. They'd better pay attention to their lives. And I do. I actually thank God every day. I realized in my head before about this, but this is a different kind of thing, I know it in my heart.

Sense of Personal Strength

People say "You're so strong." Well, yes and no. They don't see the an-guish, I do that in private. The shower is my favorite place for anguish. But, I agree that I am strong, because at the beginning, I didn't think I could make it. But I am surviving, and I really think that nothing could be as bad emotionally as this. I suppose if I got a disease and suffered great pain, that could be worse, but there is always morphine. This pain, this emotional pain, is different, and you have to live with it. I have not be-come a drug addict or anything, I faced it. So now anything else is pretty small potatoes.

Working with Reports of Growth

We have found that people express such thoughts of posttraumatic growth at various times during the grief process, sometimes fairly early on, but usually after some time has passed. Acknowledgment of these positive changes does not seem to negate any of the negative aspects of grief, and certainly does not leave people with a sense that their child's death has ended up being a positive thing. A statement from Harold Kushner, who wrote *When Bad Things Happen to Good People*, is instructive:

> I am a more sensitive person, a more effective pastor, a more sympathetic counselor because of Aaron's life and death than I would ever have been without it. And I would give up all of those gains in a second if I could have my son back. If I could choose, I would forego all of the spiritual growth and depth which has come my way because of our experiences, and be what I was fifteen years ago, an average rabbi, an indifferent counselor, helping some people and unable to help others, and the father of a bright, happy boy. But I cannot choose. (Viorst, 1986, p. 295)

It is important to speak about growth as arising out of the struggle with loss, the aftermath of it, rather than the loss itself. Make sure that you say things like,

> Having to go through this terrible grief has changed you, and now you seem to recognize some of these changes as positive.

These positive changes are important to acknowledge and discuss be-cause they allow parents to find some sense of meaning, not in the death itself, but in the life afterward. Because life as a bereaved parent can seem so devoid of meaning and purpose, recognition of posttraumatic growth can reduce the distress of this existential challenge.

Sometimes the positive changes arising from the struggle with grief can also act as living memorials to the dead child. A clinician might suggest, for example, that

> Each time you act with greater kindness, you can know that this is part of your child's legacy, making a difference in the world.

These are usually comforting notions, because they acknowledge something that is so important to bereaved parents: that their children are not gone and forgotten. They live in the memory and actions of those who have been touched by them.

For parents of infants who have died, or those who experienced miscarriages, it is sometimes necessary to live life in a way that their children did not have the opportunity to. And because other people may not have been directly touched by their children's lives, there is even more challenge in making sure that their children's existence was meaningful. You may need to help them find ways to have their child's name live in a memorial, a charity, or some other ongoing endeavor that becomes a new possibility that arises out of their terrible circumstances. But these actions are no simple matters, and there are complications that you may need to help them sort through. For example, even the naming of a child might be a problem among parents who have had miscarriages. Among parents who experienced a miscarriage, you may mention that many parents name their unborn children, even if these names are not legally recorded.

We have devoted a previous volume (Calhoun & Tedeschi, 1999) to a discussion of how to integrate this growth perspective into work with people struggling with the aftermath of major life crises. We summarize briefly some of the important aspects of this kind of clinical work as it applies to bereaved parents.

Focus on Listening, Not Solving, and Being Changed, Not Changing

This focus on listening and being changed fits with the expert companionship approach that we introduced earlier. The clinician's role is to endure the stories of the death that are heart-wrenching, without reacting in ways that usurp the affect of the story from the parent. Quiet sympathy allows the client to speak the horrific details as necessary. For clinicians who feel the necessity to solve a problem or intervene to reduce emotional distress, this may seem strangely passive, perhaps even ineffective. But we believe this focus can be a building block toward growth.

The message in this is, "I trust you have the strength to bear this, and I will bear it together with you. I'm ready to learn what you need, and be changed myself." This kind of respect for the bereaved parent is powerful. With your attention and recognition of the limitations of your abilities, you acknowledge how profound this loss is, and how much it takes to endure it. And as parents endure it, they reap the recognition that it was a great struggle that they managed. By being willing to learn and be changed, you acknowledge the value in this experience, and that their child has left a legacy for you as well. And if you are open to listening like this, you will be changed in ways that you value greatly. That is one of the reasons why people can continue to do this bereavement work for so many years, because of the vicarious posttraumatic growth that can be experienced. And as the clinician experiences this, the client can use this as a mirror, and see the positive aspects of what he or she has become as a bereaved parent.

Notice the Growth and Time Its Acknowledgment

Parents will say things in passing that you will recognize as posttraumatic growth, although they may not. We have often been struck by how often parents describe positive changes that have occurred during their bereavement experiences. Although it could be highly insensitive thing to point out that something beneficial has come from struggling with a child's death, parents themselves may see growth emerging from their struggle. *As a clinician, your job is to decide whether it is the right time for parents to acknowledge this more definitely*, and explore these changes. One way of judging if the timing is right for this is to wait for the second time this theme comes up, then say,

> I remember you saying before that you have become more compassionate since Ronnie's death.

The parent will then decide if he or she would like to elaborate.

Sometimes parents do not label the growth themselves, but it is obvious to those around them that it has occurred. For example, one mother decided that she needed to speak to church groups about how to respond helpfully when children in their congregations died. She had had a severe public speaking anxiety that she overcame in order to do this. The clinician said to her,

> I guess you'd still have the anxiety about speaking if you hadn't been so determined to be the voice for bereaved parents like yourself.

The parent responded,

I always feel like Demetria is with me when I get ready to speak. She calms me down and lets me do it. That's where I get my strength.

In fact, one of the ways that strengths experienced in the aftermath of a child's death tend to be viewed by bereaved parents is as a legacy of that child. Through this gift, the child lives on. This is an important perspective for parents to take. It allows them to view growth as a meaningful legacy rather than as a betrayal. Early on in the bereavement process, we have heard parents say,

I don't want to hear any of that junk that something good can come from this. My child is dead. What is good about that?

This is not the time to get into a debate. As a clinician, it is best to accept it. Members of support groups can respond differently than clinicians, because of their credibility. We have seen other group members clarify nicely the way that growth occurs in bereavement.

I know you feel that way now, but I have to say that this whole thing has forced me to dig down and find a me that I never knew existed. Sometimes it was an angry me, full of despair. But I also found a me that is a real survivor. I know pain. I know death. Neither one scares me anymore.

This kind of statement from another bereaved parent can be left to stand on its own, or examined a bit with the help of the clinician. A response to this might be,

So these have been the worst of times, but coping with this has also revealed the best of you.

The important distinction here is that the death of one's child is not the reason for growth, but instead it is the necessity to cope that forces parents to find a way to survive. It is often a side effect of the coping.

I wasn't looking to get anything out of this, but strangely enough, I like the person I am better than who I was before, even with all the pain in me.

Some parents make a decision to make something meaningful out of their experience, in order to honor their children.

"This is too horrible for something good not to come out of it." Or, "I want to do something that makes it easier on other families."

We point out that by coming to the group, and talking about their experiences, they are already accomplishing this. Each parent benefits from the others' presence, the others' ideas, and the others' ability to survive. This may not be something that many parents working in individual treatment can see, so the clinician might point out to them the terrible gift they have been given. After enough time has passed, you can point out that they know a lot about the bereavement experience, but that they may not recognize this until they talk with someone else who is beginning it.

> You now know some things about this process that those entering it have no idea about. Remember how confusing and frightening that was? So keep in mind that you have something to offer when you run across someone else that is going through this.

☐ Stuck Points

The process of grieving is in the short term unpredictable, although for most bereaved parents, in the long term it tends to be very predictable. In the long term, virtually all bereaved parents improve in their daily functioning, have a reduction in emotional turmoil, experience a restoration of cognitive functioning, and recognize that they are changed forever. Most also maintain some connection psychologically with the child who has died, although, as we saw in chapter 2, this is not always the case.

But most parents you encounter clinically will be mystified by what is happening to them, and perhaps frightened or disheartened by it. The emotional experience is so wrenching and so disruptive to daily functioning that they will ask early on, "How long will this last? Am I ever going to feel better?" Furthermore, they are usually unclear about *how* to feel better, because they have never felt such deep emotional pain before. One of the best descriptions we have heard was this:

> I've heard other parents say this is like a roller coaster. Well, that's true, it has its ups and downs. But the thing about it is the ups and downs come out of nowhere. I never know how I'm going to feel from one moment to the next, never mind one day to the next. It's a roller coaster, all right, but I feel like I am riding a roller coaster in the dark. I never know when the next turn is coming, or when the next up or down is coming. I feel completely out of control.

This is just one of the several points in the grieving process that mystifies, and gives the impression to bereaved parents that they are unable to do anything constructive to influence the process, or that they are stuck in it, and not moving through it.

Part of this sense of being stuck also has to do with the myths that have been promulgated about the grieving process, as we discussed in chapter 2. One of these myths is that grief is relatively short term, that the "healing" begins soon after the loss, and that "closure" will be reached. Various time frames have been mentioned to us by bereaved parents. They have read or been told, or vaguely "heard," that one should feel better in a few

ffer when parents engag
m that they are seeing thing
hat they knew at the time.
in when they might have mac
d everything. You will often fin
time appeared ordinary, and so

rnoon, and I was starting supper.
phone and I wasn't paying much
out, and I thought that I'll be
couldn't go far because it was
t out the door by then. Looking
ismissed it, or didn't even really
ld him he had to stay home, that
maybe he wouldn't have gotten

uch a typical day for you at the
t was about to happen.

omething.

aid?

oys he was mixed up with, he
would have said, "I'll be right
ybe I couldn't have changed it.
out to happen you would have

hat you know now, that would

een earlier what kind of things
ger stand.

anger?

know the whole story. I should

good kid, and his grades were
t things were basically OK.
urned out.

eality?

weeks, or six months, or a year. They have learned about stages of grief, and tried to figure out if they are in the "anger stage" or "bargaining stage." They fear that their marriages will be destroyed, because they have heard that the death of a child breaks up couples. They are encouraged to take antidepressant or antianxiety medications by well-meaning people who fear they are too sad, or too upset (which is not to say that medicine is not appropriate in individual instances). All these myths contribute to anxieties about how they will manage this grief, how well they are coping, and whether they are "normal."

One of the most useful things to tell parents is that bereavement is idiosyncratic. They will develop their own ways of grieving, and have their own experience, somewhat different from others' experiences. At the same time, you can point out that because they were pretty healthy emotionally before this happened (and in our experience this is typically the case), they will likely find a way to survive, and eventually be able to function well. Yet they will be changed forever. Bereaved parents are to a great extent challenged by the paradoxes of bereavement, and as a clinician you provide a great service by helping them hold these paradoxical elements of grief together. You can say:

> It makes sense that you wonder where this whole thing will lead you, what will become of you as you struggle through this. Life has just gotten more complicated, and you are learning some things about it at a gut level that many others don't know. Strange things like you feel terrible, but this is normal, and a sign that you are actually OK. You will survive this, although you will wonder at times if you want to. You will at some point appear to be like everyone else again, but you really won't be—you are changed forever. That there are certain efforts you can make that will allow you to feel better, primarily talking about it with supportive understanding people, but you will also need to let time and tears have their way with you. The whole thing has got to feel like a mighty strange process.

Some parents are impatient with the time frame because of the messages they have received about the grief process, but also because they wish to be done with the acute pain. They wonder, at the times the roller coaster takes them down, how they could feel several months later just as bad as, or worse than, they did at the beginning. Some parents have been helped by the message,

> You may feel like you are stuck, getting nowhere with this, when these emotional outbursts come along, but this is actually part of the process. You are really moving forward when this happens, not back.

We have heard from many parents that the second year of grieving is worse for them than the first year. This can be frightening and disappointing. But there is a way to frame this as progress, too. In support groups, many parents do this by pointing out that they were numb during much of the year. One parent who was a support group member into the second said to a person joining three months after her son died:

> You are just at the beginning of this. I'm in the second year of it, and I fe
> worse than I did before. That numbness from the beginning is starting
> wear off of you now, and I think it has totally worn off of me. Now it
> clear that he's dead, and I will never see him as a physical being again. Th
> is profoundly sad. It doesn't take my breath away like before. I really kno
> it now, and it's just very sad for me.

Even this apparent worsening is progress that can be pointed out.
clinician, you can direct the parent to memories of how it was the
few weeks. "Remember what it was like at the beginning? Do you n
any changes since then?" The answer to this is always yes, even thou
is often, "I feel worse." Still, that is movement, not being stuck. The v
ening and difficulty can make sense to parents in another way as w

> I've figured that this is the price I pay for having loved my child. If |
> weren't a treasure, then I wouldn't be reacting to losing him. My reactio
> tell me how much of a treasure he was. But sometimes I do wish for a lit
> relief.

When parents are faced with certain complications to the loss, they can e
ence a significant slowing of the process of grieving. These complication
involve legal and financial matters, such as lawsuits, criminal pro
tion, insurance issues, family conflicts, and the like. When emot
energy and attention is directed toward these circumstances, it is h
to focus on the loss itself, and the resulting sadness. Instead, parents
need to prepare for trials, and struggle with people or institutions
show little concern for their situation. For these people and institut
it is business as usual, while for the bereaved parent it is anythin
that. Your role as a clinician may be to help them make some deci
about managing these situations, and to prepare them for courtroor
pearances, depositions, and other kinds of adversarial proceedings. A
eral and important point to mention here is that the diversion o
bereaved parent into these concerns should be counterbalanced b
clinician. Sometimes it helps to remind parents of the most impo
and enduring aspects of their grief with a comment such as:

> Even though this situation with the insurance company is quite upsetti
> it is important that David not get lost in all this. You still have your re
> tionship with him, and your memories of him to look after.

With this, the parent may be able to reserve some time to focus o
sadness and loss, as well as the anger at those who treated their

One bit of perspective you can
counterfactual thinking is to remind t
hindsight, and to bring them back to
them to describe the situation they we
the intervention that would have chan
that they are describing a day that at t
it was easy to do the ordinary thing.

> *Bereaved Parent (BP):* It was late in the af
> Clark was talking to someone on th
> attention. He said that he had to
> getting supper soon, so I said that
> almost time to eat. But he was alm
> back, this was a little strange, but I
> give it much thought. I should have
> it was too late to go out then. Ther
> shot.
>
> *Therapist (T):* Of course, this was pretty
> time. You had no inkling then of w
>
> *BP:* Right, but how I wish I had just said
>
> *T:* Like what?
>
> *BP:* Don't go!
>
> *T:* What do you think Clark would have
>
> *BP:* Well, I don't know, but with those
> probably felt he had to. He probab
> back for supper," and gone out. So r
>
> *T:* Of course, if you knew then what was
> done *anything* to change it.
>
> *BP:* I would have tied him up!
>
> *T:* Of course, at that time, not knowing
> have looked a little overboard.
>
> *BP:* Yeah, of course. I guess I should hav
> he was getting into, and taken a stro
>
> *T:* You didn't think he was in this kind o
>
> *BP:* No, well, yes, I was worried. But I did
> have known better what was going
>
> *T:* I remember you said he was always
> good. Maybe that helped you think t
>
> *BP:* I think so, but I was fooling myself, i
>
> *T:* Fooling yourself? Like trying not to se

BP: I don't think that so much. I guess I just trusted him, and thought that stuff like that wasn't happening to my kid. I guess I was naive.

T: Not anymore.

BP: But it's too late for Clark. I failed him. He needed a parent who was more in touch. Tougher, maybe.

T: You didn't get a chance to adjust your parenting to these circumstances. When those boys killed him, they took away your chances as well as Clark's. I'll bet you made plenty of adjustments over the years as Clark grew up, and you figured out what he needed. I think parenting is a lot of those adjustments.

BP: Yeah, I'd think I just had things under control and figured out with him, and then he'd be on to another phase. I hadn't figured out this teen age phase yet.

T: You might have with a little more time.

In this example, we can see the therapist acknowledging the bereaved parent's feeling of guilt and failure, but putting them into a realistic framework. That framework includes the context of the day Clark died—it appeared ordinary, and she had no reason to think anything so terrible was about to happen. It also includes the context of parenting—that parents are trying to figure out what to do, and usually have the time for trial and error with their kids. It is extraordinary to have to be a parent in a life and death situation, when you do not even know you are in one. Here is part of the further conversation about this.

BP: I know I am being too hard on myself for not seeing what would happen. But as a mother, I am supposed to know how to take care of my child, to protect him from danger.

T: Of course, good parents feel this way.

BP: That's it, how could I be a good parent. Clark's dead.

T: If you met another parent whose child had died because they had not prevented the child from doing something that led to their death, would you think of them as a bad parent?

BP: It depends on what they overlooked. Like, if they left a loaded gun out for a five year old to find, I think that is pretty bad.

T: Is your circumstance like that?

BP: No, not really. The gun thing is obviously a problem. You could see that coming.

T: So you don't think parents should be able to anticipate and protect against all dangers? Like maybe the school bus will wreck? Or that a plane will crash into the school building? Or a tree will fall on him?

BP: Some things are just so unlikely, you'd drive yourself crazy trying to worry about all of them. Probably drive your kid crazy too.

T: So, in your situation with Clark, with those boys and him being involved with drugs, was that more like the five-year-old and the gun, or the school bus crash?

BP: Somewhere in between, I think.

By the end of this clinical segment, the parent has been able to explore in detail the thinking that she is utilizing in concluding that she is guilty, and comes to a moderate position. That is enough for that point. As a clinician, it is important to recognize that time is necessary to process such material. So you accept things for the time being. The advantage to this therapeutic stance, expert companionship, is that you allow bereaved parents to speak frankly and fully, and by doing so, they are free to say to you the things others do not want to hear. In the example just given, the parent had not been able to process the counterfactual thinking and guilt very well because others had tried to make her feel better by saying to her that she was a wonderful, loving mother, and that neither she nor her son deserved this. All true, but not useful given what she was cognitively and emotionally attempting to process in her own way.

At some point, most parents are able to conclude one of the following with regard to the counterfactuals. They may be able to decide that they did what they could, given what they knew at the time. Others may conclude that they made mistakes, but they are not directly at fault for their children's deaths. What is usually a minor incident turned into a major tragedy due to the confluence of other factors besides their action or inaction. Or, they may conclude that they were at fault, but that they did not intend it, and will have to seek forgiveness from themselves. Consider the situation where a mother drove off the road, and her six-year-old daughter was killed in the crash. Her husband held her responsible and divorced her. She was badly injured and could not remember what happened, including whether her daughter was belted into her seat. The police investigation found that she was not, but the mother said she always made a point to check the belt.

BP: I guess I will never know the absolute truth about this. I have decided that I belted her in, but she took it off. That is the only sense I can make of it. Maybe some people would say I'm just trying to make myself feel better, but you know, I've punished myself plenty about this for the past three years. And Charlie will continue to punish me in any way he can, even though I don't plan to see him again. But, I still drove the car off the road, and I don't know what happened there, either. Maybe I swerved to avoid another car. Maybe I slid in the rain,

Maybe I was going too fast. Who knows? Nobody. Not me. And I'll never know.

T: You have worked on this a long time. You've put yourself on trial. Is this the verdict?

BP: I guess so.

T: Was it a fair trial?

BP: I think I was a pretty tough prosecutor.

T: The charges were serious.

BP: Yeah. To live with the verdict, given the charges, it had to be rough.

T: Charlie tried you, too.

BP: And found me guilty. But I don't think that was a fair trial. Or a trial at all. That was a lynching. I think I sifted through everything carefully, and put myself through hell.

T: So that is over.

BP: I guess I decided that either I live with this or kill myself—the death penalty. And the only thing that makes sense to me is that this was a pure accident or some unintentional neglect. I don't think I deserve the death penalty for either. I loved Carly, and always tried to give her the best. If I did something wrong that day, it was just horrible luck that it had that consequence. How many times do parents make mistakes and get away with it? And I think the life sentence I'm serving as a bereaved parent is punishment enough. So, I've decided to leave it at that. That's my thinking.

T: A three-year trial is a pretty thorough one. I'm glad that's over for you.

For many clinicians, seeing a client through three years of therapy on this issue of guilt and self-forgiveness may seem like slow and inefficient therapy. But that is sometimes the time frame you will deal with when there are complicated issues in bereavement. Seldom are bereaved parents really stuck. Usually, they have a great deal of cognitive processing to do about so many aspects of the grief experience, and so much emotional turmoil has to be managed, that the process is naturally lengthy. Spiritual issues, the relationship with the deceased child, guilt and responsibility, the disappointment in the responses of others to their grief, practical issues of insurance, burial, memorials, holidays, the reactions and consequences for various family members, existential concerns with meaning, anxiety, depression, or substance abuse secondary to the bereavement experience, how to manage responsibilities such as child care or work in the aftermath of the death—all of these require a great deal of time and effort to sort through. This is not usually a brief therapy experience. It is unfortunate that many clinicians expect that bereavement, being "only" a *DSM–IV* "V-code," does not merit appreciation as a very difficult life challenge that requires much time, effort, and subtle therapeutic work.

☐ Traumatic Grief

It might be useful to consider parental bereavement as a situation that triggers posttraumatic stress symptoms, perhaps to the level of a posttraumatic stress disorder (PTSD) in some parents. We have discussed how posttraumatic growth is a common outgrowth of parental bereavement, and we have stated that the processes that engender growth have much in common with those that are involved in PTSD, especially the breaking down of fundamental worldviews.

Certainly there are some situations where it is clear that parents have had to deal with death directly and have symptoms of avoidance, numbing, flashbacks, hypervigilance, and so on that are characteristic of PTSD. For example, one bereaved parent we worked with was an emergency medical technician. One day, her son was at the school bus stop one block away, where some road construction had been taking place. The children were playing on a large drainage pipe that was awaiting installation. The pipe rolled and crushed her son. She heard the screaming of the children, and ran down the street. She applied CPR and other measures in a futile attempt to save her son.

This parent displayed some of the classic symptoms of PTSD. Not only was she confronted with grief, but also the avoidance of many reminders of her son's death. She could no longer work, because she could not tolerate the anxiety she felt in response to anything related to emergency situations, including hospitals, EMT trucks, and sirens. She had to shield herself from looking at the school bus stop one block away, and the other children in the neighborhood. She struggled with nightmares and flashbacks of her futile attempt to save her son, and was horrified at the images of his crushed skull. This bereaved parent needed a form of treatment that combined attention to the grief and also to its traumatic elements. To some extent, all parents are traumatized by their children's deaths. But only a few need treatment for posttraumatic stress in a formal sense. This mother was one who did, because of the nature of her experience with her son's death.

Clinicians who work with bereaved parents need to be familiar with trauma therapy approaches for those parents whose grief also includes elements of trauma. Trauma therapies usually incorporate relaxation procedures, graded exposure, and cognitive reprocessing. The work done in therapy with bereaved parents involves some of these elements naturally. As parents tell the story of their children's lives and deaths, they expose themselves to the trauma again, and as they search for meaning and purpose in the aftermath of the trauma, or confront feelings of guilt and regret, they have to engage in significant cognitive processing. To this, specific relaxation techniques can be added, or parents can be encouraged to find methods outside of therapy, such as yoga or meditation, to achieve anxiety reduction. Usually, parents tell the stories of their children's deaths several times in therapy, and it is useful to notice how these stories change, and how parents' emotional reactions to them change. In support groups, these stories are retold as new members join the group, and this acts as an exposure technique. Retelling of the story reduces the sense that this event is unbelievable, and gives parents practice at revisiting details, finding the right words to describe it, and managing their emotions as they confront it.

Although we think it is good to emphasize that the various aspects of the grief process are normal and understandable, people who have particularly traumatic experiences with the deaths of their children also need to realize that their situations carry this extra burden. One parent whose son was hit by a car right in front of her had this exchange with her therapist.

BP: I don't understand why I'm having so much trouble with this. Here I am still crying and choking on my words in the group, while other people seem to be so calmed down. I can't get calm about this. I don't see how they do it.

T: There are some differences in what you and the other group members have been through, you know.

BP: I know it was horrible what I went through. But I can see how everyone in the group had their own horrible part. Betsy had to watch her son just waste away for months with cancer. At least it was quick for Marty. I don't think he suffered like Betsy's boy. I'm grateful for that.

T: So in some way, you are grateful that he died the way he did, compared to what he could have gone through?

BP: I have thought that. But, still, it was so horrible to see him get hit like that.

T: Right. There is no good way to have your child die.

BP: So why am I still such a mess? This is now into the second year.

T: One thing you have to deal with that is different, is the images of Marty's death. Others didn't have to watch their children die. Or, if they did, it was something more peaceful and expected like with Betsy. The shock that you encountered is so vivid, that it has power to override your attempts to suppress it. You are in a struggle with those images, while others aren't. Witnessing something like this often produces reactions that are beyond grief, and include elements of what is called posttraumatic stress. Have you ever heard of that?

BP: Like the Vietnam vets had?

T: Yes, veterans exposed to violent deaths have often suffered this.

BP: So I'm like one of those veterans.

T: Yes, you witnessed something horrific happen to the person you loved most.

BP: So will I ever get over it?

T: Your grief and loss will always be there in some form, but not as painful. The images that come to you we can minimize, too. You have to make peace with them, be ready to look at them, rather than fear and avoid them. We can work on that together.

BP: I need some relief.

The clinician in this session is providing some basic information to the bereaved parent so that she can understand what they are going through, and not feel so crazy about it. He also gives her hope that something can be done about it, although probably not *undone. It is important not to promise too much relief from something so difficult.* You might have also noticed that the clinician was willing to share a bit more expertise here, because this is not about being a bereaved parent, but it is about a psychiatric disorder. In these unusual circumstances, it is appropriate to emphasize the expert part of the expert companionship you offer.

There are various strategies that may be useful for reducing the intrusive images based on the versions of trauma therapy that exist. The basic approach is gradual exposure and processing of the experience. Desensitization procedures can be utilized to address avoidance of activities, as was the case with this mother who had restricted her driving to avoid local hospitals, places where she would hear sirens often on routes to these hospitals, and so on. She could not avoid the scene of the accident, because it was a block away from her house, on the way out of the neighborhood, and she had developed ways to manage her anxiety at that spot.

Similar avoidance can be seen in most bereaved parents around things such as the child's room, possessions, or photographs. Here, too, gradual exposure or desensitization is useful. We do not necessarily recommend standardized systematic desensitization procedures, but rather the use of the gradual exploration of these anxiety-arousing situations, giving bereaved parents plenty of time. We emphasize that they are the experts of their own grief, and that in time things change.

☐ Time, Tears, and Talk

The combination of time, tears, and talk is a simple way for parents to keep track of the healing approach they can take. What we mean by this is patience with oneself and the process of grief, allowing emotional expression rather than suppressing it, and seeking out people who will be good, patient listeners. Good support groups allow for all three, and bereaved parents learn these lessons well in such groups.

In a culture of managed care, fast food, and individualism, this approach is frustrating for many parents, at least at some points in the process of enduring pain. And it can be frustrating for some clinicians, too. But we have found that most bereaved parents do better with a supportive, patient approach to grief that respects the nature of the process. Most bereaved parents do better when they can talk with others that have gone through a similar ordeal. Most bereaved parents do better when they have permission to allow emotional expression. If you can provide these elements, you will help the vast majority of grieving parents achieve their "new normal," a changed life that they can find useful and fulfilling, while recognizing they have been informed about life in a way that has made them experts on existential concerns such as meaning, chance, choice, and acceptance of limits.

4
CHAPTER

Bereaved Parents and Their Families

Grief fills the room up of my absent child,
Lies in his bed, walks up and down with me.
Shakespeare, *King John*

Although we have been focusing on some general, common reactions to parental bereavement in this book, we have also emphasized that there is a great deal of individual variability in these reactions. When we look at the family context of parental bereavement, this variability becomes even more apparent. In this chapter, we wish to honor the fact that each family has its own particular way of responding to grief and affecting the parents of the deceased child. But we also alert clinicians to some of the issues they are likely to face in working with parents or the larger family network, and how to respond constructively to these issues. We recognize that a volume could be written about each family member—siblings, grandparents, stepparents, and so on. We do not attempt to be exhaustive in our treatment of the bereavement of these family members. Instead, we focus on the ways the bereavement of parents interacts with the bereavement of other family members.

☐ Family as Social Support

It is understandable that couples would turn to each other in seeking support after the death of their children. Spouses can know the child intimately, usually are in close proximity, know the details of the life and death of that child, and are often present when emotional needs are great. Bereaved parents are usually confronted with the need to make plans for funerals, memorials, and the like, and to support any surviving siblings of the deceased child. They obviously can share much, and in the better marriages, couples have built a history of support and understanding on which they can rely.

It is also understandable that other members of the extended family may be counted on for social support, including the parent's own parents, siblings, or other family members. These also are people who knew the deceased child well, who might be familiar with many of the circumstances of the death, and who might be assumed to have similar feelings of loss. At the same time, bereaved parents may find themselves needing to provide support to others in the family, especially to surviving siblings and to their own spouses. Bereaved mothers may find themselves expected to provide special care for their other children, whereas bereaved fathers often speak of their role of providing support to their wives. Bereaved fathers sometimes come to bereavement support groups with the explanation that they are there to support their wives (Tedeschi & Hamilton, 1991). Despite these varied demands and expectations that bereaved parents may face about providing support to others or obtaining support from others, it is not unusual for the realities of bereavement to conflict with these demands and expectations. In the midst of some of the most difficult emotions they may ever have encountered, bereaved parents can find it almost impossible to respond in ways that others wish or expect. As a result, there may be disappointments among family members as they struggle to obtain and provide support to each other.

In grief, friction in the social network tends to be closely related to the degree of emotional well-being (Nolen-Hoeksema & Larson, 1999). When persons who are expected to be supportive create conflict at precisely the time when they are needed for support, bereavement is much more difficult. Certainly this is possible in families. The quality of the support, as described in our earlier chapters as acceptance, patience, and willingness to listen to the grief, generally determines whether family support is useful or counterproductive.

Marriage

There are many possible effects of the death of a child on a marriage. Couples may try to protect the other's feelings by being careful not to mention the subject of their child's death. Their experience with powerful negative emotions that are loosed in talking about their child may also motivate them to avoid further discussion. Bereaved parents' sexual relationship may be negatively affected, as they feel guilty about having pleasure in the aftermath of their children's deaths, or feel sex is an inappropriate return to normalcy (Rando, 1986). If one parent is held responsible in some way for the death, or is seen to have failed the child as a parent, resentment and marital distress may be severe (DeFrain, 1991).

Although we have often heard bereaved parents say that they have been told that the death of a child leads to the parents' divorce, empirical evidence does not support this contention. It appears that *although some marriages do dissolve in the aftermath of a child's death, marital relationships often do not change, and many improve* as parents struggle together to cope with the loss of a child. For example, in one study, after a period of several years, 40% of couples whose children died of cancer reported *improved* marital relationships (Martinson, McClowry, Davies, & Kulenkamp, 1994). In a study of parents whose children had died in motor vehicle accidents, some marital relationships were dissolved but some were strengthened (Lehman, Lang, Wortman, & Sorenson, 1989). In an excellent review of the empirical literature on the effects of a child's death on the parent's marriage, Oliver (1999) concluded that "the notion that the death of a child almost inevitably precipitates a severe marital crisis and/ or divorce is widespread, it is a myth which must be dispelled in light of the empirical evidence" (p. 207).

Implicit in the challenges to marriage in the aftermath of parental bereavement is the problem of gender differences in bereavement. This is one of the sources of difference that can breed misunderstanding in couples, particularly when communication involves much emotion and the difficulty of finding a way to describe one's experience. It is tempting to stereotype gender differences in communicating and relating, and we see too much of this in the popular literature already. It is also important to remember that in clinical work, individuals may demonstrate tendencies that are at variance with the group findings reported in research, and so it is important to not assume that research findings apply to each individual or family a clinician sees. But to the degree that men and women adhere to different culturally prescribed roles and are in different sociocultural contexts, we can expect to see some differences in certain responses to bereavement, there is some empirical support for this. Research generally indicates more intense experiences of grief for mothers than for fathers (Fish, 1986; Lang & Gottlieb, 1993; Sidmore, 1999–2000). This incongruity or asynchrony in the grieving of husbands and wives can be a major source of marital stress (Oliver, 1999). For example, we have seen that it is often the case that support is provided by mothers and fathers in different ways. We also have noted that bereaved fathers are sometimes prone to attempt to take some kind of action in an attempt to reduce their wives' grief. Here is an excerpt from a couples therapy session that illustrates such differences in coping styles.

Bereaved Father (BF): It doesn't seem to matter what I do, she just gets mad at me.

Bereaved Mother (BM): You just want me to get over it. You don't understand that I miss him so much. You just want to go on.

BF: I can't stand seeing you just lie around and not help yourself.

BM: I am helping myself.

BF: How? You just stay in bed a lot.

BM: I'm writing in my journal, and remembering him. And crying.

BF: But you can't go on like this.

Therapist (T): Bert, what do you do to help yourself through this?

BF: Well, I just can't stand thinking about it all the time. I try to get some exercise. I like to split wood—that helps me get it out.

T: Get what out?

BF: The pain, the pain. And my mind goes a little blank when I'm splitting wood.

T: That's a relief.

BF: Yeah.

T: [Turning to the mother] He's not so different from you about this, he has his way of getting out the pain, but he doesn't understand that you have yours.

BM: I just think we are going our separate ways on this. It's like he doesn't feel anything. I don't see the pain he's talking about and it makes me feel very alone.

T: Bert, did you hear that?

BF: Yeah, she thinks I don't care, I don't feel anything.

BM: I didn't say that.

T: Actually, Martha, you said that it's like he doesn't feel anything, and that he just wants you to get over it.

BM: Well, yeah, I guess so.

T: I can tell that you both feel that the other misunderstands you. You both loved Mitchell tremendously, and are struggling with how to deal with the pain you are feeling. [Father puts his head in his hands and begins to tremble and cry. There is a long silence.]

BM: [To her husband] I know you hurt, too. [She hugs him.]

BF: I'm OK.

BM: [To the therapist] He won't let me help him.

T: Bert, is she helping you now?

BF: Yeah, if she understands I hurt, too.

BM: I'm sorry. I just get so frustrated when you try to ignore everything and expect me to.

BF: I don't expect you to ignore everything, that'd be stupid. I can't ignore it either. I really don't know what you mean by that. Just because I chop some wood?

This excerpt demonstrates how couples can misunderstand their different ways of coping with bereavement, and how one partner can believe that the other is rebuffing an attempt to be supportive. In these circumstances, the clinician needs to educate both partners on the acceptability of individual differences in grieving, and help them appreciate the strengths of differing approaches. In the end, they might also learn from each other so that each has a more balanced way of approaching grief. In the case example here, the therapist needed to act as the expert in order to facilitate this. Here are more exchanges from the same couples session.

T: I watch and listen to the two of you, and I see two different, but capable people, in a desperately painful situation. And each of you is doing the right thing—trying to find a way to find some relief from the constant pain. You chop wood, and you write. Handling grief is about figuring out how to take doses of the pain that are not so large that they feel overwhelming. At the very beginning, you described being numb a lot—remember?

BM: I was just like a robot at the funeral.

T: Exactly. Then the real pain started to come. Often you sleep to avoid it. [To the father] And you chop wood, and it sounds like a kind of trance you go into. Both these methods bring some relief, temporarily. [To the mother] Then you write and cry.

BM: That's when my emotions really come out. But I don't see his. I know he hurts, but when I don't see it, I feel so alone.

T: I think his emotions come out when the ax hits the wood. What do you think, Bert?

BF: You know when you scream, Martha? It's like I'm screaming when I do this, but I'm using the ax to do it.

T: Do you see what he's talking about, Martha?

BM: Yes.

T: Bert, if you could remind Martha that you are going to go out and make that ax scream, she'll remember, and not feel so different, and so alone.

BF: I let the ax do the talking.

T: You can tell her that when you are going out.

BF: Will that help you Martha?

BM: Yes, but you have to talk to me too. And quit telling me to get out of bed.

BF: But you can't—

T: Bert—I think you are worried about her, and are used to making things better for her.

BF: Of course.

T: But this is a whole different kind of problem. It will demand a different kind of approach.

BF: What's that? I sure haven't got it right so far.

T: Well, Martha, correct me if I'm wrong about this, but I wonder if an important step for Bert to take would be to listen to you, with patience. He doesn't tell you what to do, how to handle it, or anything, but just reminds you that you'll get through this together, and listens.

BM: That would help a lot.

BF: I'm not sure how well I'd do with that.

T: How so?

BF: It seems like doing nothing to me.

T: Bert, what do you do before you cut wood?

BF: What do you mean—like have a cup of coffee?

T: You have some coffee before you go out?

BF: Yeah.

T: Anything else?

BF: Well, I get my stuff on—my gloves and glasses.

T: Right. You get yourself ready. And how about your ax?

BF: Sometimes I sharpen it.

T: You do these things, but no wood is getting cut. But they are important to do.

BF: If I want to have an easier job of it, and be safe.

T: Same when you listen patiently to Martha—grieving is easier and safer for her this way. You'll see the results later.

BF: That's pretty good, doc—I see what you mean.

T: Now, you still may need to get comfortable with this way of approaching things with Martha, and we can practice that here.

Notice that the therapist in this exchange steps in to prevent a repetition of misunderstanding and negotiates ways that each person can make sense of the other's reactions. In this example, the therapist cuts off the husband when he starts to tell the wife yet again that she can't lie around in bed. He then uses an extended metaphor to help the husband see the value of what initially seems to be an overly passive or inefficient way of helping his wife. The husband "gets it" and seems to enjoy the way the metaphor is used to communicate with him—he compliments the therapist. Finally, the therapist points out that this is a skill that he may need some help and experience with. They later worked on skills of listening and tolerating the wife's emotions when the husband was getting uncomfortable with their power.

This approach makes explicit that the father and mother are different in some ways in their expressions of grief, but that much of the essential emotional experience is held in common. Although there may be widely diverging ways of experiencing or expressing grief, parents almost always have healthy aspects of the experience on which the therapist can build—clinicians should be attentive to finding these and helping parents develop those ways of coping further. In this example, the clinician noted that the avoidance of each person was an appropriate manifestation of the "dosing" of grief that is necessary. The clinician made specific reference to the fact that they are "capable" people, although different. Most bereaved parents have impressed us with their capabilities in the face of their tragedy, and it may be relatively easy now to see these possibilities in the newly bereaved. We like to point out these adaptive capabilities to parents, and also to note how couples find ways to help each other. Later, with the passage of time, posttraumatic growth may become evident to the clinician, and perhaps to parents as well, and the therapist can highlight this for the couple. Bert and Martha, a few months later, talked about their marriage since Mitchell's death.

BM: I tell you I'm glad that we're still hanging together after all this. I wondered at the beginning what was going to happen to us.

T: I remember some of the trouble we had to work out.

BF: I never got Martha to try splitting wood, though [laughs].

T: But there have been other changes between the two of you, haven't there?

BF: Oh yeah, I've learned some things.

T: Like what.

BF: I think I'm more patient with Martha. Don't you think, hon?

BM: You're getting there—really, yes you are, and I appreciate that. This may sound strange, Bert, but I like you better than I used to. Not that I didn't before, but more now.

T: What do you mean, Martha?

BM: Well, he has learned to listen to me more patiently, and that I'm not going to always feel OK, and that it doesn't mean that something terrible is happening to me. It already happened, and now I'm just dealing with it my way, and he doesn't have to be afraid of that.

T: It sounds like you understand, too, that when Bert was pushing you to feel better and do things it was at least partly out of fear of what might be happening to you.

BM: And frustration and impatience, too. He has learned some patience.

T: I wish you had never had to learn this way, Bert.

BF: But I'm glad I didn't lose Martha, too.

T: I look at what has happened to your relationship since Mitchell died, and it's like the changes you've made are part of his legacy—does that make any sense?

BM: We've talked about how Mitchell wouldn't want things to go wrong between the two of us, that we need to stick together for him, too.

T: That's a way to honor him.

BM: That wasn't the initial reason, I guess, but yeah, we thought that too.

In this sequence, the clinician helps Bert and Martha focus on the growth that has occurred in the aftermath of their son's death, and links it with the idea of honoring or memorializing him. This is always a powerful motive for bereaved parents, and by connecting the positive changes in themselves and their marriage to the memory of their child, it may provide continued motivation to work on their relationship. Not all this is stated explicitly. The clinician leaves implied the idea that they will continue to be motivated by Mitchell's legacy. It is important to leave with bereaved parents a certain degree of self-discovery and sense of wonder about the process they are going through. What people do with their grief is also sometimes surprising, impressive, and a bit mysterious to us, and we prefer not to try to reduce everything to purely rational explanations.

Stepparents, Ex-Spouses, and Former Partners

Parental bereavement can be complicated by family relationships that have been changed by separation, divorce, or widowhood. Depending on the quality of relationship ex-spouses or former partners have had with each other and the deceased child, there may be difficulties to confront from the immediate aftermath of the loss. In this section we review some of the common problems that can arise in these family situations. There are many variations on these themes, and we can only illustrate here some therapeutic approaches to these complications of parental bereavement.

Whatever the problems that led to separation or divorce initially, and whatever problems that may have arisen since, these difficulties can play a role in parental bereavement from the initial reactions to, and decisions necessary after, a child has died. Depending on custody arrangements, one parent may be in a position to carry more weight in decisions after the child's death, just as it had been in life. Misunderstandings and disagreements are likely when the ex-spouses have a poor method of communicating under routine circumstances. Certain decisions, such as funeral arrangements, must be made rather quickly, and there is little time to work on improving communication and understanding in preparation for these discussions. Clinicians who are assisting families or spouses in these circumstances would be wise to focus the partners on communicating with directness and with an intention to put aside other issues in the face of this tragedy. Consider the following example of a bereaved father who is struggling to come to an agreement with his ex-wife over some of the issues that have arisen after their daughter's death.

BF: Diane just doesn't care to talk with me about Mary. I know we haven't been close for a long time, but we were parents together, for God's sake.

T: What happens when you try to talk with her about it?

BF: She pretty much just gives me the brush off and ends the conversation.

T: Any idea why?

BF: I don't know.

T: Have you asked her?

BF; Not really.

T: What could you say?

BF: I guess "Why don't you want to talk with me?"

T: That might be a good start. I wonder why you haven't done that before.

BF: I've been afraid to get into it with her. Whenever we talk too long, we seem to get into an argument.

T: Maybe she's aware of that, too.

BF: Man, that's obvious enough. I just didn't think of that before. I guess I'll tell her that I know how things have been but she's the person I really want to talk to about Mary.

T: That sounds like a nice invitation. I hope she responds in kind. It could be the start of something better between the two of you.

BF: That would be a relief.

This exchange seems quite simple. But there are some subtleties. The clinician starts with an obvious remark, rather than a complicated one.

Why not ask her? Then, when the client comes up with his own answer, the clinician simply points out that possibility, and lets the bereaved father take it from there. The clinician compliments the father's wording of things ("that's a nice invitation") and gives encouragement while acknowledging that that it may not work out ("I hope she responds in kind"), while holding open the possibility for growth as well ("It could be the start of something better"). All of this is also the modeling of simple, direct, and positive communication. From our perspective, that is the best way to respond to grief.

Complicated situations can exist in families of divorce that produce challenges to the already daunting grieving process. When there has been estrangement from the deceased child, strains over parenting decisions with the ex-spouse, or resentments held against the ex-spouse's new mate, the clinician is faced with helping the bereaved parent navigate these problems as well as their grief. Here is an example of how that might be done.

> *BF:* I realize that Sharon has been living with her mother for five years now, but I'm still her father, and I think I should be consulted before she goes ahead with these things.
>
> *T:* Like the clothes.
>
> *BF:* Yeah. And Donny thinks he can just call all the shots—like he did with Sharon's clothes.
>
> *T:* What other decisions are on the horizon that you have strong feelings about, that you wish to have a say in?
>
> *BF:* The marker for one thing. And the memorial fund. And whether we should sue the guy that hit her. I don't have any idea how that would work.
>
> *T:* It's good that you can see what things you have some preferences about, so you have a chance to work things out before Lisa and Donny go ahead with these things.
>
> *BF:* What really bugs me is they treat me like I have no standing in this. Like Donny is the father and not me.
>
> *T:* So part of it has to do with how they treat you, which is no different than it was while Sharon was alive.
>
> *BF:* True.
>
> *T:* But the other part is about how they are treating Sharon's memory.
>
> *BF:* And Lisa is real weak, as usual, and I don't trust her to do the right thing.
>
> *T:* It must feel like they still have custody.
>
> *BF:* That's what they act like.

T: Who really has custody of Sharon? And Sharon's memory?

BF: [Long pause] You know, that's a really strange thought. I'm thinking God has custody of Sharon.

T: How does that feel?

BF: Good, I guess. I mean I wish he didn't—I mean I wish she were alive—but I'd rather think of God having custody of her than Lisa and Donny. Well, Donny, especially. And you know, it makes sense. That's right. God has custody.

T: What does that mean about all these issues? Does realizing this change anything about these conflicts?

BF: I'm not sure. I still want the marker like I told you.

T: I think things like that are more about Sharon's memory, if God has custody.

BF: You mean how to remember her.

T: Right. And who has custody of her memory?

BF: I don't know. How could anyone? I mean I have my memories of Sharon, other people have theirs. That doesn't make sense to me.

T: You know, that's what I was thinking. You have your memories of Sharon. No one can take custody of those, and any way you choose to share them. Donny's always ticked you off. But maybe it's not so important to struggle with him about some things.

BF: Somehow in my mind, I guess I've been struggling with reclaiming her from him. What does that matter now? I can go ahead and remember her, and tell people about her, any way I want.

T: Of course, there are some things, like the insurance settlement, the lawsuit, her marker, that you may have to come to terms with them on. But a lot of things you can choose to do as you wish. But I'm thinking that if you keep in mind who has custody now, it will all be easier to deal with.

BF: You may be right.

Notice that the clinician in this example takes a particular stand on the issue of the conflict with the stepfather. He offers the perspective that engaging in direct conflict is not likely to be very satisfying, and that the most important issues have to do with the relationship with the deceased child. This is relatively easy for the father to see, because it fits with his schema that the stepfather is not important and that his child is. The clinician also uses the language of "custody" to offer the idea that the stepfather does not have any real control over what is most important. Furthermore, the clinician invites the father to collaborate on the custody metaphor, and this allows the father to accept this perspective more readily.

This is also an example of how working with bereaved parents requires clinicians to be accepting and flexible about what is "real" and "true." What is more important is what brings comfort to people who have enormous difficulty in finding any.

Stepparents and Bereavement

The previous clinical example also illustrates how it can be important for ex-spouses to share grief with each other, especially if they have a long shared history with the child who died. This can be threatening to the current spouses of the bereaved parents, as they may see an intimacy their spouses have with ex-spouses around this topic. This also raises the issue of the possible disenfranchisement of the grief of the stepparent of the child who died.

There is a range of reactions that stepparents may have to the death of a stepchild. These reactions are dependent on the closeness of the relationship with the child, the degree that this relationship involved parenting or some other way of relating to the stepchild, and what the biological parents permit in terms of expression of grief and involvement in the role of bereaved parent by the stepparent. Stepparents who are not particularly close to the child who has died often feel that their spouse who is the child's parent has become like a stranger in some ways, because their emotional experience is so different. And in turn, the bereaved parent may feel estrangement as well. It is best to encourage honest acknowledgment of these differences if they exist. Some stepparents have a deeper attachment to the deceased child than the family or people outside the family may acknowledge. This form of disenfranchised grief may be addressed with directness and honesty, as the clinician shows in the following excerpt from a session with a stepmother whose stepson committed suicide.

> *BM:* At work yesterday, one of my coworkers asked me what was wrong. I usually say nothing, I'm fine, but for some reason this time I just told her I was thinking about Carl. Since it's been almost a year, I don't talk about it anymore, because it seems like a long time to them, and I think they think I should just move on or something.
>
> *T:* But yesterday you told the truth about what was going on.
>
> *BM:* I should have known better. I don't really know this woman that well, and—I don't know why I even got into it.
>
> *T:* I guess she caught you at one of those vulnerable moments.
>
> *BM:* Yeah. Well, I said I was thinking about Carl and missing him, and she

said, "He was your stepson, right?" And I knew right then what she's thinking. Like I shouldn't be so upset. And sure enough, she says, "At least it wasn't your real son." And I was just speechless.

T: It is hard to know what to say to something like that.

BM: But I also felt something else. Like I should defend Carl, but I just couldn't say anything. And she was trying to be comforting I guess, and she said that I'd been doing real well, and she was sure I'd be OK. And all of this was just so confusing to me. I know she was trying to be nice, but everything she said felt so wrong, and I just felt rotten. And somehow guilty.

T: You can't quite understand that feeling of guilt?

BM: No. It's like I was betraying Carl, listening to this.

T: Now that you think about it, is there something that you could have said, so that you wouldn't feel guilty?

BM: I just don't want to get into this stuff at work, because I end up upset and can't do anything.

T: That's a good choice for you. But I was just wondering if in your heart there is some sort of response that you feel to this?

BM: Absolutely. I'd like to say that I loved Carl, and it didn't matter that he was my stepson, he was a great kid. And we had a good relationship. And that she was minimizing all of that, like it really didn't count. And I guess I resent that.

T: Making those assumptions about Carl and your relationship without knowing.

BM: Right. And I think a lot of people make these assumptions. That Carl's death wasn't that big a deal to me, because I have Kenny [her son]. And even that I'm relieved that it wasn't Kenny.

T: No one knows the feelings of another in these matters. There are just so many different reactions people have.

BM: People do it anyway.

T: Sure, we often assume that the way we feel is the way others would feel.

BM: That's kind of lazy.

T: Not too many people really want to take the time to find out now what is really going on with you.

BM: It would take a while to explain. And who wants to focus on death?

T: But somehow, if you don't tell them of the real way you feel about Carl, it feels like you betray him. You don't stand up for what a great kid he was. Maybe you could figure out something to have ready to say at these times.

BM: That might be good.

T: So you are prepared, not taken off guard completely. That's why I asked what your heart was telling you.

BM: And I said it, didn't I?

T: You said it well. You can practice saying that out loud. Or anything else you'd wish to say about him. Saying it out loud is different from feeling or thinking it. Then you'll be ready when it is the right time to tell someone about Carl and his stepmother.

BM: Then I'll decide when the right time is, and not be tongue-tied.

T: Right. And there is another thing I want to say about this guilt you feel for not defending Carl. Even if you get tongue-tied, this is no betrayal. You did have a good relationship with Carl and he knew that. What an acquaintance at work knows or believes about that doesn't change anything that you and Carl knew, and still know. Grief is tough, and sometimes other people unwittingly make it tougher. So be charitable with yourself.

In this example, there are again many things going on. The concern about keeping emotions under control in the workplace, feeling misunderstood by others, even those who mean well, the enduring sense of taking care of the deceased child and his memory. All this in addition to the issue of being a stepmother, and the way that the grief of this parent may be called into question. The clinician tackles some of these things and leaves others alone. Most of the interventions are simple validations of the parent's experiences. But the main focus is the choice of addressing the coworker's misunderstandings versus letting them stand. And finally, there is the clinician's blessing in regard to sometimes remaining silent in the tough situations a bereaved parent sometimes encounters. The reader may have also noticed something that the clinician chose not to do. You might have wondered if the stepmother's coworker had it right, that she was relieved that her biological son was not the one who died, and perhaps the guilt arose out of recognition of this. The clinician alluded to the fact that there are various reactions that people have, implying that this may be one of them. But he was not explicit about it. The judgment was made in this instance to tackle things that were easier for the stepmother to take on, and that the sense of relief might have been too difficult to admit to. Instead, the clinician first accepted the choice to remain silent rather than protest the coworker's assumptions. A more difficult topic would be validation of the sense of relief. This is a matter of timing and clinical judgment. The clinician must determine whether the client might be ready to explore something more threatening. It could have been done like this. And, at the end of this exchange, the clinician provides gentle but direct reassurance for this parent, a clinical response that we regard as appropriate in many circumstances.

T: You know that part about being relieved that it wasn't Kenny?

BM: Yes.

T: That reaction is sometimes described to me by bereaved parents. Some have said, "I don't tell anyone this, because it sounds terrible, but I'm so relieved Mary didn't die—I just realize she's always been my favorite." Or some have said, "I hate this, but the fact is that I feel like the wrong one died, Johnny was so good, and Joey's always been such a challenge." Now, they say these things in confidence to me, because they feel badly about it, but the fact is, this is just human.

BM: I don't think that's really true of me.

T: I just mentioned it in case any thoughts like that ever come to mind. A lot of bereaved parents would understand that very well.

It is very useful to refer to what one has heard from other bereaved parents in order to reassure a client that the feelings are normal and acceptable. Experienced clinicians, who have worked with or read much about the responses bereaved parents experience, will have their own storehouses of all kinds of parental experiences to which they can refer. If you are new to this field, we are presenting you with some of the experiences bereaved parents have described to us, so that you can refer to these in your work with clients. In referring to what other parents have said, there is some built-in credibility, whereas our professional reassurances on occasion may be less helpful to parents.

Another issue that arises in some blended families represents the flip side of the coin that we have just considered. Some stepparents do indeed have rather tenuous relationships with their stepchildren, and their grief reactions can be quite different from those of the biological parents. These tenuous relationships may be due to a variety of factors, such as lack of physical proximity, not having known the child for a very long time, interpersonal conflicts with the child, and the inability of the parents and child to clarify the nature of the child–stepparent relationship. These circumstances can lead stepparents to experience a variety of emotional responses that differ, and that may be less intense than what might be socially expected of a grieving parent. And stepparents may find it difficult or impossible to express these feelings to the bereaved spouse who is the biological parent. The reactions of the stepparents often involves guilt. Some stepparents have confessed that they are relieved that the child is dead because the child had been a source of such difficulty and stress. Some may feel this way because the child was a reminder of the ex-spouse, or of required frequent contact with the ex-spouse. Some stepparents may have found the child to be an obstacle in their marital relationship because of disagreements with the biological parent over child support, discipline, or other parenting issues. Stepparents may talk about the mixed emotions they have—an experience of grief mixed with some of these kinds of guilt-ridden secrets.

Another situation that can occur is the estrangement that happens when bereaved parents feel the stepparent does not share the same level of grief, and when stepparents feel that their spouses' grief is stealing them away from the marital relationship. The degree to which such issues can be discussed openly in a marriage varies. *We do not give a blanket recommendation that all these matters and issues be brought out into the open.* Instead, if the matters are clearly getting in the way of social or psychological functioning, we recommend individual counseling to clarify and thoroughly explore these kinds of reactions, *before* decisions are made to reveal them.

Surviving Siblings or Only Child

Much has been written in recent years about children's grief. There are many books for the children themselves and others for the parents of grieving children. The situation where a child loses a sibling has particular similarities to and differences from grief associated with other losses. We are not going to focus much here on these particulars, but instead discuss how parental bereavement often involves dealing with surviving children. But before we discuss this, let us turn to the situation where bereaved parents lose an only child.

Parents whose only child dies face a profound change in life circumstances and role. They may feel as if they are no longer a parent. This is understandable given that they no longer are required to engage in the activities associated with parenting, and they may not have a future that includes children. This is the case with the following parent, whose 23-year-old daughter died of leukemia.

> *BM:* I don't mean to sound like I'm that much worse off than other parents in the group, but our situation really is different from theirs.
>
> *T:* In what way?
>
> *BM:* Jennifer was our only child, and that's it for us [crying; long pause]. I guess I wouldn't say this in group, but, like Barbara, she still has her twins. I know that doesn't lessen the loss of Samuel, but she's still a mother.
>
> *T:* But you have no children to mother now.
>
> *BM:* Right. I don't know what to do with my future. Jennifer and I were so close, and you know how the leukemia brought us closer. I had so much to do to take care of her. She became my whole life the last year. Now suddenly, there is nothing to do.

T: Except take her flowers.

BM: It's the only thing I have left to do for her. But that's not the way I wanted to be a mother.

T: Of course. But there is an important distinction I think we should make.

BM: What is that?

T: Between mothering and being a mother. You can't mother her now, take care of her like you did, but you are always a mother, Jennifer's mother.

BM: That's true, no one can take that away.

T: Right. You are just as proud of her now as you always were. That sure is being a mother.

BM: You know how I love to talk about her!

T: For good reason.

BM: She was an incredible girl.

T: Now you take care of her memory, and let people know that.

BM: That's still mothering in a way.

T: I think you're right. A different way, but mothering her nonetheless.

BM: You know, I like to think she knows it.

T: Who is to say she doesn't?

BM: That's what I believe.

T: Getting back to telling the group these things, I think they would understand.

BM: I don't want to hurt anyone's feelings, or look like I have it so much harder.

T: But it is different for you than the others. I imagine you are thinking that the Johnson's, for example, could still have more kids.

BM: Exactly. But I don't want to say that, because, well, you know how people have said that kind of thing to them and it really has sounded bad, like Kevin could be replaced.

T: Sure. You are sensitive to that. I know you can find a way to talk about your situation that wouldn't be a problem. The fact is, Jennifer was your only child, and you are 55. It creates other issues.

BM: I'll never have grandchildren. And this may sound selfish, but I guess I always assumed that as I got older, if I needed some help, Jennifer would be there for me. Now, I'm going to be on my own. And, the family is coming to an end with me. There is no one to carry on. Here, I was an only child and so was Jennifer. Of course Buddy's got nieces and nephews, but I mean my side. No one will be around to remember us. It's like the memory of my parents and grandparents will die with me, too. Jennifer won't be here to carry on and tell the stories to her kids. Our family will die with me. Do you see?

T: Oh, yes. There are all kinds of losses in this. And you have some losses involved that others don't.

In this sequence, the bereaved mother brings out several issues that are specific to parents who lose only children. First, she has the sense of losing her role as a mother. Second, she senses that she will not receive special care when she grows old, and that she is more likely to feel truly alone. Third, she loses an important aspect of her future that she looked forward to—grandchildren; and fourth, she poignantly states that her entire family and all its memories, is now doomed to death.

The therapist does not sugarcoat any of these profound losses, but does point out that she will always be Jennifer's mother. This bereaved mother takes this a step farther by interpreting her remembrance of Jennifer as a way of continuing to take care of her, and her sense that Jennifer is aware of her efforts. Again we see the continuing, but changed, attachment that is common and healthy in bereavement.

Are there other comforting things a clinician can say in response to these losses? Yes. But first, it is usually important to acknowledge these changes are real and deep, and cannot be simply fixed. Many months may go by before a bereaved parent is ready to hear some suggestions about mitigating the losses. Or, the clinician may test the waters, as in the following exchange with the mother of Jennifer.

T: Nothing can make right all you have lost when Jennifer died, but I do know of what some other parents have done in similar situations. Are you interested in hearing about them?

BM: Well, yes, but I'm not sure anything can make a difference.

T: I'm not sure either, but maybe someday one of these things might make sense. For example, I know you did some writing during Jennifer's illness about how brave she was, and you have said that although some of these are painful memories, you are glad you have them.

BM: So you want me to write some more.

T: I don't want you to do anything. All these things are up to you. I'm just mentioning what some others have done. And you know from group that sometimes stuff fits and sometimes not. And sometimes stuff fits later.

BM: Yes, I know.

T: You might consider writing to Jennifer some of the family stories you wanted her to remember.

BM: Letters to Jennifer.

T: Sounds good.

BM: I'm talking to her a lot anyway.

T: You could just write any bits you'd like. Doesn't have to be a huge thing, and you'd just have to see where it takes you.

BM: Then what?

T: I don't know. But your memories are at least not totally lost that way. Your family will have some kind of life perhaps. It is hard to predict where things like that lead once you start.

BM: That might be a good thing for me to do. I'm just not sure I'm up to it now.

T: That's OK. Another thing I wondered is about Buddy's nieces and nephews. I remember you saying they adored Jennifer.

BM: Oh, yes.

T: They might be interested in remembering her, who she was like in your family, things like that. One of them might want to be your special assistant in this.

BM: Jessie might really like that.

T: I was thinking of her, too. She's written those poems to Jennifer and all. It might be an honor for her.

BM: She's a dear child. We might be able to help each other.

Our job as clinicians is often to "loosen up" the thinking of our bereaved parents who are overwhelmed by pain and cannot see possibilities. The clinician here honors the parent's reluctance, but plants some seeds that might germinate in the future. By the end of this exchange, you can sense a bit of enthusiasm developing. To an extent, this may be because the clinician is making suggestions that fit with the client's own methods of coping that she had already developed while her daughter was being treated for leukemia. He also recalls some information about her family—the nieces and nephews, in particular—that indicate that he is thinking about this suggestion in relation to her personal situation, not merely as a general approach for many parents. Finally, as we have seen in other examples, the clinician refers to the suggestions as some things other bereaved parents have tried, which encourages the parent to take them seriously.

One other point before we leave this example. At the end of this part of the exchange, the bereaved mother says that perhaps she and Jessie might be able to help each other. You can even imagine that this mother might offer Jessie some mothering that she won't be able to give Jennifer. We would not say anything about that at this moment. That might be pushing these suggestions too far. The mother is already on a good enough track in her consideration of them. Being specific about mothering Jessie might inadvertently increase her reluctance about this possibility. She might start to think that she is overstepping the bounds of her relationship with

Jessie, that she might be betraying her own daughter Jennifer by getting so close to Jessie, or that Jessie's mother might not be comfortable with their relationship. We do not know whether she might think any of these things, but this is not the moment to introduce potential complications.

In cases where an only child has died, but the parents plan to try to have another child, there are some issues of memory and forgetting as well. The children born subsequent to their sibling's death will never have known them in person. Parents often are faced with concerns about how to include the dead child in the family narrative that will be passed on to other children. Consider the following example of parents of a stillborn child, as they discuss this issue in their bereaved parents group.

BF1: I'm glad I have this place to talk about this, because I'm afraid other people would think this is morbid.

BF2: We're the death experts. Nothing is morbid to us.

BF1: Remember how we were talking about how you tell people about how many children you have? Well, Beth and I were talking about when we have more children, what we tell them about their brother.

BM1: We want them to know about him, but we don't want to upset them, either.

BM2: You'd be surprised what kids can handle. As long as you are straight with them.

BM1: You know, we have the pictures from the hospital, and they could be scary.

BF3: Yeah, that might be something you don't show until they are older. Maybe never. I don't know.

BM3: On the other hand, our kids wanted to know a lot about how Caleb died, and we got pretty explicit.

T: But they asked you about things.

BM3: Yeah, when they asked we told them. And they asked more as time went on.

BF1: I guess I'm thinking that I want our kids to know Ben—I mean know something about him. But what? How he looked? He didn't look too good. And he never had a chance to have a personality.

BM1: We just want him to be our child and their brother, too.

T: I know the others here have had to deal with this, too.

BM4: You know, in a way we have even less to remember [This couple had a miscarriage and doesn't have other children.] And you know what we've done? We've decided to imagine what Emily would have been like. What she might have looked like and been like, and we figure we can do the same when we have other kids. Kids like to imagine things. We're not worried about it. We figure if we start out talking openly about this part of our family life, our other children will be OK with it, and adopt our memories, and come up with their own ideas about their sister.

BF1: So just being open about it.

BM4: Being open isn't being morbid, I think.

BF2: Either that or we're all morbid.

BM3: I think you make it natural by talking openly with your kids. Then they'll just take it for granted that they had a brother—an older brother!

BM1: Yeah, that's a strange thing, isn't it? This baby is their older brother.

BM4: Something else for your kids to imagine. What it would have been like to have an older brother.

BM1: That's so sad, though.

T: I guess there has to be a sad part to this story. And we don't like our kids to have to go through things that are sad. But that is part of your family history now.

BF2: We tell them lots of sad stuff—like Jesus was crucified, for example.

T: I think you will all be sensitive to what your kids can handle, and be good models for dealing with the tough things in life honestly.

Notice how the group gives a great deal of latitude to the parents of the stillborn child about deciding how to respond to their other children. One couple even points out that they and their children can "imagine" what Ben might have been like. They also receive the message that they can trust their children to let them know what they would like to know. But perhaps the most important message this family receives is that they should not worry about being "morbid," and that they can be open and healthy in how they include the story of Ben in their own family.

Implicit in this example is the notion that children will vary in their wishes and needs regarding knowledge of the deceased child. They may want to know different things and to understand the situation in different ways as they get older. Individual and developmental differences will play a crucial role in parents' dealings with surviving siblings as well. Furthermore, parents themselves will be progressing through bereavement and find themselves capable of various approaches to their children's grief at different times. *Generally, the challenge for bereaved parents who have surviving children is how to provide support at a time when they often feel they have great needs for support themselves, and little to offer anyone else, even their spouses or children.*

As clinicians, our task in being expert companions to bereaved parents is to help them realize that it is understandable and common for bereaved parents to find themselves having difficulty mustering the emotional or physical energy to attend to their surviving children as they have been accustomed to doing. We also need to help them recognize what their children need in their bereavement, and how to fill these needs, either through them or through other resources. There are some general messages that we try to focus on with bereaved parents who have other surviving children:

- Previous parenting can be the foundation for their child's ability to cope with the loss of their sibling.
- Bereavement for children is a process that is recapitulated over time as they are able to understand things at more sophisticated levels during the time that they are growing up, and as they are confronted with different aspects of the loss of their sibling at different points in childhood, adolescence, and adulthood.
- Children are naturally pretty good at grieving, if we allow them to freely express themselves and answer their questions appropriately but honestly.
- Children usually take the lead on their grieving from their parents, so parents model things like appropriate open disclosure and how to manage relationships with people who are helpful and those who are not.
- Parents are not the only persons who can support your child; there are other helpers about. Adolescents, for example, may actually prefer talking to their peers rather than their parents about their grief, as many prefer to do about other matters.

As we have done with other issues, we next try to illustrate these points in some examples from clinical sessions. Here is an excerpt from a group meeting of bereaved parents that shows the wide variety of reactions from surviving siblings, and the range of parents' concern over these reactions.

BM1: Heather's [12 years old] having a lot of trouble with this, I think. Whenever I try to bring it up with her, she kind of clams up. I think she's keeping everything inside.

BM2: You never know what's going on with these kids. It's scary.

BM3: This may sound awful, but I don't feel like I even have time for Tommy [14 years old], or anything else, since this happened. I'm more worried about what Tommy feels like, sort of losing his mother, too.

T: You can't expect yourself to be the parent you used to be. Especially since it is only four months. You are just getting the full impact of this.

BF1: But we've got to go on. We still have kids to raise. It's like at Christmas, when we didn't feel like decorating, but we did it for the kids.

BM2: Yeah, I could go through the motions on that, but I know nothing about how you are supposed to help a teenager through the death of his little sister. Especially when he feels like he should have been paying better attention. I'm really afraid of how he feels about himself, guilty and responsible. I'm afraid of what that will do to him.

BM4: Have you got him some counseling?

BM2: He won't go.

BM1: That's like Heather. She's just shut down.

BF2: Does he have friends he talks to?

BM2: He has a lot of friends, but I don't know if they talk about this.

BF2: I was surprised at how much Brad [14 years old] started relying on his friends. One of his friend's mothers told me that Brad and her son had been talking a lot about it all. She heard them in their rec room one night, and asked her son later about how Brad was doing. Her son said, "Oh Brad's going to be OK. He just needs to talk it out, and we figure stuff out together." This from a 14-year-old boy. So, we were both surprised that they talked about anything else but hockey and video games.

T: That's like our kids grief groups here. You get these grieving kids together, and they really connect with each other. For teens in particular, the peer group is their natural habitat. So that's where they would like to go with their grief, too.

BM4: Shelly went to that and she loved it. She had told me that none of her friends understood. So the group was good for her. It's just like for me. No adults understood me, either, until I met you guys. And Julie [addressing BM2], you just let Luke know you love him and you will all get through this together. He might find it easier to talk with other kids, though, especially if he's feeling guilty.

T: None of you have been prepared to help yourself or your kids through this. It's just figuring it out as you go along. You may end up seeing your families grow stronger in the end.

BM4: Oh, I think that is true with us. We are much more tender with each other. But it's been longer for us than you guys.

BF3: That's right. It's been longer for us and we can see the changes. James wouldn't say anything about Sarah for about a year. Then he'd bring up things, like memories of going to a concert with her, and I'd be the one tongue-tied. He'd just catch me off guard and I wouldn't know what to say. So, I'd miss the moment, and get upset with myself. This struggle went on for a while before you [Therapist] told me to just go back to what he said. Like, "I was just thinking about what you said about the concert . . ." That made it easier, knowing I didn't have to jump at these chances to talk about Sarah with him. Then, I got more relaxed and just trusted both of us to be more natural about it. One day I said to James, "I'm glad we can talk about Sarah now. I like remembering her with you." And James said he did , too. And now it's just natural. I just had to give him time, and myself, too, I guess.

We chose to include this exchange among bereaved parents in a group because it highlights so many of the concerns that parents struggle with as they try to help their surviving children. In this excerpt, there was a good deal of discussion about how to open communication with their children, and the degree to which their children are finding an expression for their grief. But when this communication does occur, there sometimes arises another concern. Bereaved parents are often afraid that they do not have the answers to the big and small questions that their children might ask them. Sometimes these same questions are the ones that parents are asking themselves or others. Sometimes the children bring up things that the parents have not considered before. Without going into detail about the myriad of questions children may ask about dying, death, grief, and the afterlife, and what specific responses to give, we next introduce an approach that works fairly well with most questions and concerns for most bereaved parents and bereaved siblings. Following are some general messages that we believe it is helpful for clinicians to help convey to bereaved parents:

- Don't feel that you must have the correct answers.
- Invite your children to offer their own musings and understandings about their questions.
- Don't be afraid to say, "I don't know."
- Try to offer your understandings and beliefs at a level that the child will understand. Remember that young children are likely to be very concrete about things.
- It is more important to allow open, respectful communication than to provide definite answers.

Here is an excerpt that illustrates how a clinician can offer this kind of advice to a parent.

> *BM:* You wouldn't believe the questions Shawna [5 years old] comes up with. She'll say, "Mama, is Donald an angel now?" And I'll say, "I believe so, sweetie." Then she'll say, "Well, why doesn't he fly down to see us?" And I'll be stuck, 'cause I've been waiting to get a sign, too. I'm wondering why we don't hear from him somehow.
>
> *T:* So, what do you say to that?
>
> *BM:* Oh, I tell her that it's just a matter of time, we'll see him.
>
> *T:* Meaning?
>
> *BM:* That we'll get our chance in heaven.
>
> *T:* Do you think Shawna understands?
>
> *BM:* She seems to.

T: I have a hunch she may be waiting to see Donald, wings and all, make his appearance to her. Here, not in heaven.

BM: You think?

T: I'm not sure—you might ask her. And maybe she's got it right.

BM: We don't really know, do we?

T: No, we don't. And you can tell her that. Some people see angels, some don't. We don't know why.

BM: I can say I don't really know.

T: Sure.

BM: I sure have said it about a lot of other stuff!

T: That's right. She can handle it.

BM: I just don't want her to be upset.

T: What about this most upsets her?

BM: Dying, I think. Her, or me.

T: If Donald died, will I die, or you, Mama?

BM: Exactly.

T: That does make sense as the thing that might bother her most. What do you say about that one?

BM: I tell her that she won't die for a long, long time. And me neither, I hope. Although if it weren't for her, I wouldn't mind, you know. But I don't say that part.

T: Smart.

BM: I just wonder if she thinks, well, how do you know I'm not going to die for a long time?

T: You wouldn't have a neat answer to that one.

BM: Right.

T: But she hasn't said that. So you can let that be, until she does. At her age, she may not think that way—she just needs some reassurance from you. And if sometime she does ask, tell her the truth.

BM: Like I don't know?

T: That no one knows for sure, but you choose to believe that she will live to be a wise old lady. Kids can handle the truth pretty well when they are secure in your love for them. And I think you're doing great being truthful and loving.

Grandparents

The grandparents of children who have died have particular concerns that represent some challenges to bereaved parents. Like the parents, they recognize that an aspect of their legacy has disappeared, especially if this was an only grandchild and no others are expected. Grandparents may have particularly tender relationships with their grandchildren, and that shared affection is greatly missed. There is also the complication that grandparents are dealing with their own grief and their children's grief as well. They often are devastated to witness the profound sadness that their children live through, and may feel quite helpless to ameliorate it. Bereaved parents may recognize this, and may try to relieve their parents of this burden by understating their own grief reactions. In trying to minimize the pain of each other, some bereaved parents and grandparents unwittingly erect a wall of silence between them. This is an unfortunate development, and we attempt to encourage open, honest communication in this family relationship, as we have between spouses and between bereaved parents and their surviving children. Of course, the preexisting relationships between bereaved parents, their parents, and in-laws play a role in what might be attempted. And, as we indicated in chapter 3, the clinician should take care to encourage styles and types of communications that are sensitive to the specific cultural contexts of both parents and grandparents. Differences in communication styles, old hurts and resentments, and generational differences in understanding and approach to grief can all play a role in how grandparents and bereaved parents manage their bereavement together. Here is an example of this work in a session with a bereaved couple.

BM: Roger's mother just doesn't seem to get it. She'll call and ask me to go shopping with her as if nothing has happened. It drives me nuts. I tell her I don't feel like it, but she keeps calling.

BF: She's just trying to help, get you out of the house a little.

BM: But she never brings up little Roger.

BF: But your mother calls and falls to pieces, and you end up spending an hour comforting her. I don't think that's helping much.

BM: Of course. That's the other extreme. But mom and I have always been close, so I can deal with that. Your mother should know we don't get along, and not try to be the one to help me. Especially by going shopping, for God's sake. Who cares? That's why I wonder if she cares at all.

T: How about the grandfathers?

BM: They're easier to deal with. They're a lot alike. Kind of quiet. Roger will go out with his dad, and when he stops by, he'll just give me a hug. He doesn't say much, but I know he's sincere. My dad's kind of the same. He'll bring me little things he's made in his workshop. Stuff to remember little Roger, like little wooden horses because little Roger loved his horse. I think that's his way of grieving, not talking about it so much.

T: How about you, Roger. How has it been managing things with your parents and Cathy's?

BF: Me and dad do more together now, actually. I think little Roger's dying brought it home to me what being a father is about, and how dad feels about me and all, and I just have spent more time with him. It's not like we talk much about what happened. Mostly just fish. But we went on this trip on a houseboat with my brother down in Jacksonville, and my dad got into telling us all kinds of stories about the family, and it was hilarious, and he and my brother got along better than I've seen in a long time, too.

T: So things with your father have changed?

BF: Yeah. I can tell he's had something taken out of him. But he's just looser, or something.

BM: Your father's changed a lot. He never would have taken time for that houseboat thing before. It's sometimes like he's a beaten man, but then it seems that just he's more laid back. But he doesn't talk about little Roger at all, just like your mother. But at least I can see he's gone through something. Your mother, I don't know if she ever feels anything.

BF: That's just her way. She's always been a tough lady. You're just used to your mom and her breakdowns. I think she just makes it harder on Cathy. She acts like she was little Roger's mother, and no one misses him more.

BM: Well, remember, she took care of him every day for three years. What do you expect?

T: It sounds like there is a lot of history to all this. People tend to grieve like they've lived—some talk, some stay quiet, some break down, others push ahead. It's easy to fall into judgments about these styles, and you are bound to feel more comfortable with some than others. Roger, despite all these differences in expression of grief, do you have any doubt that all the grandparents are affected?

BF: No, I realize that everyone in the family is hurting over this.

T: It is hard to measure another person's pain, or another person's grief. What do you want Cathy to do about her mother?

BF: I wish she'd just tell her to remember that she's the mother of little Roger.

BM: She knows that, Roger. She just gets very emotional, and you can't change that about her.

T: I think that the ways the two of you struggle to convince each other that your mothers are OK, creates additional difficulty for you during your bereavement. It sounds to me that, as Roger said, everyone is hurting, and I think everyone has some intention to comfort others and get some comfort for themselves.

BF: I think that's right. We're not always really good at it.

T: Of course. This is a very demanding situation, and everyone is learning as they go along. I know you've talked about how you see little Roger looking down from heaven. Keep that in mind, and let him see healing in his family.

BM: My mother is not overly upsetting me, Roger. I can handle her. Don't worry.

BF: Don't you think my mom is hurting, too?

BM: Sure, but she has a strange way of showing it, or not showing it.

T: Cathy, I know you see her offers to take you out shopping as inappropriate in this situation, but that may be the only way of her saying she'd like to help you. At least she is making some contact, some effort.

BM: But that doesn't work for me, that doesn't help me.

T: You could tell her the truth, in a gracious way, like "The way I'm grieving now, I just don't feel like shopping. I don't know how I'll be feeling later, maybe there will come a time when getting out shopping will feel good to me. Thanks for the offer, and I'm sure you understand."

BM: That's not so bad. I guess I could do that. Would you be OK with that Roger? And not bug me anymore?

BF: I've got no problem with that. You do what you want, just try to remember that she's got her own way, and she doesn't mean it bad.

T: Everyone in this family is learning about how to grieve and how the others do it. To some degree you educate the others in your family about how you are doing this and what works for you.

BM: I'm still trying to figure that out myself.

T: Right! So it may change over time, too. That's why I mentioned to say to your mother-in-law that in the future you might feel differently. That's the truth. So, what will you try to remember in order to have a more peaceful way of handling grief within your family, including your parents?

BF: We're each different, and everyone's hurting.

BM: We have to accept each other the way we are.

T: And the way you are about grieving may change over time.

BM: And maybe little Roger is looking at all this and saying, you folks need to get it together!

BF: We don't want to embarrass him up in heaven.

The clinician offers the same basic messages we have seen before: there are social and individual differences in grieving and these are acceptable. The clinician also offers some advice about how Cathy might speak to her mother-in-law, as part of educating others about her way of grieving, something bereaved parents are often faced with in their families, and also with friends and coworkers. Finally, he uses a bit of the couple's understanding of their enduring relationship with their son. He is looking down from heaven, and continues to know them.

☐ Conclusions

Working with families, or with individuals about their dealings with other family members, during bereavement demands that the clinician determine where the focus of the work should primarily be. Should it be on the grief, or on the relationship issues that are played out around the grief? To a great extent, this depends on why the family or individual sought help in the first place, and whether the client expects marital counseling or support to cope with bereavement. In this book, we are focusing on the latter, but recognize that grief issues are commonplace in many other clinical encounters as well. And, in accordance with a theme we present throughout, clinicians need to be sensitive to the wide variation among parents in the way in which they experience and express their grief, and to the specific kinds of sociocultural factors that influence and shape the particular social worlds of individual parents.

Parental bereavement certainly is a traumatic event, and it therefore has the power to disrupt family relationships. This is not necessarily a bad thing. In this disruption, there can come a reexamination of these relationships, and opportunities to change and improve them. We have certainly seen many examples of the strengthening of marriage bonds, and connections across the generations, as a result of shared grief. In this grief, people usually are emotionally raw, they have difficulty maintaining façades, and they therefore may disclose more about themselves than they might have before. From these conditions and circumstances, new and better relationships can often emerge. That is a major aspect of the growth perspective from which we prefer to approach bereaved parents and their families.

Circumstances of the Loss

I only want to cradle my child,
Who lives in the darkness of the sea
Miltinho and Chico Buarque de Hollanda,
"Angelica" [translation]

The various facets of grief experienced by different people, regardless of the specific conditions surrounding the loss, tend to have much in common. But bereaved parents dealing with different situations, although they share the common fate of having to struggle with the loss of a child, may face somewhat different challenges depending on the circumstances surrounding the death and the general context in which it occurs.

As we begin a discussion of some of these different sets of circumstances, it is important to reiterate a general theme we have made explicit throughout this book—there are wide individual differences in how people in general, and parents in particular, respond to the death of a loved one. It is quite useful, however, to have some familiarity with some of the kinds of responses and problems that may be, if not unique, then certainly common to particular kinds of loss. Before we provide this general summary, a repetition of an important theme may be useful. We would caution readers once again to listen for, and when appropriate elicit, an understanding of *the ways in which the particular cultural influences and cultural context of the individual parents may prove relevant* to understanding their experience of grief. Such sensitivity will help the clinician to more fully and accurately understand the parent's narrative, and it will also make it more likely that the clinician can prove to be of assistance to the grieving parent.

We have selected some of the circumstances that the clinician is likely to face when working with grieving parents or circumstances that can represent specific, perhaps unique, challenges to the grieving parent. In this chapter we examine parental bereavement associated with suicide, homicide, accidents, and neonatal death. The particular challenges parents may face can vary somewhat according to the circumstances surrounding the child's death. Different circumstances and responses, however, should not be equated with different levels of distress and pain. Deciding if one set of circumstances is more or less difficult for parents is very much like trying to determine which form of torture is more painful—all forms are.

☐ Suicide

> Surviving the death of a dear one is to endure great pain. Surviving a suicidal death is to compound that pain with such embarrassments as public ridicule and private humiliation, and often exaggerated feelings of guilt and anger. (Bolton, 1983, p. 1)

There are many circumstances where the pain of dealing with the death of a loved one can be compounded. We have already suggested that the death of a child is one such instance, and in the case of the suicidal death of a child that burden can be even greater still.

Iris Bolton, in her book, *My Son . . . My Son . . .* , describes how she and her family responded to the suicidal death of her 20-year-old son Mitch. Although his brothers had been moving along with their education, Mitch "had been trying to find himself" (p. 2) as a musician and singer. In the weeks before he took his own life Mitch had broken up with his girlfriend and in the days before had difficulties at his job at a department store, which probably ended in his dismissal. On the day of his death he was talking on the phone with an ex-girlfriend when his comments led her to become concerned, so she called his family on a second line. His father went quickly to check, but Mitch had already ended his life with gunshot wounds from two different weapons.

In the United States in 2000, over 29,000 people took their own lives (Minino et al., 2002), and, as statistical summaries indicate, males are more likely to kill themselves and females are more likely to attempt suicide but survive. The parents of a child who chooses to take his or her own life can face a variety of challenges, above and beyond the death of a son or daughter.

In some instances a suicidal death can come as a sudden and unexpected shock, whereas in others the death is not entirely unanticipated. Where there were no evident signs of distress, depression, hopelessness, or significant social difficulties, the suicidal death of a young person can come as a calamitously unexpected shock. What parents could have imagined, for example, that the academically successful, nationally recognized star athlete at a major university, who apparently had many friends and was routinely pursued by interested young women, could be experiencing the kind of pain that would lead him to take his own life at the age of 21? For parents in similar kinds of circumstances, where the superficial appearance is that a son or daughter is apparently "doing OK" or even better than OK, how could they possibly foresee that their child was being secretly tortured by despair and hopelessness? In these kinds of circumstances the death comes as a shattering unexpected shock.

Other parents, however, may not be as surprised by the suicidal death of a child, if they have been aware of the life difficulties that the young person had been confronting. This lesser degree of shock, however, does not necessarily translate into lesser pain and distress, but it suggests that parents in these circumstances may face somewhat different difficulties in trying to survive psychologically. Sadly, some survivors (as in the obituary phrase "is survived by . . . ") of suicide also report a paradoxical sense of "relief." This experience of "relief" tends to occur when the persons who have taken their own lives have had a difficult history of crises that disrupt families, for example, previous suicide attempts, chronic and serious substance abuse, perhaps with previous overdoses, and major difficulties in coping adaptively with the demands of life (e.g., trouble keeping jobs, staying in school). Clinicians should be very cautious when such feelings of "relief" become clear, because these feelings can compound the parent's sense of guilt about the child's death.

We have seen a few parents of children who have committed suicide after chronic psychiatric problems talk about their children's courage in dealing with their emotional difficulties and in deciding to commit suicide. These were children who were in their late 20s or older, and perhaps these parents were able to see their children as capable of making these life-or-death choices at that age. One parent of a 30-year-old man with bipolar disorder, who jumped from a bridge, said:

> Aaron had gone through so much with his illness all these years. He battled it the best he could. He took the medicines, tried to be healthy, but it always came back and got him. I think this was his relief from pain, and I can understand that. I can't blame him for that. People talk about suicide as being the coward's way out. But I think it takes a lot of guts to think this through, plan it and act. I'm proud of my son, and I don't think he was a coward. I think he was courageous.

Guilt is a common component of grief experience following death from any cause, but it may be more prevalent and perhaps more intense for parents of sons or daughters who have taken their own lives (Jordan, 2001; McIntosh, 1999). One way in which parents may feel guilt over the child's death is by imagining actions taken that may have somehow contributed to the child's motivation and despair, or through actions that were not taken that might have prevented the sequence of events that culminated in the child's suicide.

Iris Bolton (1983) describes some of the guilt she felt by focusing on an interaction with her son that occurred the night before he died. He spontaneously had brought home some ice cream, which the family shared. Her son left the family group and went to his room, and his mother followed him and asked him if he was all right. His response was "No worse than any other time . . ." (Bolton, 1983, p. 33). She accepted that as reassurance and did not pursue the matter further. After his death, however, that particular incident fed her guilt:

> For months, part of my hurt . . . came from . . . not continuing down the stairs . . . to invite him to pour out his misery. I know a suicidal person can be helped greatly by a concerned and empathetic listener. . . . Talking might have helped Mitch, but I'll never know. (Bolton, 1983, p. 33)

Attempts to educate the public and publicize research about possible clues to suicidal ideation may have produced, for some parents, bitter fruit. An assumption that the publicizing of such information can produce is that suicide is both foreseeable and preventable. Such an assumption is not unreasonable for academic research and for population averages, but it is not necessarily accurate for specific persons in specific situations. More importantly, even the most highly trained and skilled clinical professionals cannot accurately identify every person who is suicidal, and they definitely do not prevent the death of every suicidal person. Certainly parents, then, whether trained or not, cannot be expected to omnisciently identify a child's internal psychological state, and then to dispassionately and accurately evaluate the severity of the child's despair and self-destructive impulses. Such unemotional logic, however, is unlikely to be successfully applied by the grieving parent.

The general cultural expectations in the United States, and perhaps in most places in the world, are that parents will protect, take care of, and watch over their children. A specific way in which the parents of a child lost to suicide may experience guilt is by *finding themselves to have failed in their role as protectors of their children* (Miles & Demi, 1991–1992). Their child has died and they may judge themselves to have failed to foresee and prevent the death, and they may judge themselves to have committed acts that somehow may have contributed to the child's death. Although this form of parental guilt is not unique to suicidal deaths, it can be a strong and central element of the parent's experience.

The general social context in which the grieving parents find themselves can also present challenges that can be accentuated in suicidal deaths. Various kinds of research have indicated that in North America the parents of young persons who take their own lives may be *viewed in a somewhat more negative way* than the parents of children whose deaths occurred from other causes (Calhoun, Selby, & Faulstich, 1980; Jordan, 2001). For example, parents may be perceived as somehow bearing responsibility for the child's death, and this may be a more likely perception when the child is not an adult (McIntosh, 1999). Others may also entertain hypotheses to explain the child's death that may include mental illness and family dysfunction. Although the perceptions may be negative in subtle ways and not communicated directly to the parents, the social environment in which many parents will find themselves may be characterized by general social attitudes and interpretations that include negative and potentially stigmatizing views.

Those who are the survivors of a loved one's death may themselves experience some degree of *embarrassment or shame* associated with the suicidal nature of the death. For example, family survivors of a loved one's suicide are more likely to report having lied or deliberately misled others about the cause of death (Range & Calhoun, 1990). And there is the possibility that parents whose child's death was suicidal *may experience less comfort and support* from others, than parents whose children died from natural or accidental causes. It is possible that parents of young persons who take their own lives are offered less support generally, or support that is less effective and producing comfort for the parent. It is also possible, however, that the lower levels of support are not the result of what others do, but of what parents *experience* in response to attempts by others to be helpful. The particular needs of parents bereaved by suicide may somehow lead to less comfort *being received*, because they may experience a type of loss that enhances the bereaved parents' sense of disconnectedness from a potentially supportive social system. For parents grieving a child's suicidal death, then, several elements can combine to accentuated their potential sense of "otherness" and of isolation from those who might have been possible sources of support, but who are now seen as dissimilar to them in many ways (Riches & Dawson, 1996). Parents grieving the suicidal loss of a child may see themselves as isolated from others because they have experienced the loss of a loved one, the loss of a child, and the loss of a child to a kind of death that has many potentially stigmatizing qualities.

Parents grieving the suicidal death of a child may also have great challenges making sense out of their loss in at least two ways (Calhoun et al.,

1982; Talbot, 2002). First, simply *achieving a satisfactory understanding of the chain of events and sequence of causes* that culminated in an irrevocable act of self-destruction may never be possible. Survivors of suicide may spend more time (compared to persons grieving deaths from accidents or natural causes) ruminating about what led the person to take the actions that produced his or her own death (Bailley, Kral, & Dunham, 1999). But the higher levels of ruminative thought do not mean that the parents of a child whose death was suicidal will actually reach a satisfactory resolution to the search for answers. On the contrary, survivors of suicide may tend to report that they have *never* reached a satisfactory answer to the question of "why did he or she do it?" As a survivor quoted by Buksbazen (cited in Bailley et al., 1999, p. 269) said, "It just remains a mystery that you can't really let go of."

A second way in which bereaved parents may have difficulty making sense out of their child's suicidal death involves broader and more abstract matters (Calhoun et al., 1982). Given the parent's general philosophy of life and understanding about the purpose of life and the general meaning of what happens to human beings, *what purpose can be found in, and what meaning can be made of, the child's death*? How can parents reconcile their general assumptions about the meaning of their lives, of the child's life, and the general principles they assume guide what happens in life, or even in the universe, with a child's suicidal death? For many parents, this is a very difficult task, and it is one that for many parents remains unfinished. A state in which the meaning and purpose of the loss can be satisfactorily understood is one that will elude many parents. For example, how will a parent reconcile a general belief in a benevolent and present God, with the senseless self-inflicted death of a teenage son? Or more broadly, echoing the question in the title of Harold Kushner's famous book, why is it that such a horrible thing happened to us, since we are good people? Although not unique to losses of children to suicide, for many parents bereaved by suicide these kinds of questions will never be resolved. The "closure" so often mentioned in the popular media is a state that for many bereaved people in general, and for many parents bereaved by suicide in particular, will never, ever be reached.

Clinicians should be aware of these various qualities of grief that are present in the typical experience of parents whose child was lost to suicide and they should be open to listening to determine if the qualities are indeed present in the experience of individual parents. Clinicians also need also to respond in ways that are helpful to parents. Although in some clinical circumstances it may be appropriate to use the word *suicide* and its various synonyms, we think that in general it is appropriate and sufficient to use words that speak of the child's death and loss, rather than to use words that accentuate the cause of death. And, as we suggested in our discussion of the cultural context of the parents' grief, clinicians also should attend to the specific ways in which loss, death, suicide, and bereavement are spoken about and understood by the parents, and by their primary reference groups. When we talk with parents who have lost a child to suicide, we tend to use words such as "the loss," "the passing," or "the death," rather than "the suicide." When working with bereaved parents, it may be desirable to *focus on the reality of the loss, and not on the specific nature of the cause of death*. We do not avoid dealing with the actual nature of the child's death, and we think it is necessary to truthfully acknowledge it. But we do not think that the main focus of clinical work with bereaved parents should be on helping parents deal with "a suicide," but it should be to help parents survive the loss. The cause of the loss is relevant, but the main source of pain for the parent usually is not how the child died, but the irrevocable fact that their physical child is gone forever.

Resources vary from community to community, but clinicians who are seeing bereaved parents should make themselves aware of any resources available to grieving parents. Survivors of suicide routinely report that among the most helpful things that was done for them was to help them to make connections with other bereaved parents whose children had died in similar ways. So a very simple but helpful step that clinicians can take is to *make parents aware of support groups or other available organizations in the parents' community*. We have found, however, that many parents whose children committed suicide fear that other bereaved parents whose children died of other causes may not accept or understand them. So, even if there are available community resources, these parents may need extra support in venturing to make use of them.

As suggested earlier, parents grieving a suicidal death may experience an accentuation of the isolation and disconnectedness from the rest of the world that can happen to any grieving parent. Because of this, *helping parents make contact with other parents bereaved by suicide can be a particularly useful step* for clinicians, or any members of the parents social support system, to take. Even if no organized support groups are available, many persons with general knowledge of specific communities or social groups (e.g., family physicians, clergypersons, hospice workers) may have knowledge of other parents who have faced similar kinds of losses. Because of the compassion for others that may have been triggered by their own struggle with loss, bereaved parents who are "veterans of the struggle" may be quite willing to talk with others who have been more recently bereaved.

It is probably unnecessary to remind practicing clinicians, but it still may be useful—*refer bereaved parents only to other parents, groups, and organizations with which you have significant familiarity*. Whenever making any kind of referral generally, but with bereaved parents in particular, do your best to learn what kinds of help and support are available, how parents will be treated, and how likely it is that parents will find responses that will be kind and useful. If services for bereaved parents are available, ascertain whether there are services that are designed specifically for parents bereaved by suicide. Although formal support systems designed for heterogeneous groups of bereaved parents can be excellent resources, parents who have lost a son or daughter to suicide may find that talking with other parents who have faced losses from the same cause may be particularly helpful.

A question that we are frequently asked by beginning clinicians is, "But as a clinician, how can I possibly help somebody who has experienced this kind of loss, especially when nothing like this has ever happened to me?" The guidelines previously proposed in chapter 3 provide a general framework, of course. In addition, *it may be useful to think of parents bereaved by suicide as similar in some ways to persons facing other kinds of highly challenging, traumatic events.* Clinicians must recognize that they are indeed powerless to undo the tragedy that has befallen the parent. But clinicians can, and perhaps must, be willing to listen repeatedly to the parent as the story of the loss is told and retold, focusing sometimes on different elements, but often returning to the themes we earlier identified—feelings of guilt, the experience of great pain, a sense of separation from others in their social world, trying to understand the causes or reasons, and trying to make sense out of the loss.

Because guilt can be a common and sometimes persistent element in the grief experience of parents, the clinician may also want to consider providing appropriate *reassurance to parents* that they are not responsible for the child's death and they did not play a causal role in the child's death. Sometimes taking the stance of "let's check out the evidence to evaluate whether or not you actually do have some responsibility" can prove useful in helping reduce inappropriate feelings of guilt, but of course the clinician must, in advance, have a very good idea about the degree to which such an examination will be helpful and not harmful. Although there may certainly be exceptions in specific instances, in general we lean toward recommending that clinicians offer reassurance to the parent that he or she is *not* culpable in the suicidal death. As with other aspects of parental grief, the matter of feeling guilty is likely to recur and, as appropriate, reassurance will need to given more than just once.

For some parents, however, the sense of guilt may be connected to specific acts, the omission or commission of which may be interpreted by the parents as indicating they somehow either failed to prevent the child's suicidal action or they somehow actively contributed to the cause of the suicidal act. If a "checking of the evidence" suggests to the clinician and to the parent that the experience of guilt may have some reasonable basis, and the clinician's good judgment suggests that addressing the guilt will prove helpful to the parent, then the clinician might want to think about the possibility of introducing the issue of forgiveness. Because a general assumption we make is that in the vast majority of cases the experience of guilt does not match "the evidence," and consequently the grieving parent's experience of guilt represents unnecessary pain, we would caution clinicians against being too quick or too facile in introducing to the parent the idea of obtaining self-forgiveness. The mere introduction of the topic by the clinician can communicate to the client that the clinician perceives the parent's sense of guilt as having a logical basis. Consequently, the clinician needs to be reasonably sure that the idea of seeking forgiveness will not be harmful to the parent and will indeed be helpful.

Here is an example of a clinician working on the issue of self-forgiveness with a mother of a child who committed suicide. In this instance the 22-year-old son had grown up with his father after his mother gave up custody after divorce. The son had lived intermittently with the mother and his stepfather, who resided several hundred miles away from the town where the boy grew up. You will see the counterfactuals that we discussed in chapter 3 show up in the mother's reflections on her son's death. And again, you will see the emphasis on what the parent knew at the time, rather than in hindsight, as a central element to the intervention. The clinician also attempts here to get very specific about what the parent may need to forgive herself for.

> *BP:* I'm sure he knew I loved him, even though I wasn't there through most of his growing up. He was always welcome, I think he knew that. But he was more comfortable back home, where most of his friends were. But in the end, I wasn't there when he was really struggling. I just wonder if I knew what was going on, I could have stopped it.
>
> *T:* That is hard to say.
>
> *BP:* I just wonder if I hadn't gotten the divorce, or had stayed in town, or had been with him that last night, whether I could have been the force to keep him alive, one way or another.
>
> *T:* If you had known this was going to happen, would you have done any of those things differently?
>
> *BP:* I would have run up there and physically put him in a hospital that night.
>
> *T:* How about the rest—the divorce, the move, and all that?
>
> *BP:* I thought I was doing what was best. He needed to stay there with the places and people he knew.
>
> *T:* So, you would have done things the same way?

BP: You mean not get divorced? If I had known the choice was, stay married and your son will live, or get divorced, and he'll kill himself, well, I would have stayed married, no doubt.

T: But of course, that wasn't a choice presented to you by the fates.

BP: I knew that it probably wasn't the best thing for the kids. But I never thought it would come to this.

T: Do you think you should have known?

BP: No, of course not.

T: And, of course, it is pretty simplistic to say Andy committed suicide because his parents divorced. Lots of factors went into this. Don't you think?

BP: Yes, I think that's right.

T: Maybe there are parts of this you are not really guilty of at all. And any parts you are, you have the choice to forgive yourself for, or keep feeling guilty about, at least for some indeterminate period of time.

BP: I still think I contributed to this, but I'm not sure exactly how. He might have committed suicide even if all the circumstances had been different.

T: We'll never know.

BP: I don't think I'll ever forgive myself.

T: For what?

BP: Just not being there for him.

T: But when we look at it specifically, it looks different to you. When you look at the fact you made specific decisions, without the benefit of hindsight, it is hard to see yourself acting any differently.

BP: I know. It's so strange. I don't think that at the time I did the wrong thing by getting a divorce, marrying Danny, or moving.

T: But if you think of any of those things related to Andy's death, then you feel very guilty.

BP: I just don't want to whitewash this.

T: Right. You have to be honest with yourself, don't you?

BP: Yes. I owe that to Andy. He's the one who suffered.

T: Did Andy ever tell you he was angry or hurt, or sad, because of your decisions? Did the suicide note refer to any of these things?

BP: No, he never said that, and like I said, he did live with Danny and me sometimes.

T: And how did that go?

BP: I think it was fine. He and Danny got along great. He just always wanted to get back home.

T: So Andy made that choice.

BP: Right. Both his dad and me left it up to him, mostly. But again, because of the divorce, he had to make these lousy choices.

T: Yes. You are responsible for that. Maybe that is something you have to live with. But that doesn't automatically translate into suicide.

BP: I think that is all true.

T: Forgiving yourself for any part of this is a work in progress, a series of careful steps. I think you are doing that examination, and we'll see where it takes you. I hope you run a fair trial, and are a merciful judge, given the time you have already served.

BP: Yeah, it's kind of like that, isn't it?

Another theme in the parent's experience that may need to be addressed is the general sense of disconnectedness from others that many parents experience. There are many ways to do this, and how it is done will vary with the specific social and cultural contexts of the parents and clinician. In many instances, however, we think that the sense of being disconnected from others can be understood as resulting from two general factors: (a) the lack of clear social guidelines for others about how they can provide support to bereaved parents in general and to the family in which a suicide has occurred in particular; and (b) the parents' own perceptions, interpretations, and expectations about what will be helpful to them.

Others may indeed feel great compassion for the parents, may engage in actions designed to communicate support and caring, and may want very much to help in whatever way they can. However, as we pointed out in chapter 1, others may not have a clear idea about what to do and how to behave to help, and may have significant worries about doing the wrong thing, doing something that will actually make things worse for the bereaved parent. And, as a result, others may do less to be supportive because pulling back socially may be seen as a way of reducing the mutual sense of social discomfort between parents and potentially supportive others. The parents can feel exiled and disconnected from others simply by virtue of being parents bereaved by a suicidal death, and potentially supportive others feel inadequate in their ability to provide comfort because they lack knowledge and clarity about how to give support and comfort.

The clinician can sometimes help parents to more clearly see where others do indeed care, love, and want to support parents, by simply helping the parent identify and acknowledge the attempts at support that have already occurred. Clinicians can also help the parents to understand that *because of the lack of experience or knowledge on the part of others, their attempts to comfort may indeed be flawed in some ways*. Clinicians can help parents see that, although specific components of attempts by others to be supportive may indeed be flawed, the general message of these attempts is that others love and care for the parents. "They could have done it better, if they had known better, but isn't the bottom line that even in their inadequate way they are trying to tell you they care about you" is a general way in which the clinician may help the parent to reframe genuine, but less than successful, attempts by others to show kindness and support. And it can also be useful to help the parent remember that indeed most of us, at least in contemporary North America, are quite ignorant about good ways to show support to bereaved people in general, and even more ignorant and awkward about showing caring for parents bereaved by suicide. Even when they fail at their goal, most people want to do what they can to provide support. It is something quite small, but helping parents realize that even if the supportive gestures do not seem to make much difference, the very fact that they are made means that others are interested in addressing their grief and in doing something about maintaining their connections with them. They may *feel* exiled and that may well be their *experience*, but others are continually trying to reach them and maintain connections. Some parents have told us that they recognize how poorly they did in offering support in the past, before their children's deaths, and this has helped them be a little more charitable about others' responses.

The suicidal death of a child can present the parent with particular challenges that take forms that may, on occasion, be somewhat different from deaths from natural causes. Although parents dealing with a child's death from any cause face great suffering, when the cause of death is suicide and there are issues involving a sense of guilt, there is greater possibility of experiencing some social discomfort related to the cause of death, and possible challenges regarding the causal sequence and meaning of the loss.

☐ Homicide

Every year in the United States several thousands of people are murdered. In 2000, for example, 16,765 people were murdered (Minino, et al., 2002). Along with deaths from suicide, those deliberately perpetrated by fellow human beings in the act of murder may present grieving parents with some specific challenges.

For most parents the loss of a child to murder can create some of the same kinds of responses typical to parents bereaved by suicide, but also others that are more characteristic of grief following a loss to homicide. Homicide is violent, and it usually occurs suddenly and unexpectedly. Under some sets of circumstance—for example, where a young person has been involved with criminal activity that is characterized by the regular occurrence of violence—the murder of a son or daughter may not be entirely unexpected. But for most parents, the murder of a child is sudden, unexpected, and shattering.

As much as death from any other cause, *the early times following the murder of a son or daughter may be disordered and chaotic*, both internally and externally (Parkes, 1993). The news comes suddenly, and information about the specific events surrounding the death may be unclear. Parents may have to interact with the police in ways and times that are out of their control. And, in many circumstances, the news media may intrude as well.

As the reality of the child's death becomes clear, parents may begin to feel strong *anger, rage, and may entertain thoughts of revenge* (Peach & Klass, 1987; Riches & Dawson, 1998) for their loss.

> If I had the chance, I could kill the son of a bitch that did this to my son with my bare hands. I find myself thinking about what exactly I would do if I was the one to find out who it was that killed him. I have already fantasized about what my hand would feel like when I closed it around his neckbone and started to squeeze. I can almost hear the bones starting to crack as I slowly strangle the bastard to death.

Although anger can occur in parents dealing with the loss of a child from any cause, rage is not an uncommon reaction when the cause of death is homicide.

Human beings tend to operate with certain general assumptions about the world and their place in it, and many human beings, especially those living in the industrialized countries, tend to assume that their daily lives are predictable, controllable, safe, and that with a certain amount of wisdom and caution bad things are unlikely to happen to them. The death of a child severely challenges or negates many of those assumptions that guide the parents' daily lives and that provide the framework for understanding the world and the place they and their children occupy in it. And *murder may be the cause of death that is most likely to lead parents to question these assumptions* (Riches & Dawson, 1998). With one overwhelming event, the parent's world has been shown to be neither safe, nor predictable, nor controllable. The chaos of the real events that swirl around the parents, involving the police, postmortem medical examinations, coroners, the courts, and perhaps the media, has a parallel in the internal assumptive world (see chap. 2) where the foundational beliefs that guided daily life are no longer applicable. The fundamental assumption that is most likely to be challenged in parents whose children have been murdered is the belief in the benevolence of the world (Wickie & Marwit, 2000–2001).

The parents' own sense of safety may be threatened. If the murderer has not been caught, then parents may worry, reasonably or not, that they themselves or their other children may be in danger. They may wonder if the assailant will come back to attack them, or their worry may be more general to include concern about their safety from criminal actions. The newsletter of a citizens' organization summarized this anxiety succinctly with the slogan *Remember All Murderers Live Next Door to Somebody* (Rock, 1998, p. 45).

Parents may also have significant feelings of *guilt*. There are widely held social assumptions that parents are responsible for the welfare of their children, and they should provide for, protect, and teach the child how to get along and survive in the world. The death of a child from murder can lead parents to question the degree to which they successfully discharged their parental responsibilities (Riches & Dawson, 1998). Gyulay (1989, p. 123) quotes bereaved parents expressing this kind of guilt:

> I keep telling myself I should have taught her never to trust anyone. We hoped we had taught her to make good decisions . . . and we failed her. . . . Nothing takes the guilt away.

When the cause of death is homicide, parents will inevitably be required to interact and deal with the police and elements of the judicial system. In most judicial settings in the United States, parents have absolutely no legal standing within the system of criminal justice. When prosecutions occur, the judicial branch that pursues the accused represents "the people" and the accused has the representation of legal counsel, but the system provides the parents with no advocate of their own. Early in the process parents may be placed in the role of people with information that may be useful to the police, perhaps as potential witnesses in a future criminal proceeding. Parents have little or no control over this process, something that may accentuate the already shattered sense of personal control over their lives. The anger that parents experience may be exacerbated by the way that they are treated by the judicial system. Although the anger may not be generated by the specific ways in which individual police or judicial officials treat the parents, the very system can contribute to anger and frustration because of the way the institutional systems operate. Parents, without any legal standing in the judicial processes, may be treated by an impersonal system as necessary nuisances at best, and as intrusive and highly unpleasant elements to which cold and rude responses are deemed appropriate under the institutional rules of operation.

For many parents, how the public responds to the murder over time is an aspect of grieving that may be unique to homicide (Dannemiller, 2002). The news media may also add to the assault on the parents' control over their lives. Sadly, the more horrible the real circumstances of the loss for the parents, the more likely it is that the press will develop an interest in the murder, and the more likely it is that the parents will be pursued for interviews and comments. Being constantly sought after by members of the news media can alone be highly stressful, but for parents of murdered children this comes at a time when they are already in deep shock or in significant pain. Parents of murdered children tend to experience their interactions with the judicial system and with the news media as unpleasant burdens that they must carry in addition to their grief (Riches & Dawson, 1998).

Homicidal deaths also carry with them the burden of a variety of uncertainties. Some murders are never solved. The parents may never know what exactly happened and the person whose deliberate actions caused their child's death may never be identified or may never be apprehended. When a person is arrested and charged with the crime, that person may or may not be found guilty. And, if a person is found guilty of the child's murder, the sentence may or may not meet the surviving parents' criteria for justice (Peach & Klass, 1987).

The nature of the death can also be the source of psychological responses that are characteristic of persons who have been exposed to other traumatic circumstances. Murder is a violent act that results from the deliberate action of another person. Parents may learn of the specific details of the crime and the child's death, and to those they may add their own imagined horrors about the terror or pain that the child may have suffered. Not surprisingly, these kinds of events and self-generated images can produce the kinds of responses seen in posttraumatic stress reactions: nightmares, intrusive thoughts and images, distress on exposure to elements associated with the crime, perhaps accompanied by some avoidance of elements associated with the child's death (Parkes, 1993).

As with any death, a death by homicide can raise general questions that for many parents will never be answered (Dannemiller, 2002). First, answers to the questions regarding the complete circumstances that led to the child's death and the events surrounding the murder itself may never be obtained. "What happened" is a question that for many parents will never be answered, but to which many parents may continue to seek an answer. Although the full answer to the question is likely never to be complete or completely satisfactory, parents may learn devastating details about what happened. As one parent said:

> I can't imagine how anyone could torture another human being. I don't think I can live through this [knowing] . . . I'll be tortured until the day I die. (Gyulay, 1989, p. 130)

A second general question or series of questions to which parents are unlikely ever to find satisfactory answers involve the abstract questions about purpose and meaning. Given what the major elements of the parent's assumptive world are, what the parent assumes about the reasons and purposes of human lives and what happens to them, what purpose or meaning can be found in the murder of a beloved son or daughter? For many parents this can represent a struggle that may last for years, and for some it is a struggle that never ends. As we have suggested to clinicians trying to be of assistance to parents bereaved by a suicidal death, parents of murdered children may need to revisit these general questions repeatedly, and a major part of what clinicians can do to be helpful is to listen, and to help parents try to restore some degree of coherence to their shattered life narratives. However, parents of murdered children generally are able to preserve their sense of meaning and personal worth (Wickie & Marwit, 2000–2001).

Parents coping with a homicide may also experience a profound, perhaps unique, sense of isolation and disconnectedness from other people in general and their social support systems in particular. There can be a "sense of isolation which comes from feeling uniquely cursed" (Riches & Dawson, 1998, p. 11). Although it is sadly more common in the United States than in many other countries, murder is still a kind of death with which most persons are unfamiliar and with which they do not have practical experience. And so, in ways similar to the parents trying to cope with the suicidal death of a child, parents of murdered children may feel they have become socially disconnected as a result of two conspiring forces. On the one hand the parents feel somehow marked, different, and separated from others, and on the other hand others may have complete ignorance about ways in which they can provide support to the grieving parents, and this may lead others to be hesitant about interacting with the grieving parents. And, of course, parents of murdered children are indeed treated differently, because unlike other forms of death, the child's death becomes part of the public proceedings of the criminal justice system, a reality that accentuates the parents' experience of otherness.

Strong emotions can be common in all kinds of bereavement, and *the murder of a child may produce particularly strong emotions*, such as rage and the desire for revenge. The experience of rage and desire for revenge are not unique to homicide; for example, they might be expected in cases of accidents or medical malpractice. The parents' experience, and perhaps expression, of such intense emotion may add to the discomfort that others, as well as the parents, may feel in social situations. This only adds to the sense of isolation that parents of murdered children can feel. The experience of parents grieving the death of a murdered child tends to be characterized by a distinct sense of social isolation, a subjective experience that is "intense, overpowering" (Rock, 1998, p. 55), highly chaotic, and that parents may believe cannot be communicated to others who have not experienced a similar loss.

What can clinicians possibly do to help? They must realize that unless the clinicians themselves have lost a child to homicide, *parents are likely to view clinical workers, quite realistically, as part of the general social world from which the death of a child has isolated them.* If this issue is raised, either explicitly or implicitly, it is appropriate for the clinician accurately to acknowledge this perspective. It will be only through good clinical work, which we believe involves primarily, but not exclusively, listening to the parents' account, that the clinician can demonstrate an ability to be of some use to the grieving parents.

Although expertise with matters related to the criminal justice system is not a requirement for the clinician to be helpful, such knowledge can be useful in this context. With such knowledge, the clinician can perhaps be of greater assistance to parents who are still in the process of dealing with the judicial system. Although this is perhaps an obvious reminder, *clinicians should accurately and respectfully acknowledge any ignorance of legal and judicial matters.*

Parents of murdered children may well want to know what happened, perhaps at levels of intensity that are even greater than for deaths from suicide. As one parent said:

> I will do anything to solve this murder. Anything. Whatever you need. You want me to bring in a psychic, I mean, I'll bring in a psychic. I will pay a reward. I will pay a detective. (Dannemiller, 2002, p. 9)

Because the reconstruction of what happened is so important to many parents, *one of the central tasks of the clinician may be, through respectful and accurate listening, to support the parent in this quest and to help the parent weave together as reasonable and coherent an account of what happened as is possible.* And, as new knowledge is added, or as the progression through the winding paths of the criminal justice proceedings unfolds, the clinician can help the parents to revise the account into a new synthesis (Dannemiller, 2002).

Clinicians also need to be prepared to hear parents' descriptions of what happened, of how they are responding to it, and how they are struggling with more general questions about purpose and meaning, *over and over again.* Not all parents will want or need to engage in this repetition of themes or stories, but this repetitive process is one that can be helpful to many parents. Clinicians should guard against the incorrect judgment that such repetitions are signs that progress is not being made or that clinical support is not helpful. Repetitions of themes may reflect the work that parents are doing to develop the most coherent and satisfying narrative of the tragic events that have befallen them and their child. Over time such repetitions may become less necessary or less likely. However, there may be some elements of the narrative that remain unknown or unknowable, and *clinicians, over time, may need to help parents bereaved by murder to try to accept the parts of the story that will likely not be completed.*

Although working with grieving parents generally can put clinicians at risk for vicarious traumatization (we address this in a later chapter), *working with parents of murdered children may be particularly challenging and stressful.* The death of a child is upsetting to most people, but the death of a child by murder can be particularly so. In addition, the parents' descriptions can involve horrific events, and on occasion parents may wish to share with the clinician somewhat gruesome particulars, for example, autopsy photos or postmortem medical reports. In order to be most helpful to the parents, the clinician needs to be prepared for these possibilities, maintaining an awareness that listening to the stories and seeing the distress of parents bereaved by homicide can be upsetting and distressing to the clinician too. Some parents may be understandably ambivalent about reading reports and viewing photos. Clinicians can play a useful role by "screening" these materials, talking to parents about what is in them, and helping them decide what they wish to see for themselves. This of course means that clinicians must be willing to face the traumatic facts themselves, in raw form.

Clinicians providing support to parents grieving a child's murder also need to be aware that although they are likely to initially be perceived as part of that social world from which the parents have been exiled, it may also be the case that the clinician can become a major source of support and stability for the grieving parents. The nature of the child's death can make the parents' usual support systems inadequate, or at least limited, in their ability to provide support and comfort. The *clinician may become, then, one of the central figures on which parents may lean* as they struggle with the aftermath of such a great loss.

Parents dealing with the loss of a child from any cause can face overwhelming challenges. The loss of a of a child to homicide can present the parent with particular challenges that can take forms that may, on occasion, be somewhat different from deaths from natural causes, including the potential chaos exacerbated by the involvement of representatives of the news media, police and judicial agencies, the possibility of strong feelings of anger and desire for revenge, a generalized disruption of the fundamental assumptions about the order, safety, and predictability of one's life, the possibility of worries about the parents' own safety, issues related to the experience of guilt, and the possible challenge of facing questions that may never be resolved in satisfactory or meaningful ways. Consider these excerpts from sessions with a parent whose 14-year-old daughter was killed in a drug-related incident. The first session is from the time when the parent was preparing for the trial of the suspects in the killing. The second session was three years later.

> *BF:* This is my chance to stand up for her, but I'm afraid I won't be able to handle it. What if I break down during court?
>
> *T:* That's why we are rehearsing this, so that under pressure, you will have all this preparation to rely on. Like training for battle.
>
> *BF:* You know, I was in the army, but this is worse.
>
> *T:* But you know what I mean about training for it.
>
> *BF:* Yeah. Absolutely. I need to be automatic about this.
>
> *T:* So we are practicing your statement, and also practicing controlling your emotions, so you can deliver it as you want to.
>
> *BF:* Forcefully. I want everyone to know what they took. And I don't want people to think she was just some druggie.

Three years later, the same father was dealing with quite different concerns now that the trial was in the past.

> *BF:* The police called and said they had some of Shawna's things that had been kept for evidence. I could have them back. Some money, her purse.
>
> *T:* Sounds like this came out of the blue.
>
> *BF:* Sure did. And you know, I kind of wish they hadn't called. I just want to leave all that stuff about the cops and the trial and those boys in the past. All that just doesn't count for much anymore.
>
> *T:* Even getting her things.
>
> *BF:* I remember being so focused on stuff like that. Couldn't give away her clothes. Wanted to know about that day. Remember how we worked on my statement to the court? Now, it doesn't really matter. That's old news. I have my new relationship with her, you know.
>
> *T:* How you talk with her now.
>
> *BF:* Right. I think of her as an angel, not as that mixed-up kid. She's at peace. And I'm more at peace. I don't want to go back to the ugliness. None of that makes any difference now. She's of another world.

Like many parents whose children were murdered, the legal matters were the early focus of the clinical work, and it seemed that to an extent, the legal issues stood in the way of dealing with the grief. After the grief was attended to, the legal issues diminished in importance for this father.

Accidents

Deaths caused by accidents represent another set of circumstances that may present particular challenges for grieving parents, and in the United States they tend to represent the most frequent single cause of death among young people. In 2000, for example, the deaths of almost 98,000 people resulted from accidental causes, and more than 31,000 of those were persons under the age of 34 (Minino et al., 2002). The majority died in motor vehicle accidents, but other causes included such circumstances as drowning, falls, accidental poisoning, and the accidental discharge of firearms (Hoyert, Arias, Smith, Murphy, & Kochanek, 2001).

By definition, accidents are sudden and unexpected. When children lose their lives as a result of such accidental circumstances, parents typically experience some degree of shock and of unreality about what has transpired. As Gary's father, whom we quoted in chapter 1, indicated:

> It happened real fast. . . . I guess I sort of blocked it out; I really didn't accept it for a long time.

As with most parents who have lost a child from any cause, parents whose children die in accidents tend to experience the full range of psychological distress and somatic complaints. And, although deaths from suicide and homicide can present the parents with some additional and unique challenges, accidental deaths also tend to produce very high levels of distress.

Accidental deaths can produce strong *guilt feelings* in parents, particularly connected to their roles as the wiser adults who are supposed to protect and provide guidance for their children. This kind of "childrearing guilt" (Miles & Demi, 1991–1992, p. 210) can lead parents whose children die in accidents to have guilt feelings fueled by the some of the same kinds of thought processes as those of parents of children whose deaths resulted from suicide or homicide. The parents' guilt may be fueled by proximate regrets and guilt about their decisions regarding where the child was, who they were with, or what they were doing —"If only I had made him take more driver's ed," "if only I had not let her date too early," "I should have reminded him not to drive fast." Or the parents' guilt may be fueled by self-recriminations about more distal childrearing matters, involving the parents' past history with the child—"I kept telling myself that I wasn't instilling enough responsibility in him, but I never did much about it; if I had, maybe this would not have happened."

It is important for the clinician to help the parents distinguish between guilt they *feel* and guilt they *deserve*. As we suggested when discussing suicidal deaths, we tend to think that it is best to provide appropriate and *gentle reassurance to the parents that they are not at fault* for the death of their children. The reassurance may need to be given repeatedly over time. Some parents may readily discount such reassurance coming from professionals, because the interpretation is that "You would say that to me no matter what, because you are supposed to say things to make me feel better—that's your job." In response, an appropriately timed identification, by the clinician, of that discounting of reassurance may be useful. The clinician can say something like, "Just because my primary job is, at least in part, to help you feel less distressed, it doesn't automatically mean that what I say is not true, does it?"

Because of the frequency of automobile accidents, people in the social networks of parents whose children die in such circumstances may be less likely to experience the kinds of social discomfort in providing support that tends to be the case of deaths from suicide and homicide. But, as we have suggested already, the death of a child represents a set of circumstances that may leave many people in the social support system somewhat unclear as to how best to provide support. Although this lack of clarity about guidelines for the provision of comfort to mourners can be more problematic when the death is ruled a homicide or a suicide, it can still be a challenge for potential comforters when the death results from accidental causes. Parents grieving the loss of a child to an accidental cause may not have to face some of the more negative social elements that can accompany deaths by suicide or homicide, but there may still be significant challenges for their social support systems. The worry about not knowing what to say or do to provide comfort to the grieving parents will be present among the friends and family of the parents whose children have died in accidents. And, as we suggested earlier when writing about deaths from suicide and homicide, the clinician may want to be alert for the possibility of helping parents accurately identify the compassionate motivation of persons who have tried to provide support, even when the specific actions may not have been perceived by the parents as particularly useful or helpful.

Some of the responses that may be present in the grief experience of parents whose children are lost to accidental deaths include issues of guilt, the difficult issue of untangling "rational" from irrational and undeserved feelings of guilt, and the other wide range of distress and pain that can be experienced by parents trying to cope with the death of a child under any circumstances. They may also be faced with certain painful pieces of evidence, such as wrecked cars or police reports. And some accidents involve the role of others in the death—for example, when a child was a passenger in a car driven by another. Generally, in our support groups, we have found that parents whose children have died in these varying circumstances usually find more in common than otherwise.

☐ Empty Arms: Miscarriage, Stillbirth, and Neonatal Death

Parents who experience miscarriage and other early infant deaths have special challenges in their grieving process. These include the personal concerns unique to this circumstance, and the interpersonal responses they may need to cope with that arise from the age of their children. The overriding personal concern for parents in this circumstance is the fact that they never get to experience their children's character, or see what they might have made of their lives. They feel deprived of the experience of being parents, and of the dreams they have had for their children. They suffer particular forms of guilt, often concerning the care with which they handled pregnancy, or the degree to which they were careful in the early care of their infants. Sudden infant death syndrome (SIDS) tends to result in much questioning of care by parents, because the death happens so mysteriously.

The parents who experience these early deaths may be more prone to gender-specific grief responses. It appears that mothers have often made closer early attachments, and may suffer grief more intensely compared with some fathers. The difference may create some challenges to the marital relationship, and the clinician's focus should be on helping the couple understand the basis of such differences and what each spouse needs as they cope with grief.

For couples who have had trouble conceiving, a miscarriage or early infant death puts a tragic end to a struggle that a couple may have endured for years. They are faced with decisions about renewing their attempts to conceive, perhaps through assisted reproduction, or giving up on their wish for a child. Some of these parents may have experienced multiple miscarriages, creating special circumstances of grief. The decision about having another baby is common for most parents who have had miscarriages or early infant deaths, and such decisions are difficult while grieving. It is may be advisable for parents to wait for a while before addressing this issue, in order to focus more clearly on grieving for their baby. But parents who have had trouble conceiving or those who are at the end of childbearing years may feel some urgency to attempt another pregnancy as soon as possible.

One of the most critical concerns of most bereaved parents is that their children will be forgotten. Parents who have suffered a miscarriage or early infant loss have even greater concerns about this, because their children were barely known, or not known at all. Because children of miscarriages have no real legal status, and there are no widely accepted rituals marking this particular kind of loss, these parents feel particularly "disenfranchised," that is, that their grief is not viewed in society as legitimate. *The clinician's job is to emphasize the legitimacy of the feelings of loss, and that the parents were indeed parents.* Here is an example of a mother who miscarried where the clinician gets this message across.

BP: My husband was saying that it was probably something wrong with the child and this miscarriage was nature's way of taking care of that. But it's like he has no feelings. I know that's not true, but it seems so cold. It's like he doesn't understand that this was a child, not a thing.

T: You were carrying this child, and you felt it move.

BP: Yeah—this was really a little human, and people think I should just move on.

T: Including your husband?

BP: He's been supportive of me, but I guess it just didn't hit him.

T: He just didn't experience this pregnancy in the same way you did. It's tough not being closer on this.

BP: It's OK he doesn't feel the same, as long as he doesn't push me so to accept it. I need a little time.

T: Have you told him?

BP: Yes, and he still doesn't get the message.

T: Perhaps he doesn't like seeing you upset. But he'll need to tolerate that. You are a mother whose child has died.

BP: You know, I've never had anyone act like that. But that's true, isn't it.

T: I think so.

BP: So it makes sense I'm upset.

T: A lot of sense.

BP: I'm just going to be upset then, and if I tell him that, maybe he'll understand.

T: I've never heard of anyone disputing that when a mother says it. They still might not accept it, but you will have made clear your position. That you've lost your child, and your grief is a mother's grief.

BP: This is so sad for me, but I feel better hearing you say that.

The reactions of others to the death can be problematical. Comments that indicate that this child could be quickly replaced with another pregnancy can be hurtful. It can be useful to help parents devise ways to deal with comments from well-meaning persons that serve to create more pain. For example, we sometimes encourage parents to claim their grief and their children with a comment such as, "This child was special to me, and another could never replace him."

Despite these problems, it does appear that most bereaved parents of very young infants or those who experience miscarriage have a briefer period of grief than parents of older children. It appears that this is at least partly because parents of older children have to engage in a process of remembering longer childhoods, and that their children have distinct personalities that sometimes created challenges. In contrast, parents of children who have died before birth, or soon afterward, are forever innocent, and without much history. There is less to reflect on, or remember, and there is not such an obvious change in life circumstances, because these children spent little or no time at home.

This is not to minimize the grief experiences of these parents, but to point out that most of them have less clinical material to work on compared with parents of older children who have died. Therefore, they tend to spend less time needing clinical help than parents of older children, although they too may find their lives forever profoundly affected by their loss.

☐ The Variety of Circumstances to Understand

We could describe many other circumstances that bereaved parents may face, such as, losing a child who is a twin, or a disabled child, or a child from whom a parent has been estranged. In these circumstances, as well as those already described, it is always best to encourage bereaved parents to thoroughly describe their experiences with grief, and their feelings about their children. Any generalizations presented here are only that, and all bereaved parents represent sets of particular circumstances that must be understood. Bereaved parents remain the best sources of information for what clinicians need to know in order to work effectively.

6

CHAPTER

Spirituality and Religion

How do we explain the death of an infant,
who couldn't possibly have sinned?
David Morrell, *Fireflies*

The death of a child brings challenges to the spiritual experience and religious understandings of many bereaved parents. Some parents have been agnostics or atheists, and now may entertain spiritual and religious questions, whereas others have had their confidence shaken in their religious beliefs. In this chapter, as we have done throughout this book, we examine these challenges primarily in terms of cognitive schemas, or belief systems, and consider the process of examination of the religious and spiritual life as part of a narrative.

At the outset, we should comment on the usage of the terms *spiritual* and *religious*. It has been commonplace in recent years to make distinctions between the two, with *religious* referring to specific beliefs and practices associated with an institutionalized entity, whereas *spiritual* represents the individual subjective experience of the connection with an entity beyond the self and humanity, a sense of community with humanity, and a worldview that incorporates some understanding or appreciation for these connections beyond the self. We attempt to maintain the distinctions in the use of these terms, recognizing they are not absolute. We generally speak more about the spiritual aspects of parental bereavement, although there are times when specific religious issues arise for parents that the clinician can help them grapple with. We also emphasize in this chapter

125

that the clinician must be able to function comfortably in the realm of the spiritual and religious, respecting the particular cultural context of the bereaved parent.

☐ Religion and Spirituality in a Multicultural World

In chapter 3 we indicated that the cultural context of parental bereavement can include the parent's religious and spiritual life, and that it is helpful for clinicians to identify and understand the spiritual and religious beliefs and activities of the bereaved parents with whom they are working. Clinicians must be ready to work with parents who are culturally connected to various versions of the religions of the world, secular agnosticism, atheism, and a wide array of individually developed amalgams of spiritual elements from varied sources and traditions. We have advocated for clinicians to use a *pragmatic religious constructivism* (Calhoun & Tedeschi, 1999) that respects the client's religious worldview and help the parents use individual spiritual and religious understandings to recover, grow, and develop. Because the death of a child can make various religious questions painfully salient, the clinician must make systematic efforts to include this dimension in the framework for understanding the individual parent's way of trying to come to terms with the death of a child. *If you work with bereaved parents, you cannot excuse yourself from discussion of these matters* with "That is something to bring up with the clergy." For most parents, the death of a child brings them face to face with the most fundamental issues addressed by religious faith: the afterlife, the meaning of living through suffering, and forgiveness. It will not be mandatory to be expert in the details of various religious faiths, but it is good to be conversant with them, especially around the beliefs and practices related to death.

The discussion that follows deals primarily with religious and spiritual experiences and views expressed by parents. As we have previously noted, however, clinicians are a bit less likely than their clients to adhere to traditional religious beliefs and traditions. In addition, a significant proportion of both clinicians and their clients in certain locations, especially in Western Europe, are likely to have primarily a secular and agnostic or atheistic orientation. That being the case, the following discussion may be a bit less directly applicable in those contexts. However, we anticipate that the same general themes will be present in the parents' attempts to come to terms with their children's death—the fundamental existential issues of the purpose and meaning of the life of the child and of the parent, and the irreversibility and permanence of death.

☐ The Afterlife

In an earlier book on posttraumatic growth (Calhoun & Tedeschi, 1999), we presented the case of a bereaved parent who was not religious who had a conversion in the aftermath of his son's death. This man realized at some point in his grief that he had been assuming his son was in heaven and that he would see him again someday. This implied to him that if he believed there is a heaven, then he had to believe in God. And if he believed in God, it mattered how he lived, especially if he wished to join his son in heaven. For many parents, it is a natural thing to think of their child in heaven, because this comforting notion corresponds to the belief system they have held for some time. But for this particular parent, this new belief represented a clear challenge to his preexisting belief system. Such challenges represent a process in which the clinician must be ready to engage the client, rather than providing ready answers or quick solutions. Options are helpful, and you can say, "Some parents have told me that . . . " when presenting ways to engage in this process or even some conclusions they have come to.

When discussing the afterlife, you should realize that you are addressing one of the most poignant concerns of bereaved parents—that is, does my child still live, are we still capable of connection, and will we be reunited? Many parents would like affirmative answers to these questions, and a belief in an afterlife can provide comforting answers. Still, it is not so simple for many to adopt such beliefs, or even maintain the beliefs they have always had about such matters. After all, the death of a child has already challenged the crucial cognitive assumption that they will die before their child, who will live on after them.

In contrast to older views on bereavement that emphasized severing the bond between parent and child, saying good-bye, and the like, the newer views emphasize the focus on the changed but continuing bonds between parent and child (Klass, Silverman, & Nickman, 1996; Klass, 1999; Talbot, 2002). What the relationship can be depends on the concepts about the possibility of an afterlife that the parent has. For example, if a parent believes that a child is being readied for reincarnation, there may be a sense that there is a window or indefinite time where some spiritual contact is possible. One parent said:

> I don't know if he is still in spirit form or if he has assumed another life yet. I feel like I am not as close to him as before, so I don't know if he can still hear me. That feeling I have in my heart isn't quite the same, not the same closeness there. But I still talk with the pond.

This parent, who eschews traditional religious practices, had developed a ritual each morning where she addressed a pond in her backyard as a conduit to her dead child, whom she thought would be reincarnated and get a second chance at life. This example can remind clinicians that they must be able to tolerate a wide variety of understandings of the spiritual and religious, without being critical of a bereaved parent.

The preceding example of a parent believing in reincarnation also raises a problem. This parent was torn between wanting her child to have a second chance, and wanting him to remain a "spirit being." She thought, as a result of her child's death, that the world was a mean place, and she did not want him to have to go through pain again. This is one of the most comforting aspects of the afterlife for many parents—their children are no longer in pain. Of course, this is particularly salient for those who had children who suffered accidents or illnesses, and associated pain and misery. Parents of children who were disabled, and had to suffer rejection, or who parents perceived to have had minimal opportunities to experience the good things in life, also tend to be able to see the afterlife as a blessing.

> I see my child as whole there. She doesn't have the problems that she had here. And she is loved and accepted for who she is.

Reaching such comforting conclusions is no simple process for many. Even though an afterlife may be conceived as a place of relief, safety, and joy, many parents are reluctant to sever the part of the parent–child bond that has to do with caregiving. One parent of a child who died of cancer said:

> I was Timmy's nurse all those years. I know he is in God's hands, but I am supposed to be taking care of him, not God, or anyone else. Maybe it's wrong, but I still feel I can take care of him better than anyone can. I'm his mother.

A useful response to this by the clinician might be

> Of course you will always be Timmy's mother. Nothing can change that, even if you can't take care of him in the same way.

Such a response acknowledges the aspect of the relationship that is changed and what endures. It also implies that there may be a different way of taking care of him, that is, caring for his memory.

For some parents, the afterlife turns the tables on this caregiving relationship. The child in heaven, or the spiritual child now is perceived as a guide or advisor. Some parents feel that their children give them guidance in their life decisions, courage, or affect their moods. A father of a girl who was noted to have a sunny personality, and a great deal of courage as she faced a terminal illness, experienced her presence.

> I think of Crystal as my sustaining force. I know she's not God or anything, and I still believe in God, of course. But I think we still have a special

connection, and I can almost hear her talking to me, telling me she's OK and I can go on. That I still have important things to do.

Again, as a clinician, it is necessary to support the parent's understanding of these experiences, without any subtle criticism.

We have seen a number of parents who report spiritual contact with their deceased children. Sometimes this happens in vivid dreams, hypnagogic states, inexplicable experiences, or through the use of mediums. We will neither try to convince the reader of the validity of such reports nor will we point out the ways in which their validity could be challenged. Instead, we encourage the clinician to accept parents' experience of the validity of these occurrences, and to be supportive of the parents' understanding. Remember, the understanding of the spiritual realm by the bereaved parent is often a work in progress, full of inconsistencies. For example, a parent who had lost his dearly held religious faith after the death of his son also reported the following.

> I went down to the basement one day in order to find some of his old yearbooks to look at. I looked everywhere and couldn't find them. So I did a load of laundry. I came back later and there was a box on the floor in front of the washer. His yearbooks. I have no idea where it came from. No one else was in the house. I would have had to stumble on it to put the clothes in the washer. I have to wonder, it must have been him.

But even though to him this seemed convincing evidence of the afterlife, this father still could not accept other parts of his religion any longer. He could no longer conceive of how God could be loving, but allow his son to die. And he remained profoundly disappointed by how the priest and the people in his congregation had given him little attention or support. This is an instance where the spiritual and religious aspects of a bereaved parent's world diverged.

Not all bereaved parents believe in an afterlife, as compelling and comforting as that belief might be, especially to this population. Some believe their children are absolutely dead. One member of a support group said:

> I know this isn't a popular notion here, but I don't think Chris is anywhere but in that box. He's really dead and there is no future for him. We get this one chance, and I feel he got cheated out of his.

It appears that for the parents who do not believe in an afterlife, the bond with their children can only exist through memory. But those memories are at the same time painful reminders of a loss that cannot ever be reconciled. Parents who take what they may term a "realistic" view of life and death are as compassionate and helpful as any parent. They report that without the comfort of the belief in an afterlife, they take on the grief full force, and they know how profound it is. Many are highly accepting of others who believe differently, and they often say that they understand how someone would seek the comfort of the belief in the afterlife. In our experience, bereaved parents who differ from each other in their beliefs about the afterlife tend to be quite tolerant of each other. It appears that the community of bereaved parents generally allows for differences of this sort, given the strength of the overall bond of the great loss they have suffered.

Many parents may look forward to some opportunity to be with their child again. They may daydream about their child walking through the door one day as if nothing had happened, and the death was only a nightmare. They may take steps to create dreams about their child. They envy those who report various kinds of encounters with their children. And sometimes, they choose to visit mediums in order to actively seek out this contact. We have seen some support groups make such visits together, but usually parents do this individually. We do not encourage or discourage these attempts to connect with "the other side," and do not criticize them. But of course, the bereaved parents themselves give their reviews of the experience in the individual or group meetings. We cannot recall when such visits to reputable practitioners were ever psychologically damaging to the bereaved parents. Some were disappointed, some skeptical, but we have not seen parents actively hurt by these attempts to reach their children. Some parents return greatly relieved, and assured that they have been in communication with their children, and therefore assured of the afterlife, and the fact that their children are thriving in this afterlife. Parents who reach these conclusions are convinced that they have been told things by the medium that are so specific that only their deceased children could have shared them. It is striking to us that among this group of "believers" few return to the medium. It appears that the assurance that their child lives and is content is enough. They can then proceed with their private conversations with their deceased children with confidence that they are getting through to them somehow.

Although the "contact" with their deceased children through mediums has been a relief and reassurance to many bereaved parents, it has not alleviated their pain. They still miss their children's physical presence and experience with them in this world.

> I am sure that the medium was in touch with Barry. She talked about the fact that he wanted me to know about the rust on the chair. This was a chair he bought for the garden, that I had been worrying had been getting rusty. How could she know that? There were other things, too. So now when little strange things happen in the house, I am sure it's him, I just say, "OK, Barry, I get the message." But it isn't like him really being here. I still miss him, cry for him, that hasn't changed.

Mediums can give some bereaved parents a version of the afterlife that seems reassuring. For example, we have heard parents return from visits to mediums convinced that the dead retain their personalities, that there is work to do in the afterlife, that there are familiar objects and animals, that they can recognize other people, that there are spiritual tests of sorts, or levels of spirituality to ascend, and that they can affect life here through manipulation of objects by electrical or gravitational forces. Mediums tend to give messages that are symbolic, leaving room open for some interpretation or misunderstanding. Parents have told us that the mediums usually ask parents for clarification, and some parents wonder about the extent to which this guides the mediums' conception of what is being said and their reports to parents.

We cannot recall many bereaved parents asking either of us if we believed in such phenomena. When they have, we have been noncommittal, and again refused to be experts on such matters.

> I have heard many bereaved parents who have visited mediums come back with similar stories. It is a bit mysterious, but I certainly don't arbitrarily dismiss them.

Generally, what they have experienced in such a session with a medium seems to be enough for them to reach their own conclusions. In the spirit of pragmatic religious constructivism referred to above, and as expert companions, we symbolically accompany the parent on this aspect of the journey, and see how they use this aspect of their grief experience. We try to help them use it as positively as possible. For example, in response to what Barry's mother had reported, the clinician could say

> Even though you don't have the joy of him being here, it is a relief to feel that he exists, that he still knows you, and is with you.

Such nonjudgmental reflections serve to keep the clinician together with the parent without getting into nonproductive conversations about the validity of these reports from mediums.

Because you must be able to entertain the spiritual and religious ideas of bereaved parents to work as expert companions, it can get sticky when parents ask very directly about your religious and spiritual beliefs. We recommend that *you allow for possibilities when you have the slightest doubt in order to accommodate a parent, but be direct about what you do hold clearly in your own religious and spiritual life.* Most parents are certainly mature enough to understand that the world contains people of different faiths and cultures. Still, it may be somewhat more challenging for a strongly committed atheist or skeptic to do this clinical work that calls for some acknowledgment of the validity, or at least the clinical utility, of the spiritual aspects of the parent's life. Some bereaved parents would find it difficult to feel you truly were an understanding and trusted companion if your beliefs precluded a spiritual life for their children.

Belief in the afterlife that their children now experience also produces another important change that many bereaved parents report: a decrease in death anxiety. Many parents have told us they no longer fear death. They believe their children are waiting for them, and they look forward to the reunion. When they die, they will be joining their children, not leaving them. So death comes to be a paradox that parents may not have considered before. It is the terrible thing that stole their children from them, and it is also the key to reunion.

Some clinicians who are not experienced in working with bereaved parents might be alarmed to hear such talk, and think that the parent was suicidal. In all but the most extreme circumstances where the parent discusses suicidal plans, this lack of death anxiety is common for many for bereaved parents. Clear signals of suicidal ideation must always be assessed. However, it is probably not helpful to the rapport you are trying to build as the expert companion to launch into a suicide assessment in the midst of the discussion of the parent's comfort with joining his or her child in heaven someday.

We have seen some parents become uninterested in taking care of themselves, at least over a certain period of time after their children's deaths. They may eat poorly, not visit their physician or dentist, give up exercise, or make other lifestyle changes that are detrimental to their health. The motives behind these behaviors are varied. Some parents seem to be paying penance for their failure to protect their children. Some have so little energy that they do not bother with taking care of themselves. In some, there may be some signs of depression. Some start to drink in an attempt at self-medication for their anxiety or insomnia. It is wise for the clinician to voice concern about any of these behaviors that threatened clients' health and well-being, while understanding the source of these reactions.

☐ Meaning and Suffering

All parents, whether or not they anticipate a reunion in the afterlife, are faced with the question—what meaning does life have now? To the outsider, there may be obvious answers. What about your surviving children? Your spouse? The important work you do? Often these obvious answers provide little solace. So, the clinician would be wise not to suggest them. If you think it is important to talk about them, do not suggest that they are your answers to their problem. Try instead to word your statements along the lines of, "I'll bet there are people who think, she still has another child to raise." Most parents have either heard this said, or imagined others thinking this. Those who have suffered miscarriages, stillbirths, or early infant deaths may deal with the variation, "They can have another child." Parents recognize in some fashion that one of the problems with such statements (besides their unfortunate insensitivity) is that they fail to acknowledge the uniqueness of the life the child who has been lost. That particular life can never be replaced by another. To bereaved parents, the impression can be that their children are being dismissed as unimportant. One of the most important and meaningful parts of life after the loss is protecting and nurturing the memory of the deceased child, not just in oneself, but especially in others. "I never want him forgotten." This prompts parents to do things that end up carrying additional meanings: starting scholarship funds, organizing blood drives, giving talks, all in the memory of their children. These activities provide opportunities to keep the child's name in public, for parents to say their children's names, and to hear their children's names spoken.

Such activities can be part of the possible growth experiences of bereavement that we have spoken about throughout this volume. These activities are usually begun some time after the death, perhaps years in some cases. Because they often require good emotional regulation and cognitive focus, many parents are not ready for them initially. But the suffering tends to be mitigated when it can be channeled into meaningful activities that benefit others, keep the child's name alive, and provides an activity for parents who cannot simply return to life as if nothing has changed, and they are doing nothing different.

The major religions of the world examine suffering and consider the purpose of it, as we have discussed elsewhere (Tedeschi & Calhoun, 1995). Some bereaved parents can accept the child's death as God's will or part of God's plan, in ways that they are not wise enough to understand. They expect that in their death, this plan may be revealed. Other bereaved parents, although equally religious, find this to be a highly unsatisfactory answer, and they may agree that they will not know what the purpose might be. Some consider their children's death to be merely bad luck, being in the wrong place at the wrong time, or getting the wrong piece of DNA. Some wonder if they are being punished, perhaps for committing an immoral act, or for being a poor parent, and not a good enough follower of their religion. Parents ultimately reach their own conclusions about why their children died, and why they have had to suffer. Coming to some kind of answer is useful, so that bereaved parents do not need to exert energy on examining this question indefinitely. If the parents' conclusion that they are being punished by their children's deaths seems psychologically damaging, the clinician might cautiously disagree.

> I understand that right now you see Meagan's death as punishment for your affair. Of course, neither of us knows for sure. I consider it just as possible that there is no connection between the two.

This is no proclamation of certainty about this spiritual matter of God's intentions, but rather an invitation to keep the processing open for the time being. And of course, bereaved parents do change their minds over the course of the grief process, and it is especially valuable to see this in support groups where veterans of the process share with newcomers the twists and turns in the cognitive processing. Other parents can also elicit the "I never thought of it that way before" that clinicians love to hear.

☐ Bereaved Parents' Experiences with Clergy and Religious Groups

We have found bereaved parents to have a range of experiences with their religious organizations in the aftermath of the children's deaths. Of course, a great many families do not have connections to religious communities, and some begin to seek them out, whereas others do not. Among those previously committed to a congregational group, some are fortunate enough to be well supported. This takes the form of consistent attention from the clergy and friends at their houses of worship, without platitudes that bereaved parents often resent. Clergy who are willing to grapple with the spiritual challenges parents face as well as their emotional turmoil are usually appreciated. Making contact beyond the standard first few months is also a signal for parents that they are understood and accepted.

Even when the clergy and friends in the congregation do everything right, there still may be certain painful aspects of the experience that make it hard to continue attending a house of worship.

> Every time I go to church, all I think of is her, I remember when she was baptized, and how she looked sitting in the pew. I try to keep myself from crying, and in fighting that battle, I miss most of the service. I sit at the back so I can escape if I need to, and so I can get out without having to mingle with people. I just don't think going is helping me.

Parents' experience at their houses of worship can involve the same dilemmas they encounter in other social settings. They notice that everything is going on the same as before their children died. Their emotional logic tells them that this is wrong, there must be more acknowledgment of their children's deaths. They see other intact families, and envy them, or are pained by the reminder of what they lost. They may be afraid that someone will act tenderly toward them, and they will start to cry. Or they may be afraid that someone won't treat them with a recognition of their grief, or mention their child, and feel slighted. One place that they hope would be most comforting can become anxiety arousing or disappointing. Some parents think that changing their house of worship would be the best solution. When they try this solution, sometimes they find that in addition to the difficulty of being new, they also face other dilemmas. Because other people are unaware of their children's deaths, they may need to tell this story, perhaps making themselves or others uncomfortable. They may miss the place where their children walked and worshiped. They may feel guilty leaving those who tried to support them. Changing houses of worship, disconnecting altogether, or changing relationships within a congregation are special cases of the general experience of feeling disconnected from others. We have heard parents refer to this as the "changed address book." Bereaved parents may often find that those they expect to support them do not, whereas others they had not counted on, do. The death of their children changes their address books.

As in most aspects of parental bereavement, there are no easy answers to these difficulties. Bereaved parents move by trial and error, traveling a path they have never expected to travel, and looking for signs from other bereaved parents and from you, the clinician. Trying to lay out the greatest range of options and being accepting of the bereaved parents' readiness or unreadiness to try them seems to be the best strategy.

☐ Talking with the Clergy

The people who are experts on many of the spiritual and religious issues bereaved parents have are usually the clergy within their individual cultural contexts. Where we have done our work, these religious leaders are typically highly trained clergypersons. Some parents are members of congregations and have clergy they are familiar with, and it is natural for them to seek out these persons in order to discuss these questions. Other bereaved parents do not belong to any religious organizations, and for them, it is often uncomfortable to find clergy to whom they can address their concerns, should they wish to do so. It is useful to know about members of the clergy in the community who are open to these discussions with people who may be unfamiliar with the basic tenets of the faith. Even among this group of parents, there is usually a preference for discussing religious issues with clergy of one faith or another. This is sometimes based on the religion of their childhood, or positive or negative general impressions of religious faiths. However, for parents whose views are primarily secular, the clinician may need to assist the parents as the expert companion who helps parents examine the fundamental existential questions of meaning and purpose.

By the time the bereaved parent has come to a clinician, it is usually some time after the funeral and the initial discussions with others who have been involved in planning these kinds of rituals. These initial *discussions about the funeral service and such are seldom occasions for exploring the kinds of concerns about the afterlife we are discussing here*. Most parents have had time to reflect and develop particular questions by the time they are choosing to meet with clinicians. The clinician's role in these situations is to help parents frame the issues they wish to discuss, and deal with the responses they may get.

We have found that many parents wish to address with clergy issues related to their children's status in the afterlife, not the existence of the afterlife. They expect that clergy are going to support the concept of the afterlife, at least in some form. What they wish to know are the religious details in situations where their children may not have been so clearly equipped to make the transition the parents hope for. These situations include suicidal deaths, children who were not baptized or not raised in a religious tradition, and children who were engaging in behavior the parents fear was "sinful," such as promiscuous sexual behavior or drug use.

Some clergy find themselves in the difficult position of delivering further bad news to a bereaved parent. In some forms of conservative Christianity, for example, perhaps the message is that because the child had not been "saved" through a baptism and profession of Jesus Christ as a "personal savior," the child will not have been able to enter heaven. Some members of the clergy may adhere rather dogmatically to the tenets of their faith, at least as they interpret them, even if that interpretation leads to some unsupportive responses to bereaved parents. In these cases, the clinician will need to help the parent absorb the message and decide what to do with it. The parents who have received messages that their children are "not saved" from death may well be those who have not raised their children in a specific religious framework. They may be able to dismiss these messages from clergy by deciding that this confirms their decision not to be involved with such a harsh and unsympathetic institution. The implicit contradiction parents may experience, of course, is that they sought out clergy to talk to, indicating some notion that the religious institution has credibility. As a clinician, you can point out to these parents that they have weighed what the clergy member has said and come to their own conclusions about God and the afterlife.

> *BP:* So the preacher told me that Albert was not in heaven because I hadn't got him baptized. So I said, "Do you mean he's in hell?" And he told me that he didn't mean to cause me more pain, but that is what his church believes and teaches.
>
> *T:* I think that was the response you feared.

BP: Right, I was worried about not raising him in the church, and my mama always told me I was not doing him any good by not getting that going.

T: So, were you surprised by what the preacher said?

BP: Not really. I guess I sort of expected it. My mama always told me about her preacher, so I knew him without knowing him.

T: Do you accept that?

BP: That Albert's in hell? I just can't accept that a boy as good-hearted as Albert would be condemned to hell. He hadn't hurt nobody.

T: So, what do you believe at this point, now that you talked to the preacher?

BP: Well, I think God knows Albert's heart. Albert believed in God. We just hadn't gotten part of a church. That wasn't his fault. I think that when Albert got to talk with God, or whatever the judgment is, then God saw his soul as good. He's God's child, right?

T: God's and yours.

BP: If God has to punish someone, it should be me, not Albert. And I sure am going through punishment now.

T: You mean you interpret this loss is punishment for you not getting Albert to church.

BP: No, I just don't think of God like that. God is love is how I learned it.

T: It sounds like you actually are pretty clear on a lot of things about God. Makes me wonder why you asked those things of the preacher in the first place.

BP: Yeah, me too. There are a lot of preachers, and lots say different things. I sure don't have to believe that Albert's in hell. But you know, I'm going to ask Mama if she thinks like the preacher about this. How could she?

☐ Shattered Beliefs About God

It appears that the split between what is intellectually understood and what is emotionally logical is clear in many bereaved parents. They usually realize intellectually that other children die, and that their child was unlucky in some sense, to catch the disease or be in the accident. But still, for religious parents it may not make sense that this happened to their children, and that God did not provide protection. This shattering of the beliefs some parents have in God's benevolence produces a great deal of discussion about bereaved parents' relationships with God. Here is an excerpt from a support-group discussion that illustrates some of the issues parents may grapple with:

BP1: I've been feeling that I don't want to have anything to do with a God that allows this to happen.

BP2: Well, I think we just don't understand the big picture, and that this must be part of God's plan, even though it looks horrible from where we sit.

BP1: Well, if this is part of the plan, God is not the loving God I thought of. I don't want to have anything to do with a God that has such plans.

BP2: You know, whether you want to have anything to do with Him or not—that's not your choice. God is there and that's that. There is nothing we can do about that, and he's going to have his way.

BP3: I don't think this has anything to do with God's plan. I don't think he plans these things out. We go about making our choices and sometimes they lead to tragedy. I think Mitch decided to drink that night, and that was a factor in the wreck. I don't think God arranged for Mitch to drink, that was Mitch's doing.

BP1: Whether it was planned by God or not, it still stinks. And it looks to me that the world and life and everything is pretty much just misery. Maybe this is hell, maybe we are in hell. Maybe that's how this is part of God's plan.

BP2: I'm not saying God directly caused our kids to die and that everything is arranged like that, our every move or anything. We have free will. It's just that each of us has a life to live, and some of us do what we need to do, and then we are ready to go.

BP4: I don't think Sarah even got a chance to do what she needed to do. She needed to go to college, get married, have kids. But I don't blame God. She just had the wrong gene or something, and so the leukemia took her, not God. I don't think we are all like little Jobs, getting tested, with God making a mess of our lives to prove some point.

T: Have those of you who have been through this for a while noticed a change in your perspectives on God during your grief?

BP5: I was really furious at the start. At God, and a lot of other people—that hunter, the doctor—but I finally realized that no matter what, it wouldn't bring Andrew back. And I was becoming a bitter person, and the anger was making everything worse for me. I needed to go back to God to find some peace. And I figured that he can take my anger, so I didn't give it up, I just trusted him to listen to me about it, and take it. And after a while I wasn't so angry anymore. I'm not sure what happened to it all. Some is still there sometimes.

BP3: Maybe because I was never really religious, I just don't think much about God having a role. I just think that we've got to deal with it as it is. No matter how much you get into this stuff, it doesn't change that our kids are dead. I always get back to that. Mitch is dead and I'm alive. So now what?

BP2: I just have to trust God. Always have, and I've got to go ahead, no matter what happens. I don't turn my back on God just because bad things happen—no matter how bad. I'm God's child, not God's spoiled brat.

BP1: I guess I agree that God can take anything, including my anger. I'm just not sure He knows I can't take this. It doesn't seem like it. I'm just saying I'm angry with Him, and I do think that's OK. We're not through with each other yet. But I don't know how it will be between me and God in the future.

BP2: I think God understands everything, and is OK with you. He lost His own son, you know.

BP1: He got Him back. What loss was that?

BP2: His son had to suffer, and I think God suffered for that.

BP5: Basically, we are all pathetic little creatures who don't understand much about any of this, so I just seek some comfort in God, and his angels, like everyone here, and try to go on. I don't try too much anymore to make sense of everything. Letting that go has helped me a lot.

BP6: Listening to all this, I have to say that struggling to make sense of it has actually been good for me. This whole thing has stopped me in my tracks and made me think about life and death like I haven't before. Maybe I've got a little depth I didn't have, though some of you might argue that one. But, really, I've thought about spiritual life when I didn't really before. I guess I thought I'd get around to it later. When Angie died, later had arrived.

In the preceding discussion, several different viewpoints were aired, but it is clear that there are some parents who preserve certain religious positions and others who are questioning them and find that the deaths of their children represent challenges to their beliefs. These challenges are distressing, but also are possible precursors of posttraumatic growth.

As demonstrated in the exchanges between support group members just shown, clinical work with bereaved parents can be striking in the way that religious and spiritual concerns are much more commonly discussed than with other clients. In support groups, parents may talk about and sometimes debate these issues, when in most social situations, they are reluctant to make known religious views. Bereavement calls forth these concerns, and they cannot be resisted by parents or clinicians. We see in the exchange by these support-group members: those parents who believe quite literally in God's hand intervening in human affairs, those who reject God's role in the deaths and see God as having no real role in coping with children's deaths, and those with various views that fall in between these. It is usually these bereaved parents who are struggling with changes in their religious perspectives and may change the most in the process. When they are angry at God, it is a sign that they remain convinced that God is a powerful force in life.

☐ Rituals and Ceremonies

All cultures have sets of general rituals and ceremonies surrounding death that allow those who mourn and wish to support the bereaved a way to come together and enact certain behaviors that have meaning and provide comfort. Because they are ritualized, they have the advantage of not having to be designed on the spot. They are ready to be enacted by all in the culture because of their familiarity. Most parents report that the rituals in the immediate aftermath of the death were experienced during a state of emotional numbness, and they may have only vague recollections of these times. They often recall people guiding them through them, and going on in almost robotic fashion through much of it. By the time most bereaved parents reach clinicians, the numbness may be wearing off. Bereaved parents then find themselves without the comforting religious rituals and ceremonies that are most focused on the loss they are enduring, at the time when their emotions are becoming more distressing.

As a clinician, you can help by working with parents to design their own rituals that acknowledge the spiritual experiences and religious beliefs they may have (or not), and that fit with the parents' belief systems. There is a little ritual in this area that seems to help parents start and end our support group meetings. It involves a candle lighting and a reading at the start, with the candle extinguished after another reading at the close. Parents can establish daily rituals that are outgrowths of the usual spiritual practice in which they have always engaged, or create new rituals that comfort them. These rituals need not be religious to be helpful to parents. We mentioned in chapter 3 the parent who communed at the pond in her backyard each day. Others carry on conversations with their children, kiss lockets bearing pictures of their children, or visit grave sites. Our position is that whatever brings comfort is usually acceptable, with exceptions for obviously undesirable acts such as severe abuse of alcohol.

Rituals and ceremonies become especially important during anniversaries and holidays. Personal versions of the meaningful, comforting rituals for these occasions typically involve a way to remember and acknowledge the deceased child. These rituals we usually term "family traditions" to give them a comforting connotation, and emphasize that they can be carried on into the future. Knowing that there is something that can be enacted at each of these times—the child's birthday, the anniversary of the death, Thanksgiving, Mother's Day, and so on—provides bereaved parents with the security that they do not have to determine how they are going to deal with their children's deaths during each holiday. There is something they can rely on to include their children's memories at these times, allowing them to proceed with the rest of the events of the day with less preoccupation, guilt, or anxiety.

Clinicians can be ready to suggest ideas to bereaved parents about things they can do, based on what other parents have done. It is important to emphasize that whatever ritual or ceremony they would like to enact be suitable for them and their families. We encourage families to work together to decide what would be appropriate. Siblings of the deceased child can be especially engaged in this planning, and often have ideas that parents find surprising and appropriate. We recall one example where at Thanksgiving dinner, when the family came to the table for the meal, there were little pieces of paper placed by each person's plate. The 8-year-old sister of the child who had died announced that during dinner, each person was to answer the question on the paper at his or her plate. Each question was about her older brother who had died that year. They included things like, "What was the funniest thing that Ben did?" and "What was Ben's favorite shirt?" The young girl included her brother during that Thanksgiving in a way that was lighthearted. She solved a problem the parents had not been able to manage themselves, as they struggled with the recognition of the empty place at the table.

☐ Maladaptive Spirituality and Religion?

Our perspective is that the clinician should be an expert companion to bereaved parents. Clinicians should try to work with parents within the concepts and understandings of their cultural contexts, and more narrowly within the parameters of their existential and spiritual beliefs and practices. *Are there any circumstances where the clinician should not passively accept a particular spiritual practice or conceptualization?* We believe there are. It is obvious that if the parents' ways of conceptualizing their experience or the behavior that they engage in requires that the clinician violate his or her own professional code of ethics, then it would be wrong for the clinician to support the parent in those instances.

In addition, certain kinds of spiritual conceptualizations in which parents may engage may have an actively destructive and maladaptive impact on their psychological well-being. For example, there is some indication that when parents interpret their child's death as the result of some kind of punishment, perhaps from God, for their own "sinful" behavior, their psychological adjustment may be harmed (Pargament, 1997).

When the clinician's judgment is that a particular spiritual stance taken by the parent is likely to be detrimental to the parent's psychological well-being, then we believe the clinician should address the matter. It may be useful for the clinician to gently draw attention to what the parent is doing, and to encourage the parent to examine his or her spiritual or religious stance from different perspectives and to help the parent evaluate the likely consequences of what he or she is doing. Congruent with the expert companion clinical style that we advocate, we are not suggesting that the clinician engage in active confrontation or in active condemnation of the parent's perspective. We are suggesting that if we see the possibility of danger in what the parent is doing, we should draw attention to it and help parents make their own evaluations. The hope is that the combination of the clinician's attention to the matter, and the collaborative evaluation, will lead to a helpful and ethical outcome. The following exchange between a parent and a clinician provides an example of the style we recommend. In this instance, a 17-year-old boy had taken the mother's car out late at night and had a fatal accident.

BP: I know that I hadn't been doing right, I mean as a parent, but also in general, the way I was living, so I guess this is the result.

T: You mean those affairs and partying.

BP: I know I wasn't paying attention to what was going on like I should. I was just stupid and selfish, acting like a teenager myself. I can't believe it. After the divorce, I went crazy. I guess getting married at 16, I didn't get it out of my system or something. But now look what I've done.

T: What did you do?

BP: Killed him!

T: What do you mean?

BP: God knows I've done wrong all along. He knew I wasn't fit. So he took Brian away. He knew I got pregnant at 16. He knew I drank. He knew I committed adultery. He knew I left my husband. He said, "That's enough! You've had your chances and you still don't learn. Now you'll see!"

T: Brian's death was God's way of getting your attention, or punishing you?

BP: God knows I was a bad mom. He couldn't stand to see me be Brian's mom anymore, what I was doing and all.

T: So God took Brian from you?

BP: God figured He had to take over, since I wasn't doing it.

T: God's version of foster care. Like when Social Services took Brian that time.

BP: But he's not coming back!

T: Right, he's not coming back this time. This is a terrible punishment.

BP: God says that children will suffer for the sins of their parents.

T: Brian's paying the price for your sins.

BP: Right. This is what I deserve, but Brian didn't deserve this. He shouldn't have to pay with his life for how I've lived!

T: But that's God's way in this situation?

BP: They've been warning me. Like my sister said, if I didn't straighten up, God would step in, and then I'd be sorry. She was right. She was right. And I knew it, but I didn't heed it. I guess I thought I had time to get it together or something. I don't know what I was thinking. But it wasn't right.

T: I'm confused about a few things.

BP: What?

T: You're thinking that Brian's paying the price for your sins. Right?

BP: Yeah.

T: I thought that Jesus did.

BP: Well, yeah, but I mean that Brian's dead because of all the things I did that have been sinful.

T: I guess I'm thinking that there are three sources of responsibility for what happened. You, Brian, and God.

BP: I'm not sure what you mean.

T: Well, we've agreed before that you should have been paying closer attention to Brian's activities.

BP: Yeah, right.

T: And if you did, maybe, possibly, you might have caught him going out that night.

BP: I so wish I did, I so wish I did.

T: But Brian is also responsible for going out when he shouldn't have. He made a bad choice.

BP: I know, but I didn't teach him like I should have.

T: Yes, but I think Brian still knew right from wrong here, when he took the car out, didn't he?

BP: Sure. He knew he wasn't supposed to take the car.

T: Right. Now the third area of responsibility has to do with God. His will, His action in this. To me, that is less clear.

BP: What God did?

T: Right. You say that God took Brian to punish you for sin, and you may be right about that. Then again, God may be broken-hearted watching both you and Brian make your mistakes, leading to this tragic accident. He may already be sending angels to help soften your grief, and help you go on. I know you've run into some wonderful kindness, too.

BP: Oh, that's true, you know. Those people are my angels.

T: I think maybe they believe they are doing God's will. Maybe He's using them.

BP: Oh, yes, He can be merciful like that.

T: I don't pretend to know all about God's will and ways. He can be a mystery to me sometimes. But I'd encourage you to keep considering carefully God's responsibility in all this, as well as yours and Brian's, and over time, we'll perhaps see the whole picture.

BP: I just know I don't like my part of the picture.

In this exchange between the therapist and the bereaved parent, the therapist determines that the parent's idea that God is punishing her with the death of her child is gently challenged. The clinician acknowledges the parent's beliefs, and stays within her religious framework, referring to Jesus, God, and aspects of God's will. By mentioning Jesus paying the price for sin, angels in the form of humans, and that God is a mystery, the clinician tries to introduce some flexibility into a religious system that the parent is beginning to make rather rigid and punitive. The clinician doesn't attempt to debate or convince, but just to keep the options open for the time being, recognizing that in so doing, the parent may eventually arrive at an understanding that produces a little less suffering.

☐ A New Community: Bereaved Parents

Bereaved parents often seem to form new communities that contain some spiritual elements. We see this often in the bonds that are forged in support groups, and bereaved parents sense a special connection to others who have lost a child as well. The depth of emotional experience seems to be bonding like that seen in combat veterans. One parent told a story of sitting next to a man on an airplane, and discovering during their conversation that the man was also a bereaved parent who had lost his daughter 30 years before. They were struck by the fact that although they were of different generations, and one man was 30 years down this road while the other was in his first, there was much they had in common. They discovered they shared membership in the same group; they were citizens of the same country.

The community of bereaved parents reaches beyond many differences that often divide people, because coping with the death of one's child has a strong existential element that for many parents is experienced as having a spiritual dimension. By that, we mean that there is mystery, rawness of emotion, and a concern with the essential issues of living—attachment and loss, life and death. Because these are fundamentally human concerns, all can relate to them, so one bereaved parent can feel that at the core of this experience is a common understanding that all the other bereaved parents also have.

7 CHAPTER

Issues for the Clinician

> *In the event of decompression in the cabin,*
> *oxygen masks will automatically drop down.*
> *Make sure you put yours on first,*
> *before you try to assist others.*
> —Preflight safety instructions

How can you do that kind of work? It must be amazingly tough to have to sit and listen to all those problems people have. And when you are talking about people who have horrible things happen to them, things that you can't undo, things that are just awful . . . like with parents whose kids died. . . . It would just be more than I could take. How do you keep all that from affecting you?

These kinds of questions are probably quite familiar to many clinicians and they are the general focus of this chapter. We first look at the kinds of issues that can arise in clinical work with bereaved parents, focusing on countertransference, and such particulars as whether the clinician is a parent or not and the specific cultural influences that may impact how the clinician responds to grieving parents. Then we look at the issue of vicarious traumatization and the possibility of vicarious growth resulting from work with bereaved parents. Finally, we will offer some suggestions for the self-care of clinicians who work with bereaved parents.

☐ Issues in Clinical Work with Bereaved Parents

Countertransference

The word *countertransference* has its origins in traditional psychoanalysis, but the word is currently used in broader ways than was Freud's original intent. As the word is used here, countertransference can be thought of as the set of general attitudes, feelings, fantasies, and responses that the clinician experiences toward clients, which originate primarily from the clinician's own needs, assumptions, biases, and conflicts, and not from what is actually present or occurring in the relationship with the client. In work with bereaved parents these matters are especially relevant if they are connected to parenthood, the loss of a child, and views about grief and death generally.

The specific psychoanalytic assumptions on which Freud originally based the concept of countertransference may not currently be viewed as very useful. But the idea that traits or states of the clinician, and the various forces that influence the clinician, can have unintended and sometimes unnoticed detrimental effects on the process of counseling is quite useful. Work with bereaved parents is not unique in this possibility, but there may be some elements specific to this kind of clinical work that merit attention.

Some clinicians are themselves parents and some are not. Neither of these particular states confers greater competence or liability. Each can present the clinician with its own kinds of challenges. Our experience suggests that bereaved parents tend to feel most similar and most closely connected to clinical workers or volunteers who are also parents who have lost a child, especially if the circumstances of the loss are similar. We discussed this when we talked about deaths from suicide. In a similar way, parents may attribute some degree of higher credibility to clinicians who are themselves parents, because the perception may be that the clinician at least has the possibility of *imagining* what the bereaved parent is going through. Clinicians who are not parents may face a slightly higher level of skepticism from bereaved parents, on the assumption that when clinicians are childless they may not be able to comprehend what the parent is experiencing.

It is unlikely that any of these particular parenthood categories conveys a distinct advantage to the clinician's ability to provide support to grieving parents. Although being a parent or having suffered a similar loss may lead parents to *perceive* the clinician in somewhat more favorable ways, at least initially, the very similarities may present unique challenges as well. Childless clinicians lack direct experience with parenthood on which to draw, but that lack also means that in some ways the clinician is less likely to have had experiences that may inadvertently bias the way in which the parent's grief is viewed. The clinician's own experience with parenthood and loss can provide a framework that may limit, or in some cases distort, the way in which the clinician understands the experience of the parent. Being a parent oneself, then, may sometimes create the possibility of problems with countertransference. So clinicians who are parents need to be particularly careful to maintain a good awareness of the ways in which their own situations may affect how they engage the bereaved parent. Being a parent, or more specifically being a bereaved parent, gives the clinician a unique opportunity to help other parents, but it also means that there are unique opportunities for the clinician's own perspective to distort the accuracy with which the parents who are clients and their experiences are viewed.

Clinicians who are parents, however, may also have the advantage of being able to more easily understand the parent's descriptions of the experience both as parents generally and as bereaved parents in particular, because the clinician and parent share the many experiences of the parenthood journey. Clinicians who have themselves experienced the loss of a child can have a unique credibility in the eyes of many parents. This unique credibility offers the possibility for clinicians to be of greater influence on grieving parents. But, as all good clinicians know, that influence must be used with great care, and only in highly ethical ways, in the service of helping the bereaved parent to cope in the best way possible with the death of a child. To be a fellow bereaved parent means that the clinician and client are citizens of the same country. But, as we have indicated, that similarity can produce some special challenges. Simply being in the same category, or, using the metaphor, in the same country, does not necessarily mean that clinician and client arrived in the same way, or that their experience is identical, or even very similar. All clinicians must stay alert for issues related to countertransference, but when the clinician has faced the same kind of major crisis as the client, this admonition is particularly appropriate.

The longer we live, the greater the likelihood is that we will ourselves face highly challenging life circumstances that involve significant loss. The losses may not necessarily involve the death of a loved one, but we are likely to encounter them. The same general cautionary note that we provided about clinicians who are themselves parents applies to clinicians who have experienced major losses. The particular ways in which clinicians experienced, coped with, and successfully or unsuccessfully adapted can color the ways in which the bereaved parent's loss is understood and experienced by the clinician. On the one hand, that personal history of crisis can provide the foundation for an enhanced empathetic grasp of the parent's pain and general experience. On the other hand, the clinician's own losses can also serve as a source for the kinds of distortions that represent problems with countertransference.

In addition to the clinician's status as a parent and personal history of loss, additional elements can contribute to the possibility of problems with countertransference. One of these is the influence of what might be called the *general culture of North American psychotherapy*. As we saw in chapter 2, there are some ideas that can generally be regarded as myths that still have significant influence over the way many clinicians think about and work with bereaved persons. In addition to distorted assumptions about the bereavement process that clinicians may hold, there are some general norms and rules about the psychotherapy process that may influence, perhaps in ways that clinicians themselves are not quite mindful of, how clinicians work with bereaved parents.

A general assumption that is widely made about how psychotherapy and counseling should proceed is that the client should do most of the talking. This is not a bad or incorrect assumption. In general, it probably is an important component of many effective ways of helping clients cope with difficult problems. In addition to doing most of the talking, however, clients are usually expected to engage in a high level of self-disclosure about a host of highly personal and intimate things, and to focus primarily on the world of internal experience. There are some clients, and in our experience these are more likely, but not exclusively, to be adult men, for whom these expectations may not be quite appropriate. We suggest that if individual bereaved parents have difficulty with high levels of self-disclosure, that clinicians respect that reluctance. In such situations clinicians should take care to work with parents in ways that respect that reluctance and that are appropriate to the individuals. It would be unfortunate to uncritically follow the rule that tells some clinicians that, in order to get better, clients must always disclose all of the highly private elements of their internal experience, which may involve a great deal of pain for some persons.

Clinicians are not exempt from the same kinds of social and cultural influences that come to bear on bereaved parents. Clinicians working with grieving parents must also be accurately aware of the ways in which their own cultural contexts, past and present, may influence the ways in which they respond to bereaved parents. A useful exercise, for example, is for clinicians to look at the elements for understanding the parent's grief in cultural context (see chap. 3). Then, examine what particular cultural factors influence them and what the particular content of those influences is. For example, what are the general cultural traditions, the primary reference groups, the rules and norms (especially about grief and bereavement), values, views and experiences regarding spirituality and religion, idioms of grief and bereavement, and the main assumptions as to what is most helpful to grieving parents that are held by the clinician? And to what degree is the clinician aware of the way such cultural elements may serve as guides, helpfully or not, to the way the clinician approaches each grieving parent who becomes a client? Cultural similarities, in our view, are not a requirement for good work with bereaved parents, and cultural similarities do not necessarily convey any special therapeutic advantage. But to the extent that the clinician's own context and cultural influences have an impact on the course of treatment, accurate awareness of those influences may be a helpful preventative step to take toward avoiding undesirable distortions of the counseling process.

When work with bereaved parents creates anxieties about death for the clinician, this can also raise the possibility of countertransference distortions. When clinicians become anxious about topics related to death generally, or the deaths of children in particular, they may respond in ways that may be designed more to reduce their own distress, rather than to contribute to the well-being of the bereaved parent. This kind of work can raise the anxiety of clinicians in individual sessions with clients. One undesirable way in which the clinician can manage his or her own anxiety is to guide the client away from talking about the anxiety-producing content. This can reduce the clinician's anxiety, but it may also represent a potentially unhelpful clinical reaction. The clinician may inadvertently communicate to the client that certain topics or experiences should not be discussed. Many bereaved parents do need to narrate their stories of pain and survival over and over again, and clinical responses that do not support this process can be unhelpful to the parent. As we have suggested, clinicians' accurate awareness of their anxiety may be a helpful step to ensure that their own discomfort does not lead them to conduct counseling in a way that reduces its potential helpfulness to the parent.

Ideally, clinicians should maintain accurate self-awareness at all times. The best strategy is for the clinician to strive to identify responses that may be driven or distorted by his or her own needs. However, no clinician is omniscient. As a general preventative strategy, it is probably very useful for therapists to meet regularly with clinical colleagues to review their cases. This does not need to be a formal supervisory relationship, but it should be professional and characterized by sufficient trust so that difficult issues can be presented and reviewed.

Although we generally think of clinician emotional involvement in this work as a positive aspect of the work, and a sign that the clinician is empathic, this emotional involvement must be balanced with some perspective and detachment that allows for clinical planning and decision making in the session. There are certainly going to be moments of profound sadness or horror that the clinician shares with bereaved parents, but recovery from that reaction in the session should be fairly rapid. We think that it is perfectly acceptable to shed tears, but not to cry and wail uncontrollably as a client might need to do.

Some signs that the clinician might be having reactions that compromise his or her ability to work effectively with grief include basically two kinds of responses—inordinate distancing, from the bereaved parent and one's own emotional responses, and inordinate closeness or involvement with the parent and one's own emotional responses.

Inordinate distancing occurs when it is difficult to share the bereaved parent's grief and loss. This may be because of the parent's presentation or something about the circumstances of the loss. For example, if a clinician sees the parent as bearing some responsibility for the death, perhaps by failing to place a young child in a restraint seat in the car, it might be more difficult than usual to feel concern for the parent. This might be revealed in the clinician's choice to focus on this aspect of the tragedy:

> *BP:* I just can't remember for sure if I buckled her in. But I always do. I just can't account for how she was found unbuckled after the wreck.
>
> *T:* Can you retrace your steps and try to figure out what you did with her carseat that morning?
>
> *BP:* I've tried that and I just can't get it straight.
>
> *T:* You'll always wonder unless you can get that memory back.
>
> *BP:* But it won't seem to come. I wonder if the trauma of the accident and my injuries messed up my memory.
>
> *T:* Or maybe you are repressing it, because it is too difficult to face.

A clinician who approaches an issue like parental responsibility for a child's death in this way has his or her own agenda in mind, and is not able to muster much empathy for the parent because of judgments that the clinician is making. This clinician is not a companion in this grief, but rather a prosecutor. Nonetheless, we can sometimes convince ourselves that we are still doing good clinical work when we do such things from the perspective that we know better than the bereaved parents we wish to serve.

The primary indication of *inordinate closeness* is preoccupation, in session or out, with the story of the bereaved parent and continuing emotional reactions to it. Such reactions may include putting oneself in the parent's place, recurring thoughts about the parent and the parent's situation, sleeplessness, applying the parent's situation to oneself and imagining being in it, and so on. Although we believe these reactions can be within the parameters of good practice, at least to a degree, we are warning of recurring, constant reactions such as these. Having these reactions does not mean that a clinician is unhealthy or unsuited for this work. It may merely indicate that as a human being, you are affected, and could use a chance to talk about it and receive some support. Working in groups with a cotherapist is helpful in this regard. It may be helpful for cotherapists to spend time after group meetings discussing some of the experiences of the session, because this can help them to be better able to leave feeling whole.

In sum, the psychoanalytic term *countertransference* provides a useful perspective to remind clinicians about the ways in which factors to which they may not be attending can adversely affect their work with bereaved parents. In order to guard against these potentially negative effects, clinicians need to maintain accurate self-awareness in their work with parents. Clinicians need also to be aware of the ways in which their own cultural contexts and social influences may mold their responses to clients. The clinician's own status as a parent or not, as a bereaved parent or not, anxieties about death, and the culture of psychotherapy within which most clinicians are trained and remain immersed are all factors that may affect how they are perceived by grieving parents and that may influence their clinical work. And again, two signs that the clinician's effectiveness may be compromised are inordinate distancing or inordinate closeness from the bereaved parent.

Negative Effects and Vicarious Traumatization

The possibility that work in any field involving emotional work with people can produce negative psychological responses has been recognized for some time. The word *burnout* (using the metaphor of the rocket that crashes back to earth once the fuel is exhausted) has been used to describe a general cluster of negative psychological reactions that are produced by the chronic stress of being in professions that involve working with people in highly challenging situations—for example, teachers, social workers, or mental health workers. In general terms, burnout is an unpleasant psychological state that is characterized by physical and emotional fatigue or exhaustion, brought about by the demands and conditions of one's work. Clinical work with clients who have experienced major life difficulties and losses, for example, grieving parents, can also put the clinical worker at particular risk for more specific kinds of negative psychological responses.

Several terms have been used to describe essentially the same general cluster of negative psychological effects of working with clients who have suffered major life crises: *vicarious traumatization* (Pearlman & Saakvitne, 1995), *secondary traumatic stress,* and *compassion fatigue* (Figley, 1995; Jenkins

& Baird, 2002). Some of these phrases were developed to designate specific and highly negative sets of responses that are similar in many ways to the kinds of stress-induced problems listed in classification systems of mental disorders (e.g., American Psychiatric Association, 2000). Although we employ one of these terms, *vicarious traumatization*, in our usage the term designates a broader set of negative responses that do not necessarily reach the threshold of a either a clinical or a subclinical "disorder" and that are broader than the disturbances originally articulated by Pearlman and Saakvitne (1995).

When parents describe experiences that are horrible and extremely distressing, these images can have a significant psychological impact on the clinician. Although the clinician does not personally observe or directly experience the events, the client's description can in itself lead the clinician to experience posttraumatic-like responses. In chapter 3, for example, we described the death of a young boy who had been playing on top of construction pipes when they collapsed, crushing and killing him. These are painful and disturbing images, and although readers did not see or participate in the tragic events directly, images may have occurred to them that were very upsetting. When the horrible events clinicians hear about involve harm that has befallen children, such vicarious exposure to trauma may be particularly distressing.

As a consequence of listening to parents describe the deaths of their children, clinicians may indeed experience some of the same kinds of responses that characterize posttraumatic stress disorder and similar kinds of clinical difficulties. There may be intrusive thoughts and images, increased physiological arousal, and perhaps some avoidance of reminders associated with the tragic events described by the parents.

As one clinician said:

> Once she talked about what had happened, even though she did not go out of her way to provide any gory details, the scene of that cute little kid playing on the pipes and then losing his balance as the pipes started to move, then falling, and then being crushed under them kept sort of creeping into my consciousness. It was as if I could see it kind of in slow motion, even though it was less of a visual than a visceral experience. And in describing her valiant but futile attempts to put life back into his destroyed bloody little body . . . it's an image slash experience that haunts me whenever something cues it for me.

As we have suggested, parents' descriptions of the loss of their children may lead clinicians to become anxious about their own safety and the safety of loved ones, and, if they are themselves parents, the safety of their own children. Some years ago, the local paper reported the lethal results of a tragic accident in a grandparent's backyard. A grandson had come for a visit, and he was playing in the backyard as the grandparent watched him from a picture window. As he was running across the yard, the boy fell, and hit his forehead on the sharp end of a pecan nut that was on the ground. The pecan shell penetrated his skull and caused his death shortly thereafter. When clinicians listen to such accounts by parents or grandparents, their own assumptions about control, predictability, and safety may be challenged or shattered. In addition to disrupting the clinician's general understanding of his or her own world, the disconfirmation of the accuracy of such assumptions can cause significant emotional distress (Janoff-Bulman, 1992).

> To some extent, particularly when my children were younger (they are in college or beyond now), when I would have a client describe something bad happening to a kid, then my level of anxiety about my own kids' safety would go up. In some ways, I think it was in the ballpark of *DSM* kind of stuff. Just really minimal things could trigger what I knew in my head to be irrational anxiety, but even though I would really try all that adaptive self-talk stuff we use with clients, which is supposed to really work, I would still stay more worried than I should have. One of the things that would help was to just articulate the experience I was having, either to my husband or to a close clinical friend, and that would help a lot. But, the next time a parent would tell me about a loss that represented a kind of cause that *could* happen to my kids, then it could trigger that worry about their safety again. I guess that as I got more experience the frequency and intensity of that kind of apprehension sort of diminished.

Clinicians working with bereaved parents can themselves experience a wide range of distressing emotions—sadness, depression, anger, and anxiety can be common reactions to the account of a child's death. For most clinicians, these are more likely to be temporary, and to be particularly intense on hearing about the loss for the first time. But unless clinicians are highly insensitive, most will experience some degree of sympathetic pain each time a parent speaks of the loss of a child.

In sum, clinical work with bereaved parents can present unique challenges to the psychological well-being of the clinician, and can expose the clinician to various psychologically distressing responses, which, if they are intense and persistent, can constitute burnout or vicarious traumatization. The distressing responses clinicians experience can include the following: a range of distressing emotions, a disruption of the general assumptions that are used to organize one's understanding of how the world works, and sometimes responses that are similar to those that characterize posttraumatic stress syndromes.

The problematic reactions that can result from vicarious exposure to the narratives provided by bereaved parents are very well captured by the phrases *vicarious traumatization, compassion fatigue, secondary stress disorder,* and the like. There is a word of German origin, probably familiar to many, that seems to capture the potential difficulties we are describing a bit more broadly: *weltschmerz*. This word describes a general state of weariness of the soul, a general state of pessimism and melancholy about the state of the world. Clinicians whose work involves exclusive or primary work with people exposed to tragic and traumatic events generally, or grieving parents in particular, may be at risk for this general loss of vocational satisfaction and for the experience of the melancholy sense of a sadness and weariness of soul (Pearlman & Saakvitne, 1995).

Risk Factors for Burnout and Vicarious Traumatization

One of the important factors that can place clinicians at risk for problems resulting from their work with grieving parents is *the presence of unrealistic expectations* about their ability to help clients change themselves, their circumstances, or their psychological pain. It is possible that this is more likely to be a problem for beginning clinicians, but it is not limited to them. The psychologist Julian Rotter, one of the developers of what became known as social learning theory, developed a concept that he called *minimal goal level* (Rotter, 1954). These minimal goals represent the minimal level at which individuals are willing to give themselves rewards for their performance on specific tasks. Or, as applied to the present context, the minimal goal level represents the degree of progress, experienced by a client, that the clinician will regard as reflecting satisfactory clinical work. The wisdom, of course, is to find the most practical and realistic level at which to set one's minimal expectations. This concept can serve as a general reminder to clinicians to be wise about the level of power they assume they have to help clients adapt and change for the better. A risk factor for burnout, and perhaps for some forms of vicarious traumatization, is unrealistically high expectation about the amount of reduction of suffering that it is possible for a bereaved parent to experience. As we said in chapter 2, for example, the data clearly indicate that for some bereaved people "recovery" will never occur. When clinicians expect that most or all grieving parents will "reach closure" or "recover," or even that all clinical sessions will lead parents to "feel good," disappointment is inevitable. We urge clinicians to utilize the best wisdom they can as they set their expectations for the amount of power they have to provide comfort and relief to bereaved parents.

Just as with the development of posttraumatic symptoms resulting from direct exposure to highly challenging events, there is something of a "dose and response" relationship in the development of vicarious traumatization. *The greater the tragedy and horror of the parents' accounts, and the more often* clinicians hear stories of parents' losses, the greater is the risk for the clinician to develop psychological troubles arising from vicarious exposure to loss and trauma (Pearlman & Saakvitne, 1995). In addition, the greater the proportion of the clinician's caseload that involves helping people who have experienced trauma and loss generally, and the loss of a child in particular, the greater is the long-term risk for vicarious traumatization.

Some characteristics of the clinician may also raise the risk of developing vicariously induced stress symptoms. *Beginning clinicians* may be at greater risk than experienced clinicians who have developed adaptive ways of coping with the stress associated with clinical work (Pearlman & MacIan, 1995). Clinicians at the beginning of their careers have to cope with various challenges that more experienced clinicians no longer face (e.g., building up caseloads, learning the general art and practice of clinical work), and the added challenge of doing a great deal of work with persons who have suffered personal tragedies can add to the amount of pressure experienced from clinical work. Further, our experience suggests that *clinicians who themselves have children* may be more vulnerable in some ways than those who do not have children. When they repeatedly hear stories describing the various ways in which children can die or be killed, clinicians who are parents may be a bit more vulnerable to the psychological distress that can accompany the contradiction of their assumptions that their own personal worlds are predictable, controllable, and safe.

Regardless of the particular level of experience of the clinician and of the number of bereaved parents he or she sees, it is important to keep in mind that *working with persons who have experienced tragic loss carries with it an element of risk*. The risk is that clinical work may begin to be more than the clinician can take—that is, the experience of burnout—or that the clinician may vicariously develop some of the same kinds of psychological difficulties that are often experienced by traumatized persons in general, and bereaved parents in particular.

Positive Aspects and Vicarious Posttraumatic Growth

In the interest of clearly pointing out the risks involved in clinical work with bereaved parents, it is possible to inadvertently imply that this kind of work offers nothing but the possibility of negative effects for the clinician. On the contrary, this kind of work can be highly rewarding, and there is also the possibility that this kind of work can lead the clinician to develop in ways that would not have occurred without being engaged in this kind of work (Saakvitne, 1997, November). As we indicated in chapter 1, parents who have lost a child may experience significant positive changes emerging from their struggle with tragic loss. Vicarious exposure to their experiences may also lead clinicians to experience *vicarious post-traumatic growth.*

Working with bereaved parents can offer uniquely rewarding experiences for the clinician. Offering support and participating in the process whereby grieving parents struggle with, and experience some reduction in, their pain can be a source of great satisfaction to clinicians. After they have gained experience in this area, we find that clinicians point to particular sources of satisfaction. One is the privilege of being close to a person who is in his or her most honest state. The grief of losing one's child seems to make it very difficult for people to manage their impression, or keep a façade. This kind of emotional honesty can allow a clinician to bypass some of the usual efforts necessary to open people up emotionally, and can permit rapid progress to a strong therapeutic relationship and good clinical work. Furthermore, clinicians who work with bereaved parents often refer to the hopefulness they see in this process. With enough experience, the clinician learns that people improve significantly over time, despite the desperation that appears at the start.

Another rewarding aspect of this work can be experienced in *group settings.* Bereavement support groups allow for rapid bonding of group members, and it is especially satisfying to see *people from different life circumstances find common ground in the fundamental human experience of grief.* Clinicians can also be greatly rewarded when they see parents experiencing elements of posttraumatic growth, and helping others learn from their insights. One clinician who works with bereaved parents said:

> In all my clinical work over the years, I don't think I have ever seen the range of responses, at an emotional level, that I typically see with bereaved parents. There is nothing more satisfying to me than a good group meeting, where parents validate each others' experiences, are comfortable with crying, encourage members to tell stories of horror, address the deepest religious and philosophical issues with passion, and manage to come up with some of the funniest comments about their situations that I have ever heard. It can be an amazing look at what good people are capable of, when they feel at their lowest.

Clinicians may be strongly affected by the experience of their clients' descriptions of heroic struggles with loss, and *may find themselves inspired by their clients' simple ability to survive and continue with life* (Pearlman & Saakvitne, 1995). On a more general level, working with persons who face great adversity can lead some clinicians to increase their appreciation and admiration for the strength and resilience of the human spirit. As one therapist put it, "I think that the thing that I know . . . is that the human spirit is very resilient. And we rebound, and we come back" (Arnold, 1998).

Clinicians working with persons who have experienced great loss can themselves experience what they perceive as significant changes in who they are—*changes in their levels of compassion, insight, and tolerance.* These can be experienced by clinicians as enduring and fundamental changes in their character and personality, brought about by the challenging work of providing support to persons who have undergone profound and tragic losses. As one clinician said about working with people who had faced traumatic circumstances, "I think I am more knowledgeable, more sensitive, more tolerant of difference in people and differences in situations" (Arnold, 1998, p. 30).

Working with bereaved parents can also lead some clinicians to *experience significant development in their own spiritual lives.* This kind of clinical work forces the clinician to consider the fundamental questions about the purpose of human lives and what happens after death. The vicarious reminder about existential issues leads many clinicians to wrestle with these fundamental matters and to develop answers and perspectives that, for them, are more meaningful and more deeply satisfying than the answers they previously had.

Working with grieving clients can lead some clinicians to experience a deepening of their spirituality or of their religious lives. As one experienced clinician said:

> People who are healing after some kind of trauma know very, very well that there is a God, or some sort of higher power. And the more they work through it, the closer they get to whatever that spiritual part of themselves is, and you can't sit there in the room with a person who is getting in touch with that and not know that there's some similar kind of thing going on in yourself. (Arnold, 1998, p. 41)

As they are confronted with the tragic losses experienced by the parents with whom they are working, *clinicians can also develop a deeper and stronger appreciation for their own good fortunes.* By listening to the accounts of the losses reported by grieving parents, clinicians may come to regard themselves as blessed in many ways. Some may be reminded that they have been spared the suffering undergone by others, and may count themselves fortunate. The general experience is a realization that "I am really lucky." As another clinician said of this kind of clinical work:

> I go home and count my blessings—it's affected me that way. . . . By the time I get home, I realize I've got a lot to be thankful for.

One clinician summed up the possibilities of vicarious posttraumatic growth this way:

> I think it was Richard Belzer [the actor and comedian] that said that for him cancer was like a cosmic slap in the face. That quote has always stayed

with me, because he also went on to say that you either get discouraged or ennobled by it. Well, working with clients who have been traumatized, or lost a child, or had something really bad happen to them, things like that, for me is sometimes like getting slapped. Sometimes that slap just discourages me, and makes me worried and sometimes it just makes me depressed. And other times, I don't think that it really ennobles me or anything, but working with clients who have themselves lost much makes lots of things salient for me and in some ways that indirect slap reminds me to pay attention. It reminds me to pay attention to how fortunate I am, it reminds me to work on keeping my priorities straight, it makes some existential and spiritual things more salient and it makes me think of some important things. I guess that occasional slap provides me with opportunities and reminders that people who do other kinds of work just don't have. This work changes you, and I think most of it is for the better.

☐ Taking Care of Ourselves

Many clinicians are motivated, at least in part, by their interest in being of service to fellow human beings. The daily clinical work of helping bereaved parents is focused, appropriately, on the development and well-being of the client. With the general motivation to help others, and the professional focus on the well-being of the client, it is possible for clinicians not to attend as much as they should to their own psychological welfare. As we have previously indicated, work with bereaved parents, although it offers great rewards, carries with it an inherent risk of distressing psychological responses. In what follows, we provide some general reminders and suggestions for clinicians to utilize to minimize the likelihood that their own work with grieving parents will lead to burnout or to significant kinds of vicarious traumatization.

Considerations in Clinical Work

One of the most important decisions clinicians must make, in order to reduce their chances of burnout or vicarious traumatization, is to *control their caseloads*. The constraints of clinicians' employment and work demands may restrict the degree to which they can control their caseloads. Nevertheless, in order to engage in appropriate professional self-care, we recommend that clinicians exercise as much control as they can in two general ways: monitor, and set limits on, the maximum number of direct, clinical service hours done each week.

Clinical work is often psychologically demanding and can on occasion be significantly distressing for the clinician. There are individual differences in the stamina clinicians have, but clearly there is a limit on the number of hours any person can work. As the individual clinician begins to reach his or her upper limit of clinical hours, not only will the quality of care provided to clients suffer, but the clinician develops a greater risk of suffering negative effects from clinical work. How many hours of direct clinical service in a week is too much must be determined by following the guidelines provided to the clinicians by professional associations and by the clinicians' own knowledge about their own stamina. As the provision of direct services (working with clients) begins to *reach upward of 30 hours per week, then the clinician should exercise caution*. The more hours that the clinician spends in direct services, the more important it becomes to carefully monitor the level of stress experienced and to systematically employ self-care measures, such as those we describe next.

Clinical work with clients who have suffered tragic losses can be highly demanding. And work with bereaved parents can certainly qualify as challenging on many occasions. It is important for the clinician to *monitor and, to the extent possible, control the proportion of clients seen whose problems include narratives of great suffering*, particularly if the suffering also involves descriptions of horrible events. Because of their particular pattern of interests and skills, some clinicians choose to specialize in trauma work or bereavement counseling. Most clinicians, however, work in settings where they see a wider range of psychological problems and life challenges. As a general rule of thumb, the greater the proportion of clients in the caseload who present with highly traumatic histories, the greater the risk for the clinician to experience adverse effects from clinical work. Another general suggestion, then, is that, to the extent that it is feasible, clinicians should control, and perhaps limit, the proportion of their caseloads devoted to clients dealing with major losses and traumas—for example, bereaved parents.

We have already mentioned that setting unrealistic goals about the effects of one's clinical work can be a risk factor for professional burnout, and perhaps even worse kinds of difficulties. Another way in which clinicians can exercise good self-care is *to set appropriately realistic goals about the impact they can have on clients*—this is neither simple nor easy. Our experience has been that clinicians still early in their professional careers may be more likely to entertain unrealistically high expectations about their abilities to induce change in clients. One consequence of unrealistic expectations is that the clinician will often be disappointed with the progress clients make. The disappointment then leads clinicians to conclude that they are not doing good work, or that they are somehow deficient in their skills. And, as such judgments multiply, the likelihood is great that individual clinicians will begin to experience significant personal distress resulting from their interpretations of the quality of their work.

How can the clinician decide, in ways that are at least partially objective, that clients are indeed being well served by his or her clinical support? One very rough measure is simply to assess the percentage of clients who return after one session. The greater the proportion of clients who return for subsequent sessions, the greater is the likelihood that they have experienced the kind of clinical response that can be psychologically positive. Clearly, there can be other reasons for clients returning (e.g., the clinician inappropriately begins to foster dependence on the part of the client), but a high percentage of clients who do return after the first session can be a rough indicator that the clinician is probably doing something right.

Although the need for regular supervision is greater for clinicians who do not yet have a significant amount of experience, *regular consultation with colleagues is a good practice for all clinicians*. Some clinicians find that maintaining a regular supervision relationship with a trusted fellow clinician is helpful throughout their careers. For most experienced clinicians, formal relationships may not be necessary. But we recommend that all clinicians regularly meet with colleagues and talk over cases, elements of their clinical practice, or even of their lives in general that may be the source of stress (of course, appropriate client confidentiality must always be maintained). We have found that regularly scheduled, but informal, meetings with fellow clinicians offer a good way to obtain a different perspective on both clinical work and real life. An easy way of doing this is to set a regular social appointment with a trusted colleague, and, as the need arises, to use this opportunity to discuss clinical matters that are bothersome or about which the clinician would like some feedback.

> The way I do it is simple, but I think it really works. A clinical buddy of mine and I get together once a week for about one hour. We schedule it weeks ahead of time and we keep that time locked in. We usually have some kind of business stuff to talk about, but we almost always talk about particular clients that we want some advice about, and sometimes we just talk about stuff. Having that regular time, which is like an appointment really, I think is a really good preventive stress buster for both of us.

In addition to talking things out with a colleague, clinicians may also find it useful to *write about matters about which they have a concern*. There is some good evidence that writing about difficult challenges may have a beneficial effect on health (Pennebaker, 1997). When clinicians write about their challenges, either in their clinical work or in their everyday lives, it may prove useful to include a focus on the cognitive and emotional aspects of the challenges faced (Ullrich & Lutgendorf, 2002). Such writing, which many clinicians may already do in the regular journals they keep, may help generally with both physical and mental health, and may also enhance the likelihood of experiencing vicarious posttraumatic growth.

A general set of instructions for writing about challenging circumstances that may prove useful is as follows (modified from Ullrich & Lutgendorf, 2002, p. 246):

> Keep a journal of your deepest thoughts and feelings about the challenges of your clinical work and any other challenges you face in life. If the circumstances on which you are focusing do not make sense to you, or they are difficult to deal with, write about how you are trying to understand them, make sense of them, and deal with them, and how your feelings may change about those circumstances.

An additional way in which clinicians may need to engage in self-care is by *protecting their time away from clinical work.* Clearly, different kinds of clinical work present different challenges for protecting time off. The various new technologies that allow individuals to be reached, no matter where they may be, can add to the challenge. However, it is a desirable goal to be able to have a "time territory" away from clinical work that the clinician does not allow to be encroached on by the demands (or even the satisfactions) of work. It is important, particularly for clinicians who work or life situations place them at risk for negative responses, to defend the away-from-work "time territory" with some degree of zealotry. All clinicians, at one time or another, will need to be on call 24 hours a day, may need to carry beepers and cell phones, and may have to work at times that culturally may be traditionally viewed as times that people should be away from work (e.g., holidays, weekends). To the extent that the opportunities arise, it is important for clinicians to take measures to ensure that the demands of work do not unnecessarily invade the periods of time that are devoted to matters that in some ways may well be much more important than work: friends, children, family, and so on.

It is important for clinicians to make sure that they indeed *do take time away from their clinical work.* It is highly desirable to clinicians to build in breaks during every working day, that they build in breaks from work every few days, and that they take significant time away from clinical work at least several days each year. All clinicians should have built into their daily work routine periods of time where they leave the space in which they do clinical work, go to a different location, and do something other than meet with clients. In fact, doing nothing for several minutes each hour or two is probably a very good stress managing idea.

As anybody who has seen the tables summarizing the average number of yearly vacation days knows, the United States routinely ranks among the countries that offer workers the fewest number of yearly vacation days. The general cultural context in which clinicians in the United States find themselves is one that tends to discourage taking time off. Nevertheless, it is important for clinicians to have several consecutive days each year where they take a vacation, or at least a sabbatical from clinical work. As one of our clients from another country said, *"You Americans work too much! You need to take time way from your work more—go to the beach!"* Clinicians may work too much, and they should make sure that, at least once a year, they indeed take two or three weeks away from their clinical routine. And, even if the beach is not a possibility, then at least stay away from clinical work and defend the "time-away territory" from encroachment.

One clinical psychologist described some feelings that are similar to the client just quoted:

> We failed to do it one year, and my husband and I talked about it all year, how somehow we had missed something and we were less energetic as a result. Ever since the children were little we had been renting a house at the beach and spending a week there. Over time it has become really expensive but it is clear that the time away is something that we *need*. When we are there, after about four days both he and I can just feel the stress drop off. What we like is the ability to just do nothing. I know that would probably make some people kind of antsy, but it works great for me. It's a week where my primary concern every day is what I am going to have for dinner!

Considerations Beyond Clinical Work

The research on the helpful influences of positive social relationships is plentiful. There are various ways in which social support may serve as a psychological buffer against the negative effects of major life challenges and also as a helpful coping resource during difficult times. A very important measure that clinicians need to take is to *consciously maintain and nurture the important relationships in their lives.* Although probably a bit less likely to be held by clinicians, a common myth that many laypersons can have is the assumption that if one attends to one's relationships, in attempts to nurture and maintain them, then somehow one is being manipulative. This myth of spontaneity (that good intimate relationships must evolve spontaneously) may inhibit the maintenance of intimate relationships, but it may be more likely that for many clinicians the major inhibitor may be simple neglect. The demands of clinical work may not leave sufficient time and energy for the important relationships in life, so clinicians may inadvertently not place sufficient priority on them.

An important step that clinicians can take in their own self-care is to routinely remind themselves of who the important people are in their lives beyond their professional clinical work, and, in addition, to engage in the kinds of actions that are needed to keep important relationships active and nurtured. Although clinicians already know this, the reminder may be appropriate for those who work regularly with traumatized or grieving clients—*spend time with, stay in touch with, and actively seek out the important people in your personal life.* It is particularly important for clinicians to apply this reminder to partners, spouses, children, and good friends and family members with whom they have positive, healthy relationships. Clinicians may well have greater skills than laypersons regarding the maintenance of good and intimate relationships, but those skills are not always exercised. It is important to do so.

Another, and certainly very familiar, resource for managing stress and for preventing the negative psychological effects of the demands of clinical work is *physical exercise.* Physical activity must be appropriate for the individual's particular physical status and health condition, but the evidence is quite convincing as to its utility. Appropriate physical activity can have long-term benefits for physical health. With regard to managing the stress of clinical work and preventing the potential negative psychological effects of highly challenging clinical work, regular physical exercise tends to reduce anxiety and depression, and to improve self-esteem, in addition to more immediate effects such as increasing alertness and energy. Regular physical exercise can be a highly beneficial component the clinician may want to add to effective self-care.

A good way to maintain the habit of regular exercise is to engage in it with other people, particularly people who will encourage the clinician to participate even on days when he or she may be tempted to not participate.

> I am fortunate to work with a group and there are several of us who get together and play what I call age-adjusted-basketball. There are plenty of days when my temptation is to stay at my desk and, instead of exercising, to stay at my desk and catch up on my paperwork. But at least one of them will come by and talk me into going to the gym. There is no doubt in my mind that it helps me be more energetic, helps prevent stress from getting to me, and all those other health benefits we hear about all the time.

The work of many clinicians can sometimes tempt them to eat unwisely. The demands of work may lead them to skip lunch breaks and to eat the kinds of unhealthy foods that lend themselves to ease of preparation and fast consumption. We suggested earlier that taking time away from work is an important part of looking after oneself. It is important for clinicians to take sufficient time to have meals at appropriate times, to do so away from their desks and offices, and, in addition, to also have diets that are health promoting. It is probably a good investment to take sufficient time to consume meals in a slow and relaxed fashion, and to take the opportunity to also use the time to get away from the immediate physical environment where the clinical work is done—leave your office, go outside, make it at least to the lobby of the building, or have lunch with a friend at a nearby restaurant. These are surely commonsense suggestions, but clinicians may gradually be shaped into other kinds of habits, which are less healthy and less likely to protect them against the potential negative effects of demanding clinical work.

For most human beings, a *good dose of the natural world* can be a helpful resource to manage stress. Even in highly urbanized environments, open spaces, trees, and sometimes gardens or parks are easily accessible. To the extent that they are available, regular visits to such small urban bits of nature may prove useful additions to the resources available for keeping the stress of work manageable.

Finally, a crucial component of good clinician self-care is *the periodic evaluation of the level of stress experienced*. It may be wise to think of stress as occurring in at least two broad domains: environmental and psychological. A very simple and easy way to check your current level of stress is to think about these domains separately, and to ask one question for each domain. To evaluate the level of environmental stress you have experienced, simply enumerate the tough things that have happened to you in the past few months. Although there are various scales that have been developed to assess stressful events, a simple inventory of challenging circumstances you have had to face may be sufficient. The more there are (and don't neglect daily hassles) of them and the more demanding they are, the higher is the level of environmental stress to which you have been exposed

One general way to evaluate the level of psychological stress you may have been experiencing is to ask yourself the extent to which you have felt that you have been readily meeting the demands placed on you by your job in particular and your life in general. To the extent that you feel that there are many demands over which you have no control, that you are not going to be able to meet demands in the time allotted, then your level of psychological stress is higher. The more you feel and believe that the demands of life are more than you can handle, the higher is the level of psychological stress you are experiencing. For clinicians, it is important to ask this question in the context of their clinical work. To what extent are the demands of the work, both in its quantity and in its nature (e.g., large proportion of clients with highly distressing experiences), starting to feel as if they are more than you can handle?

When the clinician's monitoring of his or her own level of environmental or psychological stress indicates that the stress level is going up, or is high, then it becomes imperative to employ adaptive methods for dealing with the challenge. Working with bereaved parents offers great rewards to the practicing clinician, but it can also, under some circumstances, place a strain on the clinician's own adaptive resources. It is important to be aware of the levels of stress experienced, and to employ a wide array of strategies both to prevent the potential negative effects of difficult clinical work and also to enhance the likelihood that the clinician will reap the great satisfaction and potential personal growth that can come from being of help to clients who have suffered much.

Resources for Bereaved Parents and Their Expert Companions

*In the depths of winter, I finally
learned that within me there lay
an invincible summer.*
—Albert Camus, quoted by
McCracken & Semel (1998, p. 273)

This book has focused on understanding the concerns of bereaved parents and offering some ways to respond to these concerns as expert companions. Clinicians who are expert companions see their primary role as a comforting presence, but are able and willing to intervene with individuals and couples to promote healthy ways of responding to grief when it is too painful and confusing for bereaved parents to discern a constructive path. As clinicians provide expert companionship, it is sometimes helpful to learn more about the experiences of bereaved parents, not to become more expert in terms of having answers and claiming to know what the experience is like, but in order to develop empathy and become more comfortable with the variety of situations, reactions, and concerns that bereaved parents present. This chapter provides some information on some resources that will be valuable for clinicians who wish to become expert companions. Most of the resources we list here are primarily for bereaved parents. Clinicians may suggest some of these resources to parents who thrive on informing themselves like this. We find that many parents are greatly comforted to know that others have struggled with similar situations and had similar reactions, and many get good ideas about how to take perspective and cope with their children's deaths. *Clinicians should thoroughly preview the resources before recommending them, and do so with a good understanding of both clients' needs and the social contexts in which the client is immersed.* We are giving you some thumbnail sketches of some resources we think can be helpful to get you started. When clinicians read the materials written for bereaved parents, it can help heighten their awareness of the experience of parental bereavement.

We divide the resources into materials primarily for professionals— materials that have theory, research, and interventions with bereaved parents as their focus—and resources that are meant to comfort and accompany bereaved parents on their confusing and painful journey, providing information about what they can expect and how they can respond. Finally, we provide information about some starting points clinicians may use to access more information about bereavement. We have chosen some high-quality clearinghouses, publishers, and organizations that should allow a clinician to learn about all the important developments in this field.

☐ Resources Primarily for Professionals

In order to assess grief experiences, researchers have developed some instruments that clinicians may wish to use directly with clients, or as a format for clinical interviews. We present some information about available instruments here, but it would be wise to read the references we give you in order to determine if any of these instruments might be useful in your practice.

The *Grief Experience Questionnaire* (Barrett & Scott, 1989) has not been used widely, but may have some usefulness for clinicians who want to have a way of quantifying the extent to which different aspects of grief are present. Although the scale can be used with persons coping with any kind of loss, it may be most useful for parents coping with bereavement in the aftermath of a suicidal death (Bailley, Dunham, & Kral, 2000). The *Grief Experience Inventory* (Sanders, Mauger, & Strong, 1985, 1991) and the *Texas Revised Inventory of Grief* (Faschingbauer, Zisook, & DeVaul, 1987) measure symptoms that can be associated with grief as well as efforts to process or cope with grief. The Texas Revised Inventory of Grief is much shorter. The *Perinatal Grief Scale* (Toedter, Lasker, & Alhadeff, 1988) was developed to assess reactions to perinatal deaths. A short version followed (Potvin, Lasker, & Toedter, 1989).

To find out more about assessment of grief and other aspects of theory and research, we recommend consulting the *Handbook of Bereavement Research—Consequences, Coping and Care*, edited by M. S. Stroebe, R. O.

Hansson, W. Stroebe, and H. Schut (2001a) a comprehensive, excellent general source on grief and bereavement. Professionals, both those whose interest in grief and bereavement is primarily scholarly, and those whose interest is primarily clinical, will find useful and important information on current perspectives on the process of grief and on the ways in which others may provide assistance to people who face bereavement.

In order to understand the cultural context of bereavement, clinicians might wish to consult *Death and Bereavement Around the World* (Morgan & Laungani, 2002), which presents views of several religious traditions. Even if you are not working with people who adhere to these traditions, it is useful to consider the various perspectives that may be taken on death and grief so that these may be integrated into your work. In *The Spiritual Lives of Bereaved Parents* (1999), Dennis Klass, who has made great contributions to our understanding of grieving persons generally and bereaved parents in particular, provides a comprehensive overview of the ways in which parents attempt to reorganize their spiritual lives in the wake of the loss of a child. This book provides rich descriptions of the experience of parents and of concepts that can help others understand the spiritual processes in the lives of grieving parents.

Parent Grief—Narratives of Loss and Relationship, by Paul Rosenblatt (2000), another major contributor to our understanding of parental grief, offers professionals another rich source. In addition to the organizing ideas provided by the author, this book's major strength is the wide variety of experiences of parental grief that are provided in the parent's own words.

Gordon Riches and Pam Dawson (2000), two scholars who have done work on bereavement in the United Kingdom, made a major contribution with their book *An Intimate Loneliness: Supporting Bereaved Parents and Siblings*. The book focuses on the grief process of different members of the family. The book is very well written and includes useful information, for both clinicians and researchers.

The book *Meaning Reconstruction & the Experience of Loss*, edited by Robert A. Neimeyer (2001), offers readers chapters written by a variety of experts, focused on four major areas: general theoretical ideas about the grief process, an understanding of relationships in the grief process, possibilities for growth and transcendence in coping with loss, and the roles of meaning making in grief therapy.

In order to learn more about particular religious perspectives on grief, varying cultural approaches to mourning, and the grief experiences of particular groups such as the deaf, developmentally disabled, or gay people, a book edited by Kenneth Doka and Joyce Davidson entitled *Living with Grief: Who We Are, How We Grieve* (1998) provides much useful information, although it is focused on bereavement in general rather than on parental bereavement.

Our own book, *Facilitating Posttraumatic Growth—A Clinician's Guide* (Calhoun & Tedeschi, 1999), provides a general overview of the process of how growth may arise from the struggle with loss. The book also provides various clinical suggestions that we believe are sensitive and temperate, as to how the possibility of growth sometimes can be a part of the clinical process of helping clients who have faced major crises and losses. We include two extensive descriptions of growth work with bereaved parents. In this book, we also describe some resources that are fine autobiographical accounts of posttraumatic growth. To learn about trauma therapy approaches in general, Judith Herman's modern classic *Trauma and Recovery* (1992) is an excellent source.

Linda Goldman's (2000) book *Life and Loss—A Guide to Help Grieving Children* is easy to read and provides a general aggregate of suggestions that are both specific and concrete. It offers suggestions that are specific to helping children, and also includes helpful lists of community and national resources. Depending on the clinician's own specific approach, either the whole book or only portions of it may offer helpful guidance to what clinicians might do to help children, or advice on how laypersons, including grieving parents, can provide help to grieving children. The wide range of listed resources may be one of the book's greatest strengths.

☐ Resources Primarily for Laypersons, Including Grieving Parents

In *Give Sorrow Words—A Father's Passage Through Grief*, Tom Crider (1996) provides, in journal form, his struggle to cope with the death of his only child, a daughter, in a fire at her university room. This is a poetic, eloquent, and elegiac book that may do for grieving parents what the best poetry can do—put into beautiful language the reality of what they themselves are experiencing, but which they may not be able to articulate in such a beautiful way. A clinician who gets the voices of the bereaved parents right is Barbara Rosof in her book, *The Worst Loss: How Families Heal from the Death of a Child* (1994). She does a good job in making her clinical experience accessible to the lay person while providing a great deal of insight for clinicians who want to understand bereaved parents more deeply.

For parents who have suffered the deaths of young children or who have had miscarriages, there are several books that provide a roadmap for getting through the confusion and shock of a baby's death. *A Silent Sorrow* by Ingrid Kohn and Perry-Lynn Moffitt (2000) provides specific information about many situations encountered in pregnancy loss, and addresses the dilemmas of mothers, fathers, grandparents, and siblings.

The authors cover infertility problems and pregnancy loss, subsequent pregnancies, and, to their credit, devote a chapter to therapeutic abortion and grief. Other books provide information to both bereaved parents and the clinicians who may be working with them. Two fine examples are *Help, Comfort & Hope After Losing Your Baby in Pregnancy or the First Year,* by Hannah Lothrop (1997), and *The SIDS Survival Guide* by Joani Nelson Horchler and Robin Rice Morris (1997). This volume is a combination of first-person accounts of the experience of having a baby die of SIDS, and advice and information from a variety of professionals who work in the field. Lothrop's book has a similar purpose, but is meant to cover perinatal losses in general, rather than specifically SIDS. The first part is an explanation of the grieving process through the words of bereaved parents, and the second section provides some guidance for professionals who work with this group.

Just as *The SIDS Survival Guide* focuses on a particular cause of death, there are books that focus on other circumstances of death. Iris Bolton (1983), in her book *My Son . . . My Son . . . A Guide to Healing After Suicide in the Family*, describes her journey of grief and coping following the suicidal death of her 20-year-old son Curtis Mitchell (Mitch) Bolton. Although written more than 20 years ago, the book is still a timely first-person narrative of a bereaved parent's experience with the aftermath of suicide. This book is likely to be most helpful to persons interested in the account of one parent coping with the death of a son from this specific cause.

When a Child Has Been Murdered: Ways You Can Help the Grieving Parents by Bonnie Hunt Conrad (1998) is useful for both professionals and family members. It is based on the descriptions of parents whose children were murdered, and therefore provides vivid accounts of the aftermath of these losses. As clinicians who have worked in this field for many years, it is striking to us that the accounts in this book and many others written by bereaved parents seem to echo just the sort of things we have heard from our clients in therapy and our support-group members.

A first-person account of the grief over a murdered child is also found in *Surviving the Death of a Child* (1995) by John Munday and his wife Frances Wohlenhaus-Munday. This book is written from a Christian perspective, with much discussion of the struggle to understand God's role in such situations. Another autobiographical book on parental grief written from a Christian perspective is *Roses in December* (1987), by Marilyn Willett Heavilin. Many of our clients who have been trying to understand their experience through their Christian faith have found comfort in this book.

Catherine Sanders is a bereaved parent as well as a clinician, and has written several books on grief. *How to Survive the Loss of a Child: Filling the Emptiness and Rebuilding Your Life* (1998) is a good book for bereaved parents, in that it combines a professional and personal perspective addressing the various difficulties that bereaved parents are likely to face, and provides some specific advice on how to manage grief. Alan Wofelt's *Healing a Parent's Grieving Heart: 100 Practical Ideas After Your Child Dies* (2002) provides just what the title promises: much sound advice for handling the various decisions and difficult situations that grieving parents have not anticipated. Another book that provides specific advice, although it is not specifically about parental bereavement, is *The Mourning Handbook* by Helen Fitzgerald (1994). Some of our clients have remarked that they like how this book is arranged so that they can look up particular situations of interest, such as "Visiting the Cemetery," "When There Is No Body," or "Dreams, Nightmares, and 'Visions.'"

For a focus on marital difficulties in the aftermath of a child's death, a good resource to recommend is Paul Rosenblatt's *Help Your Marriage Survive the Death of a Child* (2000). It focuses on honoring different forms of grieving and on making use of support groups and counseling.

One of our favorite books that describes the experience of parental bereavement is *A Broken Heart Still Beats: After Your Child Dies* (1998) by Anne McCracken and Mary Semel. In this remarkable book, the authors have gathered accounts of parental bereavement in many well-known people and important historical figures: Victor Hugo, Mark Twain, Eric Clapton, George McGovern, Frank DeFord, Dwight Eisenhower, Anne Morrow Lindbergh, and many others. Also included are fictional and biographical accounts of parental grief. We have found that bereaved parents are surprised to find that so many people have gone through this loss, and they didn't realize these people were bereaved parents. Many come to the conclusion that "if they lived through this, so can I." The sad and beautiful descriptions of grief allow many parents to say, "That's it—that's what I was trying to say."

☐ Clearinghouses, Publishers, and Organizations

Our list of resources just given is brief. There are many excellent books, audiotapes, CDs, and videotapes that are available on bereavement in general, parental bereavement, and very specific kinds of parental bereavement. You will find much more beyond what we have mentioned by contacting publishers, organizations, and individuals who have collections of information on bereavement that are easily accessed. Going to these sources can help clinicians, grieving parents, and others who wish to support them find a great selection of useful information. Some of our favorite sources for materials and information we list next. Many grieving parents will use the Internet to find this information, as well as many sites devoted to sharing experiences of grief and honoring deceased children.

The Centering Corporation (www.centering.org) has a large catalog of resources, some in Spanish. The catalog is conveniently divided into sections that represent different populations and concerns. For example, in the section on the death of a child, there are books and videos on subjects such as fathers, teenage deaths, suicide, and adult children.

The publisher of this book, Brunner-Routledge of the Taylor & Francis Group, has been building an extensive collection of resources on bereavement. Its web site (www.eBookstore.tandf.co.uk) and catalog are worth examining for many of the works cited in this book, and others that would be of interest to clinicians working with the bereaved. Baywood Publishing Company (www.baywood.com) has a series on "Death, Value, and Meaning" that is worth keeping up with.

Among the authors of books on grief with their own useful web sites are Alan Wolfelt, Jim Miller, and Tom Golden. Wofelt's Companion Press (www.centerforloss.com) publishes books, CDs, and videos, for all family members, that provide many good ideas for coping with loss. Wolfelt's "100 Ideas" series that we mentioned earlier can be found here. Miller (www.willowgreen.com) has a fine selection of audiotapes, videotapes, and books on grief, dying, and caregiving. He publishes a series of very small books that give concise and accurate advice to grieving persons and those close to them. His videos are sources of comfort, using beautiful photos and poetic narration. Golden's web site (www.webhealing.com) offers bereaved parents a chance for interaction by publishing concerns and comments.

Richard Gilbert, of the World Pastoral Care Center in Elgin, IL, has a book review service and bibliography on death, grief, and religious and spiritual concerns that is truly remarkable. By getting on his list (www.wpcc.org), a clinician will enjoy the luxury of having an expert find and sort through about every conceivable resource that a chaplain would be interested in. Gilbert provides frequent updates of his bibliography so that you may be constantly aware of what is being published that is of interest to chaplains, and therefore many others who serve bereaved parents.

The Compassionate Friends is a well-known international organization devoted to providing support to the bereaved. On their web site (www.compassionatefriends.com) they provide information about almost 600 local chapters that arrange support meetings for bereaved parents and other bereaved persons.

An innovative, local nonprofit organization that has been growing in Charlotte, NC, for 25 years is called KinderMourn (www.kindermourn.org). It serves bereaved families and provides information and a model for local action for the bereaved. The senior author of this volume has facilitated support groups for this organization for over 15 of those years, and has received his education on which this book is based from the staff of KinderMourn and the families it serves.

The Association of Death Education and Counseling (www. adec.org) is a multidisciplinary organization that is dedicated to professional development for those serving the dying, the bereaved, and their caregivers. Their conferences and publications will be of great interest to readers of this book. They offer professional certifications as well as continuing education. Members may receive the premier journals in the area of bereavement, *Omega* and *Death Studies*. In addition to empirical articles, these journals feature extensive book reviews, and *Death Studies* has a useful "News and Notes" section that lists materials and organizations of interest.

The International Society of Traumatic Stress Studies (www.istss.org) is also a multidisciplinary organization that is devoted to empirical research, the development of interventions, and advocacy for survivors of trauma. There is a significant number of members in this organization interested in grief, and the ISTSS publication, *Journal of Traumatic Stress*, carries some articles on bereavement.

Clinicians who utilize the resources we have listed will have access to all the information one could want in order to develop skills as an expert companion to bereaved parents. These starting points open up a world of rapidly expanding literature on bereavement that is allowing bereaved parents to benefit from better understanding and more compassionate care. We hope that this volume also can play an important role in helping to develop the expert companions many bereaved parents need.

REFERENCES

American Psychiatric Association. (2000). *Diagnostic and statistical manual of mental disorders* (4th ed.). Washington, DC: Author.

American Psychological Association. (1993). Guidelines for providers of psychological services to ethnic, linguistic, and culturally diverse populations. *American Psychologist, 48,* 45–48.

Arnold, D. A. (1999). *Vicarious transformation in psychotherapy with trauma survivors: A description investigation of the views of practicing clinicians.* Unpublished Masters Thesis, University of North Carolina at Charlotte.

Bailey, S. E., & Dunham, K., & Krall, M. J. (2000). Factor structure of the Grief Experiences Questionnaire. *Death Studies, 24,* 721–738.

Bailey, S. E., Kral, M. J., & Dunham, K. (1999). Survivors of suicide do grieve differently: Empirical support for a common sense proposition. *Suicide and Life-Threatening Behavior, 29,* 256–271.

Barrett, T. W., & Scott, T. B. (1989). Development of the Grief Experience Questionnaire. *Suicide and Life Threatening Behavior, 19,* 201–215.

Bolton, I. (1983). *My son . . . my son . . . : A guide to healing after a suicide in the family.* Atlanta, GA: Bolton Press.

Bowlby, J. (1980). *Attachment and loss: Vol. 3. Loss: sadness and depression.* New York: Basic Books.

Bowlby, J., & Parkes, C. M. (1970). Separation and loss in the family. In E. J. Anthony (Ed.), *The child in his family* (pp. 197–216). New York: Wiley.

Calhoun, L. G., Abernathy, C., & Selby, J. W. (1986). The rules of bereavement. *Journal of Community Psychology, 14,* 213–218.

Calhoun, L. G., Selby, J. W., & Faulstich, M. (1980). Reactions to the parents of the child suicide: A study of social impressions. *Journal of Consulting and Clinical Psychology, 48,* 535–536.

Calhoun, L. G., Selby, J. W., & King, H. E. (1976). *Dealing with crisis.* Englewood Cliffs, NJ: Prentice Hall.

Calhoun, L. G., Selby, J. W., & Selby, L. (1982). The psychological aftermath of suicide: An analysis of current evidence. *Clinical Psychology Review, 2,* 409–420.

Calhoun, L. G., & Tedeschi, R. G. (1989–1990). Positive aspects of critical life problems: Recollections of grief. *Omega, 20,* 265–272.

Calhoun, L. G., & Tedeschi, R. G. (1999). *Facilitating posttraumatic growth: A clinician's guide.* Mahwah, NJ: Lawrence Erlbaum.

Calhoun, L. G., & Tedeschi, R. G. (2001). Posttraumatic growth: The positive lessons of loss. In R. A. Neimeyer (Ed.) *Meaning reconstruction and the experience of loss* (pp. 157–172). Washington, DC: American Psychological Association.

Calhoun, L. G., Tedeschi, R. G., Fulmer, D., & Harlan, D. (2000, August). *Parental bereavement, rumination, and posttraumatic growth.* Poster session presented at the meeting of the American Psychological Association, Washington, DC.

Conrad, B. H. (1998). *When a child has been murdered: Ways you can help the grieving parents.* Amityville, NY: Baywood.

Crider, T. (1996). *Give sorrow words—A father's passage through grief.* Chapel Hill, NC: Algonquin Books.

Dannemiller, H. C. (2002). The parents' response to a child's murder. *Omega, 45,* 1–21.

Dees, D. (2001). *Death and bereavement. The psychological, religious and cultural interfaces* (2nd ed.). Philadelphia: Whurr.

De Frain, J. (1991). Learning about grief from normal families: SIDS, stillbirth, and miscarriage. *Journal of Marital and Family Therapy, 17,* 215–223.

Doka, K. J., & Davidson, J. (1998). *Living with grief: Who we are, how we grieve.* Philadelphia: Brunner/Mazel.

Donnelly, K. F. (1982). *Recovering from the loss of a child.* New York: Macmillan.

Faschingbauer, T. R., Zisook, S., & DeVaul, R. (1987). The Texas Revised Inventory of Grief. In S. Zisook (Ed.), *Biopsychosocial aspects of bereavement* (pp. 111–124). Washington, DC: American Psychiatric Press.

Finkbeiner, A. K. (1996). *After the death of a child.* New York: Free Press.

Fish, W. (1986). Differences in grief intensity in bereaved parents. In T. Rando (Ed.), *Parental loss of a child* (pp. 415–428). Champaign, IL: Research Press.

Fitzgerald, H. (1994). *The mourning handbook.* New York: Fireside.

Fraley, R. C., & Shaver, P. R. (1999). Loss and bereavement. In J. Cassidy & P. R. Shaver (Eds.) *Handbook of attachment* (pp. 735–759). New York: Guilford.

Freud, S. (1957). Mourning and melancholia (J. Riviere, Trans.). In J. D. Sutherland (Ed.), *Collected papers* (Vol. 4, pp. 152–170). London: Hogarth Press. (Original work published 1917)

Goldman, L. (2000). *Life and loss: A guide to help grieving children.* New York: Brunner-Routledge.

Gyulay, J. (1989). The violence of murder. *Issues in Comprehensive Pediatric Nursing, 12,* 119–137.

Heavilin, M. W. (1987). *Roses in December.* Eugene, OR: Harvest House.

Herman, J. L. (1992). *Trauma and recovery.* New York: Basic Books.

Horchler, J. N., & Morris, R. R. (1997). *The SIDS survival guide: Information and comfort for grieiving family & friends & professionals who seek to help them* (2nd ed.). Hyattsville, MD: SIDS Educational Services.

Hoyert, D. L., Arias, E., Smith, B. L., Murphy, S. L., & Kochanek, K. D. (2001). Deaths; Final data for 1999. *National Vital Statistics, 49*(8), 1–114.

Janoff-Bulman, R. (1992). *Shattered assumptions: Towards a new psychology of trauma.* New York: Free Press.

Jordan, H. (2000). *No such thing as a bad day.* Atlanta, GA: Longstreet Press.

Jordan, J. R. (2001). Is suicide bereavement different? A reassessment of the literature. *Suicide and Life-Threatening Behavior, 31,* 91–102.

Kanfer, F. H., & Saslow, G. (1969). Behavioral diagnosis. In C. M. Franks (Ed.), *Behavior therapy—Appraisal and status* (pp. 417–444). New York: McGraw-Hill.

Klass, D., Silverman, P., & Nickman, S. (Eds.). (1996). *Continuing bonds: New understandings of grief.* Washington, DC: Taylor & Francis.

Kohn, I., & Moffitt, P. (2000). *A silent sorrow: Pregnancy loss guidance and support for you and your family* (2nd ed.). New York: Routledge.

Kübler-Ross, E. (1969). *On death and dying.* New York: Macmillan.

Lang, A., & Gottlieb, L. (1993). Parental grief reactions and marital intimacy following infant death. *Death Studies, 17,* 233–255.

Leahy, J. M. (1992–1993). A comparison of depression in women bereaved of a spouse, child, or a parent. *Omega, 26,* 207–217.

Lehman, D. R., Lang, E. L., Wortman, C. B., & Sorenson, S. B. (1989). Long-term effects of sudden bereavement: Marital and parent–child relationships and children's reactions. *Journal of Family Psychology, 2,* 344–367.

Lewin, K. (1936). *Principles of topological psychology.* New York: McGraw-Hill.

Lindemann, E. (1944). Symptomatology and management of acute grief. *American Journal of Psychiatry, 101,* 141–148.

Lindeman, E. (1979). *Beyond grief—Studies in crisis intervention.* Northvale, NJ: Jason Aronson.

Lipsyte, R. (1998). *In the country of illness: Comfort and advice for the journey.* New York: Alfred A. Knopf.

Lothrop, H. (1997). *Help, comfort & hope after losing your baby in pregnancy or the first year.* Tucson, AZ: Fisher Books.

Martinson, I. M., McClowry, S. G., Davies, B., & Kulenkamp, E. J. (1994). Changes over time: A study of family bereavement following childhood cancer. *Journal of Palliative Care, 10,* 19–25.

McCracken, A., & Semel, M. (Eds.). (1998). *A broken heart still beats: After your child dies.* Center City, MN: Hazelden Information and Educational Services.

McIntosh, J. L. (1999). Research on survivors of suicide. In M. T. Stimming & M. S. Stimming (Eds.), *Before their time: Adult children's experiences of parental suicide* (pp. 157–180). Philadelphia: Temple University Press.

Miles, M. S., & Demi, A. (1991–1992). A comparison of guilt in bereaved parents whose children died by suicide, accident, or chronic disease. *Omega, 24,* 203–215.

Minino, A. M., Arias, E., Kochanek, M. A., Murphy, S. L., & Smith, B. L. (2000). Deaths: Final data for 2000. *National Vital Statistics Reports, 50*(15), 1–120.

Morgan, J. D., & Laungani, P. (2002). *Death and bereavement around the world: Major religious traditions.* New York: Baywood.

Munday, J., & Wohlenhaus-Munday, F. (1995). *Surviving the death of a child.* Louisville, KY: Westminster John Knox Press.

Neimeyer, R. A. (Ed.). (2001). *Meaning reconstruction & the experience of loss.* Washington, DC: American Psychological Association.

Nolen-Hoeksema, S., & Larson, J. (1999). *Coping with loss.* Mahwah, NJ: Lawrence Erlbaum.

Oliver, L. E. (1999). Effects of a child's death on the marital relationship: A review. *Omega, 39,* 197–227.

Pargament, K. I. (1997). *The psychology of religion and coping.* New York: Guilford.

Park, C. L. (1998). Implications of posttraumatic growth for individuals. In R. G. Tedeschi, C. L. Park, & L. G. Calhoun (Eds.). *Postraumatic growth* (pp. 153–177). Mahwah, NJ: Lawrence Erlbaum.

Parkes, C. M. (1970). Psycho-social transitions: A field for study. *Social Science and Medicine, 5,* 101–115.

Parkes, C. M. (1993). Psychiatric problems following beravement by murder or manslaughter. *British Journal of Psychiatry, 162,* 49–54.

Parkes, C. M. (1998). Conclusions II: Attachments and losses in cross-cultural perspective. In C. M. Parkes, P. Laungani, & B. Young (Eds.), *Death and bereavement across cultures* (pp. 233–243). New York: Routledge.

Peach, M. R., & Klass, D. (1987). Special issues in the grief of parents of murdered children. *Death Studies, 11,* 81–88.

Pearlman, L. A., & MacIan, P. S. (1995). Vicarous traumatization: An empirical study of the effects of trauma work on trauma therapists. *Professional Psychology: Research and Practice, 26,* 558–565.

Pearlman, L. A., & Saakvitne, K. W. (1995). *Trauma and the therapist: Countertransference and vicarious traumatization in psychotherapy with incest survivors.* New York: Norton.

Pennebaker, J. W. (1997). *Opening up: The healing power of expressing emotions.* New York: Guilford.

Perry, P. L. (1993). Mourning and funeral customs among African Americans. In D. P. Irish, K. F. Lundquist, & V. J. Nelsen (Eds.), *Ethnic variations in dying, death, and grief: Diversity in universality* (pp. 51–65). Washington, DC: Taylor & Francis.

Potvin, L., Lasker, J., & Toedter, L. (1989). Measuring grief: A short version of the Perinatal Grief Scale. *Journal of Pscyhopathology and Behavior Assessment, 11*, 29–45.

Rando, T. (Ed.). (1986). *Parental loss of a child*. Champaign, IL: Research Press.

Rando, T. (1993). *Treatment of complicated mourning*. Champaign, IL: Research Press.

Range, L. M., & Calhoun, L. G. (1990). Responses following suicide and other types of death: The perspective of the bereaved. *Omega, 21*, 311–320.

Riches, G., & Dawson, P. (1996). Communities of feeling: The culture of bereaved parents. *Mortality, 1*, 143–162.

Riches, G., & Dawson, P. (1998). Spoiled memories: Problems of grief resolution in families bereaved through murder [Electronic version]. *Mortality, 3*, 143–160.

Riches, G., & Dawson, P. (2000). *An intimate loneliness—supporting bereaved parents and siblings*. Philadelphia: Open University Press.

Rock, P. (1998). *After homicide—Practical and political responses to bereavement*. New York: Oxford University Press.

Rosenblatt, P. C. (2000a). *Help your marriage survive the death of a child*. Philadelphia: Temple University Press.

Rosenblatt, P. C. (2000b). *Parent grief: Narratives of loss and relationship*. Philadelphia: Brunner/ Mazel.

Rosof, B. D. (1994). *The worst loss: How families heal from the death of a child*. New York: Henry Holt.

Rotter, J. B. (1954). *Social learning and clinical psychology*. Englewood Cliffs, NJ: Prentice Hall.

Rubin, S. (1981). A two-track model of bereavement: Theory and application in research. *American Journal of Orthopsychiatry, 51*, 101–109.

Saakvitne, K. W. (1997, November). The rewards of trauma therapy for the therapist. In R. G. Tedeschi (Chair), *Posttraumatic growth in survivors, therapists, researchers, and communities*. Presented at the meeting of the International Society of Traumatic Stress Studies, Montreal.

Sanders, C. M. (1998). *How to survive the loss of a child: Filling the emptiness and rebuilding your life*. Rocklin, CA: Prima.

Sanders, C. M. (1999). *Grief—The mourning after* (2nd. ed.). New York: John Wiley & Sons.

Sanders, C. M., Mauger, P. A., & Strong, P. A. (1985/1991). *A Manual of the Grief Experience Inventory*. Palo Alto, CA: Consulting Psychologists Press/Charlotte, NC: Center for the Study of Separation and Loss.

Sarason, I. G., & Sarason, B. R. (2001). *Abnormal psychology: The problems of maladaptive behavior*. Upper Saddle River, NJ: Prentice Hall.

Shay, J. J. (1996). "Okay, I'm here but I'm not talking!" Psychotherapy with the reluctant male. *Psychothrapy, 33*, 503–513.

Sidmore, K.V. (1999–2000). Parental bereavement: Levels of grief as affected by gender issues. *Omega, 40*, 351–374.

Stroebe, M. S., Hansonn, R. O., Stroebe, W., & Schut, H. (Eds.). (2001a). *Handbook of bereavement research—Consequences, coping and care*. Washington, DC: American Psychological Association.

Stroebe, M. S., Hansson, R. O., Stroebe, W., & Schut, H. (2001b). Future directions for bereavement research. In M. S. Stroebe, R. O. Hansson, W. Stroebe, & H. Schut (Eds.), *Handbook of bereavement research—Consequences, coping and care* (pp. 741–766). Washington, DC: American Psychological Association.

Stroebe, M., & Schut, H. (1999). The dual process model of coping with bereavement. *Death Studies, 23*, 197–224.

Stroebe, M., & Schut, H. (2001). Meaning making in the dual process model of coping with bereavement. In R. A. Neimeyer (Ed.), *Meaning reconstruction & the experience of loss* (pp. 55–73). Washington, DC: American Psychological Association.

Talbot, K. (2002). *What forever means after the death of a child: Transcending the trauma, living with the loss.* New York: Brunner-Routledge.

Tedeschi, R. G., & Calhoun, L. G. (1988, August). *Perceived benefits in coping with physical handicaps.* Paper presented at the meeting of the American Psychological Association, Atlanta.

Tedeschi, R. G., & Calhoun, L. G. (1993). Using the support group to respond to the isolation of bereavement. *Journal of Mental Health Counseling, 15,* 47–54.

Tedeschi, R. G., & Calhoun, L. G. (1995). *Trauma and transformation: Growing in the aftermath of suffering.* Thousand Oaks, CA: Sage.

Tedeschi, R. G., & Calhoun, L. G. (1996). The posttraumatic growth inventory: Measuring the positive legacy of trauma. *Journal of Traumatic Stress, 9,* 455–471.

Tedeschi, R. G., & Calhoun, L. G. (2001, August). *Posttraumatic growth in parental grief? A qualitative study.* Poster presented at the meeting of the American Psychological Association, San Francisco, CA.

Tedeschi, R. G., Calhoun, L. G., & Cooper, L. (2000, August). *Rumination and posttraumatic growth in older adults.* Paper presented at the meeting of the American Psychological Association, Washington, DC.

Tedeschi, R. G., Calhoun, L. G., Morrell, R., & Johnson, K. (1984, August). *Bereavement: From grief to psychological development.* Paper presented at the meeting of the American Psychological Association, Toronto.

Tedeschi, R. G., & Hamilton, K. (1991). Support group experiences of bereaved fathers. *Thanatos, 16,* 25–28.

Tedeschi, R. G., Park, C.. L., & Calhoun, L. G. (Eds.). (1998). *Posttraumatic growth.* Mahwah, NJ: Lawrence Erlbaum.

Toedter, L. J., Lasker, J. N., & Alhadeff, J. M. (1988). The Perinatal Grief Scale: Development and initial valication. *American Journal of Orthopsychiatry, 58,* 435–449.

Ullrich, P. M., & Lutgendorf, S. K. (2002). Journaling about stressful events: Effects of cognitive processing and emotional expression. *Annals of Behavioral Medicine, 24,* 244–250.

Viorst, J. (1986). *Necessary losses.* New York: Fawcett.

Walter, T. (1996). A new model of grief: Bereavement and biography. *Mortality, 1,* 7–25.

Wickie, S. K., & Marwit, S. J. (2000–2001). Assumptive world views and the grief reactions of parents of murdered children. *Omega, 42,* 101–113.

Wolfelt, A. (2002). *Healing a parent's grieving heart: 100 Practical ideas after your child dies.* Fort Collins, CO: Companion Press.

Worden, J. W. (1991). *Grief counseling and grief therapy: A handbook for the mental health practitioner* (2nd ed.). New York: Springer.

Wortman, C. B., & Silver, R. C. (1989). The myths of coping with loss. *Journal of Consulting and Clinical Psychology, 57,* 349–357.

Wortman, C. B., & Silver, R. C. (2001). The myths of coping with loss revisited. In M. S. Stroebe, R. O. Hannsson, W. Stroebe, & H. Schut (Eds.), *Handbook of bereavement research—Consequences, coping and care* (pp. 405–429). Washington, DC: American Psychological Association.

Younoszai, B. (1993). Mexican American perspectives related to death. In D. P. Irish, K. F. Lundquist, & V. J. Nelsen (Eds.), *Ethnic variations in dying, death, and grief: Diversity in universality* (pp. 67–78). Washington, DC: Taylor & Francis.

INDEX

Abernathy, C., 6
"Absent grief," 27–29
Accidents, 4, 120–121
  guilt, 120–121
  statistics, 120
Acknowledging growth, 56–58
Afterlife, 127–132
Alhadeff, J. M., 168
American Psychiatric Association, 66, 152
American Psychological Association, 41
Anniversaries, 140–141
Appreciation for life, 52–54
Arias, E., 1, 102, 112, 120
Arnold, D. A., 156–157
Association of Death Education and
  Counseling, 174
Assumptions
  about what helps, 45–46
  clinicians', 148–149
Attachment
  continuing, 9–10
  perspective, 20–21
Ausman, M., xv

Bailley, S. E., 106, 168
Baird, 151–152
Baker, J., xv
Barrett, T. W., 168
Baywood Publishing Company, 173
Belzer, R., 157
Bereavement
  gender differences, 73–78
  marriage after, 72–78
  resources, 169–172
The Bible, 1, 14–15
Bipolar disorder, 103–104
Blended families. See Stepparents
Bolton, C. M., 102, 104, 171

Bolton, I., 102, 104, 171
Bonds
  Bowlby's theory, 20–21
  continuing, 9–10
  revised after death, 23
Bowlby, J., 9, 20, 24, 29
  attachment perspective, 20–21
Brabham, S., xv
Brunner-Routledge, ix, 173
Bryant, J., xv
Buarque de Hollanda, Chico, 101
Buksbazen, 106
Burnout, 151–154
  risk factors, 154–155
Busch, D., xv

Calhoun, L. G., ix–xi, 6, 10, 28, 31, 33–
  35, 47, 52, 55, 105–106, 126–127,
  133, 170
Camus, A., 167
Cann, A., xv
Centering Corporation, 173
Ceremonies, 140–141
Change
  focus on being, 55–56
  sociocultural consequences of, 46
Children
  death of siblings, 86–95
  death statistics, 1–2
Circumstances of death, 3–4, 13, 101–123
  accidents, 4, 120–121
  homicide, 112–119
  illness, 3–4
  miscarriage, 122–124
  neonatal death, 122–124
  stillbirth, 122–124
  suicide, 102–112
Clapton, E., 172

Clearinghouses, 172–174
Clergy
  clinician interaction with, 135–137
  parents' experiences with, 134–135
Clinician
  as "expert companion," xiii–xiv
  beyond clinical work, 162–165
  clinical work considerations, 158–162
  countertransference, 146–151
  dealing with homicide, 117–118
  inordinate closeness, 150–151
  inordinate distancing, 150
  issues for, 145–165
  learning about trauma therapy, 66–68
  resources for, 168–170
  risk factors, 154–155
  self-care, 158–165
  status and social role, 44–45
  stresses for, 117–118
  talking with clergy, 135–137
  vicarious posttraumatic growth, 155–158
  vicarious traumatization, 117–118, 151–154
"Closure" myth, 31–32, 58–59
Cobb, A., xv
Coconut Grove fire, 19–20
Companion Press, 173
Compassion fatigue, 151–154
Compassionate Friends, 173
Conrad, B. H., 171
Continued connections, 9–10
  afterlife, 127–132
  attachment theory, 20–21
  case example, 88–90
  legacy of the child, 56–58, 123–124
Counselor. See Clinician
Counterfactuals, 61–66
Countertransference, 146–151
Crawford, C., xv
Crider, T., 5, 22, 170
Cryder, C., xv
Cultural perspectives
  affected by circumstances, 102–123
  after homicide, 113–116, 125–144
  afterlife, 127–132
  assumptions, 45–46
  clinician's status and role, 44–45
  continuing connections, 9–10
  dealing with the bereaved, 6–7
  experience of grief, 26–27
  experiences with clergy, 134–135

faith issues, 46–48
Freud's, 17–18
growth in, 12–13
identifying primary groups, 41–42
idioms of distress, 48–49
language of, 48–49
maladaptive, 141–144
meaning and suffering, 132–134
multicultural context, 41–50
new communities, 144
of this book, 1–2
parents' sociocultural context, 49–50
pragmatic religious constructivism, 47–49
questioning, 12–13, 137–140
religious beliefs, 47–49, 125–144
rituals and ceremonies, 140–141
social rules and norms, 42–44
sociocultural issues, 46, 49–50
struggling with grief, 15–16
suicide, 105–106
talking with clergy, 135–137
Cutler, B., xv

Daily functioning, 8–9
Dannemiller, H. C., 114–115, 117
Davidson, J., 169
Davies, B., 73
Dawson, P., xiii, 6, 35, 105, 113–116, 169
Death idioms, 48–49
Dees, D., 47
DeFord, F., 172
DeFrain, J., 73
"Delayed grief," 19–20, 28–29
Demi, A., 104, 120
Denial
  defined, 28
  Freud's perspective, 18
  myth of, 27–29
DeVaul, R., 168
Disbelief, 32–33
Disenfranchised grief, 82–86
Disorientation, 4–5, 13
"Distorted reactions," 20
Distress idioms, 48–49
Divorce. See Ex-spouses; Marriage; Stepparents
Doka, K. J., 169
Donnelly, K. F., 6
Dual process model, 24–25
Dunham, K., 106, 168

Eisenhower, D. D., 172
Empathy, 50–52
Evans, K., xv
Exercise, 163
"Exiles," 6–7, 13–14
Expert companionship, 37–41
    assumptions, 45–35
    clinician's status and role, 44–45
    faith issues, 46–46
    growth perspective, 52–58
    identifying primary groups, 41–42
    idioms of distress, 48–49
    in multicultural context, 41–50
    listen, don't solve, 55–56
    notice growth, 56–58
    parents' sociocultural context, 49–50
    primacy of, 38–41
    social rules and norms, 42–44
    sociocultural issues, 46, 49–50
    traumatic grief, 66–68
    uniqueness of grief, 50–52
Ex-spouses, 78–82

Faith matters
    after homicide, 113–116, 125–144
    afterlife, 127–132
    continuing connections, 9–10
    experiences with clergy, 134–135
    growth in, 12–13
    language of, 48–49
    maladaptive, 141–144
    meaning and suffering, 132–134
    multicultural issues, 46–48, 126
    new communities, 144
    pragmatic religious constructivism, 47–
        49, 126
    questioning, 12–13, 137–140
    rituals and ceremonies, 140–141
    struggling with grief, 15–16
    talking with clergy, 135–137
Family support, 71–99
    ex-spouses, 78–82
    former partners, 78–82
    marriage, 72–78
    only children, 86–95
    siblings, 86–95
    stepparents, 78–86
Faschingbauer, T. R., 168
Faulstich, M., 105
Figley, 151
Finkbeiner, A. K., 5
Fish, W., 73

Fitzgerald, H., 172
Fraley, R. C., 20
Freud, S., 21, 23–24, 28–29
    perspective of, 17–18
Friends
    growing closer, 12, 35
    social norms, 42–44
    support groups, 41–42
    uncertain how to help, 6–7
Fulmer, D., 52
Funerals. *See also* Ceremonies; Rituals
    social rules, 42–44

Gilbert, R., 173
Golden, T., 173
Goldman, L., 170
Gottlieb, L., 73
Grandchildren
    anticipated loss, 86–88
    loss of, 95–99
Grandparents, 95–99
Grief Experience Inventory, 168
Grief Experience Questionnaire, 168
Grief
    "absent," 27–29
    acknowledging, 56–58
    affected by circumstances, 102–123
    amid pain, 10–13
    Bowlby's perspective, 20–21
    case examples, 3–4
    categories of, 19–20
    circumstances of loss, 3–4, 13
    contemporary models, 23–25
    continuing connections, 9–10
    "delayed," 19–20, 28–29
    "denial," 27–29
    disenfranchised, 82–86
    disorientation, 4–5, 13
    "distorted reactions," 20
    dual process model, 24–25
    early modern perspectives, 15–22
    Freud's perspective, 17–19
    from struggle, not from loss, 54–55
    growth through, 10–13, 33–36
    idioms of, 48–49
    influence of models, 22
    isolation, 6–7, 13–14
    Lindemann's perspective, 19–20
    listen, don't solve, 55–56
    loss of daily functioning, 8–9
    models, 15–25
    "morbid," 19

Grief (*continued*)
  myths, 25–33
  "normal," 19–20
  pain and suffering, 7–8
  parents' experience of, 1–14
  Parkes's perspective, 21–22
  perspectives, 15–25, 51–58
  possibility of growth, 33–36
  priorities change, 12, 35
  "recovery" myth, 31–32
  relationships, 11–12, 34–35
  sense of self, 11, 34
  shock, 4–5
  spiritual matters, 12–13, 35
  stages" of, 20–21, 32–33
  stepparents and, 85–86
  traumatic, 66–68
  two-track model, 23
  uniqueness of reactions, 13–14, 25–33,
    50–52
  "universality" myth, 25–27
  "working through" myth, 29–31
"Grief work," 29–31
Growth
  acknowledging, 56–58
  clinicians', 155–158
  possibility of, 33–36
  reports of, 54–58
  self, 11, 33–36, 52, 54
Guilt, 61–66
  after accidents, 120–121
  after homicide, 114–115
  after suicide, 103–105, 108–111
  maladaptive beliefs, 141–144
  stepparents and, 73–74
Gyulay, J., 114–115

Hagan, M. S., xv
Hamilton, K., xv, 72
Hansonn, R. O., 16, 25, 32–33, 169
Harlan, D., xv, 52
Heavilin, M. W., 171
Herman, J. L., 38
Holidays, 140–141
Homicide, 112–119
  disconnectedness, 116
  guilt, 114
  legal issues, 114–115, 119
  resources, 171–172
  thoughts of revenge, 113–114, 116–117
Horchler, J. N., 171
Houseman, A. E., 37

Hoyert, D. L., 120
Hugo, V., 172

Idioms, 48–49
Illness, 3–4
International Society of Traumatic Stress
    Studies, 174
Intervention framework, 37–69
  clinical stance, 37–41
  expert companionship, 37–41
  growth perspective, 52–58
  multicultural context, 41–50
  stuck points, 58–66
  traumatic grief, 66–68
  uniqueness of grief, 50–52
Isolation, 6–7, 13–14
  after homicide, 116
  after suicide, 111–112

Janoff-Bulman, R., 21, 153
Jenkins, 151–152
Johnson, K., 52
Jordan, H., 32
Jordan, J. R., 104–105
Journal of Traumatic Stress, 174
Journaling, 161

Kanfer, F. H., 41
Kilmer, R., xv
KinderMourn, xv, 173–174
King, H. E., 31, 33
Klass, D., 7–8, 10–11, 113, 115, 127,
    169
Kochanek, K. D., 120
Kochanek, M. A., 1, 102, 112, 120
Kohn, I., 170
Kral, M., 106, 168
Kübler-Ross, E., 20, 32
Kulenkamp, E. J., 73
Kushner, H., 54, 106

Lang, A., 73
Lang, E. L., 73
Language
  after suicide, 106–108
  using parents', 48–49
Larson, J., 72
Lasker, J. N., 168
Laungani, P., 169
Leahy, J. M., 25
Legacy, 56–58
  after infant death, 122–124

Legal issues, 50
    after homicide, 114–115, 119
Lehman, D. R., 73
Lewin, K., 41
Lindbergh, A.M., 172
Lindemann, E., 29–30
    perspective of, 19–20
Lipsyte, R., xiii, 6
Listening
    to language of grief, 48–49
    vs. solving, 55–56
Loss vs. restoration orientation, 24
Lothrop, H., 171
Lutgendorf, S. K., 160–161
Lyons, S., xv

MacIan, P. S., 155
Maladaptive religion, 141–144
Marriage
    after bereavement, 72–78
    ex-spouses, 78–82
    former partners, 78–82
    growth in, 11–12, 33–36
    resources, 172
    stepparents, 78–86
Martinson, I. M., 73
Marwit, S. J., 113, 116
Mauger, P. A., 168
McAnulty, R., xv
McClowry, S. G., 73
McCracken, A., 167, 172
McGovern, G., 172
McIntosh, J. L., 104–105
McMurray, L., xv
Meaning. See Faith matters; Growth;
    Religious beliefs; Spirituality
    matters
Mediums, 130–131
Miles, M. S., 104, 120
Miller, J., 173
Mills, E., xv
Miltinho, 101
Minino, A. M., 1, 102, 112, 120
Miscarriage, 122–123
    acknowledgment of loss, 55, 122–124
    multiple, 122
    resources, 170–171
    suffering and meaning, 132–133
    underreported, 1
Models, 15–25
    Bowlby's, 20–21
    contemporary, 23–25

defined, 16–17
    dual process, 24–25
    early modern, 15–22
    Freud's, 17–19
    influence of, 22
    Lindemann's, 19–20
    Parkes's, 21–22
    two-track, 23
Moffitt, P., 170
"Morbid grief," 19
Morgan, J. D., 169
Morrell, D., 125
Morrell, R., 52
Morris, R. R., 171
Multicultural issues, 41–50
    assumptions, 45–46
    clinician's status and role, 44–45
    faith issues, 46–48
    identifying primary groups, 41–42
    idioms of distress, 48–49
    parents' sociocultural context, 49–50
    religion and spirituality, 126
    resources, 169
    social rules and norms, 42–44
    sociocultural issues, 46, 49–50
Munday, J., 171
Murder. See Homicide
Murphy, S. L., 1, 102, 112, 120
Muscular dystrophy, 3–4
Myths, 25–33
    absence of distress, 27–29
    closure, 31–32, 58–59
    need to "work through" grief, 29–31
    recovery, 31–32, 58–59
    stages of grief, 32–33
    universality of distress, 25–27

Neimeyer, R. A., xi, 169
Neonatal deaths, 122–124
    resources, 170–171
    suffering and meaning, 132–133
New life paths, 52–53
Nickman, S., 127
Nolen-Hoeksema, S., 72

Oliver, L. E., 73
Omega and Death Studies, 174
Only children, 86–95
Organizations, 172–174
Oscillation, 24–25, 33
Overidentification. See
    Countertransference

Pain, 7–8
    continues, 9
    experiencing differently, 26–27
    metaphors of, 7–8
Paralysis, 8–9
Parents
    assumptions of, 45–46
    circumstances of loss, 3–4, 13
    continuing connections, 9–10
    disorientation, 4–5, 13
    exiles, 6–7, 13–14
    experience of grief, 1–14
    ex-spouses, 78–82
    family support, 71–99
    former partners, 78–82
    grandparents, 95–99
    growth through pain, 10–13
    language of grief, 48–49
    loss of daily functioning, 8–9
    marriage, 72–78
    only child, 86–95
    pain and suffering, 7–8
    priorities change, 12, 35, 52
    reactions, 13–14
    relationships, 11–12
    religious issues, 46–49
    resources for, 170–172
    role changes, 86–88
    sense of self, 11
    shock, 4–5
    siblings, 86–95
    sociocultural context, 41–50
    spiritual matters, 12–13
    stepparents, 78–86
    uniqueness of response, 13–14
Pargament, K. I., 47, 141
Park, C. L., 33–34
Parkes, C. M., 20, 47, 113, 115
    perspective of, 21–22
Peach, M. R., 113, 115
Pearce, E., xv
Pearlman, L. A., 151–152, 154–156
Peer consultation, 159–161
Pennebaker, J. W., 160
Perinatal Grief Scale, 168
Perry, P. I., 43
Perspectives, 15–25
    Bowlby's, 20–21
    contemporary, 23–25
    defined, 16–17
    dual process model, 24–25
    early modern, 15–22

Freud's, 17–19
    influence of, 22
    Lindemann's, 19–20
    Parkes's, 21–22
    two-track model, 23
Photographs, 39–40
Positive change. *See* Growth; Post-
    traumatic growth
Posttraumatic growth, 33–36, 52–58
    acknowledging, 56–58
    clinicians', 155–158
    possibility of, 33–36
    reports of, 54–58
    self, 11, 33–36, 52, 54
    vicarious, 155–158
Posttraumatic stress disorder, 66–68
Potvin, L., 168
Pragmatic religious constructivism, 47–49,
    126
Priorities change, 12, 35, 52
Proffitt, D., xv
Psychological investment
    ending, 17–19, 23
Psychological problems, 27–29
Psychosocial transitions, 21–22
Publicity, 114–115
Publishers, 172–174
Pulmer, D., xv

Questions, 50
    about God, 12–13, 137–140
Quidley, E., xv

Rage, 116–117
Rando, T., 22, 73
Range, L. M., 105
Reactions to grief, 13–14
    circumstances, 13
    disorientation, 4–5, 13
    isolation, 6–7, 13–14
    uniqueness of, 13–14, 50–52
"Recovery" myth, 31–32
Reference groups, 41–42
Reincarnation, 127–128
Relationships
    difficult, 61
    ex-spouses, 78–82
    friends, 6–7, 12, 35, 41–44
    growth in, 11–12, 33–36, 52–53
    marriage, 72–78
    siblings, 86–95
    stepparents, 78–86

support groups, 107–108
Religious beliefs
after homicide, 113–116, 125–144
afterlife, 127–132
continuing connections, 9–10
experiences with clergy, 134–135
growth in, 12–13
language of, 48–49
maladaptive, 141–144
meaning and suffering, 132–134
multicultural issues, 46–48, 126
new communities, 144
pragmatic religious constructivism, 47–
49, 126
questioning, 12–13, 137–140
rituals and ceremonies, 127–128, 140–
141
struggling with grief, 15–16
talking with clergy, 135–137
Reports of growth, 54–58
Resources
for bereaved parents, 170–172
for clinicians, 168–170
for laypersons, 170–172
organizations/publishers, 172–174
Revenge, 113–114, 116–117
Riches, G., xiii, 6, 35, 105, 113–116, 169
Rituals, 7, 127–128
religious, 140–141
social rules, 42–44
Rock, P., 114, 116
Rosenblatt, P. C., 5, 7–9, 12, 21, 169, 172
Rosof, B. D., 170
Rotter, J. B., 154
Rubin, S., 31
two-track model, 23

Saakvitne, K. W., 151–152, 154–156
Sanders, C. M., 21, 23, 168, 171
Sarason, B. R., 28
Sarason, I. G., 28
Saslow, G., 41
Schut, H., 16, 23, 27, 32–33, 169
dual process model, 24–25
Scott, T. B., 168
Secondary traumatization, 151–154
risk factors, 154–155
Secular humanism, 47
Selby, J. W., xv, 6, 31, 33, 105–106
Selby, L., 105–106
Self-care, 158–165
beyond clinical work, 162–165

in clinical work, 158–162
Self-growth, 11, 33–36, 52, 54
Semel, M., 167, 172
Severe distress
universality myth, 25–27
absence of, 27–29
Shakespeare, W., 15, 71
Shaver, P. R., 20
Shay, J. J., 45–46
Shock, 4–5, 13, 32–33
Siblings, 86–95
Sidmore, K. V., 73
Silver, R. C., 21, 28–31, 33
myths about grief, 25
Silverman, P., 127
Smith, B. L., 1, 102, 112, 120
Social rules, 6–7, 42–44
Society of Traumatic Stress Studies, 174
Sorenson, S. B., 73
Spiritual matters
after homicide, 113–116, 125–144
afterlife, 127–132
clinicians' growth, 155–158
continuing connections, 9–10
experiences with clergy, 134–135
growth in, 12–13, 35, 52–53, 155–158
language of, 48–49
maladaptive, 141–144
meaning and suffering, 132–134
multicultural issues, 46–48, 126
new communities, 144
pragmatic religious constructivism, 47–
49, 126
questioning, 12–13, 137–140
resources, 169
rituals and ceremonies, 140–141
struggling with grief, 15–16
talking with clergy, 135–137
"Stages" of grief
Bowlby's perspective, 20–21
Kubler-Ross, 20–21
myth, 32–33, 59
Stepparents, 78–82
bereavement and, 82–86
Stillbirths, 122–124
acknowledgment of loss, 55
bereavement, 90–91
resources, 170–171
suffering and meaning, 132–133
underreported, 1
Stoebe, M., 16, 23, 27, 32–33, 169
dual process model, 24–25

Stroebe, W., 16, 25, 32–33, 169
Strong, P. A., 168
Stuck points, 58–66
    closure myth, 58–59
    complications to the loss, 60–61
    counterfactuals, 61–66
    stages myth, 59
    uniqueness of grief, 59–60
Sudden infant death syndrome, 122–124
    resources, 170–171
Suffering, 7–8
    and meaning, 132–134
Suicide, 102–112
    disconnectedness, 111–112
    guilt, 103–105, 108–111
    making meaning of, 105–107
    relief after, 103–104
    statistics, 102
Support groups
    after suicide, 107–108
    ex-spouses, 78–82
    family as, 71–99
    for clinicians', 162–165
    former partners, 78–82
    grandparents, 95–99
    identifying, 41–42
    only child, 86–95
    other bereaved parents, 144
    siblings, 86–95
    spouses, 72–78
    stepparents, 78–86
    stillbirths, 90–91
"Symptomatology of normal grief," 19–20

Talbot, K., 21, 106, 127
Tedeschi, R. G., ix–xi, 10, 28, 33–35, 47,
        52, 55, 72, 126–127, 133, 170
Texas Revised Inventory of Grief, 168
Theories. *See* Perspectives
Therapist. *See* Clinician

Toedter, L. J., 168
Traumatic grief, 66–68
Twain, M., 172
Two-track model, 23

Ullrich, P. M., 160–161
Unconscious
    Freud's theory, 17–10
Uniqueness of grief, 13–14
    acknowledging, 59–60
    expert companion and, 50–52
University of North Carolina, Charlotte, xv

Vicarious posttraumatic growth, 155–158
Vicarious traumatization, 117–118, 151–
        154
    risk factors, 154–155
Videotapes, 40–41
Violence. *See* Homicide; Suicide
Viorst, J., 54

Walter, T., 23
What-ifs. *See* Counterfactuals
Wickie, S. K., 113, 116
Wohlenhaus-Munday, F., 171
Wolfelt, A., 172–173
Worden, J. W., 30
"Working through" loss
    Freud's perspective, 17–19
    Lindemann's perspective, 19–20
    myth of necessity, 29–31
World Pastoral Care Center (Elgin, IL),
        173
Wortman, C. B., 21, 28–31, 33, 73
    myths about grief, 25

Yeats, W. B., 5
Younoszai, B., 43

Zisook, S., 168